A FU[illegible] [illegible]HE NHS? HEALTH CARE FOR THE MILLENNIUM

A Future for the NHS? Health Care for the Millennium

Wendy Ranade

SECOND EDITION

LONGMAN
London and New York

Addison Wesley Longman Limited,
Edinburgh Gate, Harlow,
Essex CM20 2JE, England
and Associated Companies throughout the world.

Published in the United States of America
by Addison Wesley Longman Inc., New York

First published 1994
Second edition 1997

ISBN 0 582–28993–9 PPR

British Library Cataloguing-in-Publication Data
A catalogue record for this book is available from the British Library

Library of Congress Cataloging-in-Publication Data
Ranade, Wendy, 1940–
A future for the NHS? : health care for the millenium / Wendy Ranade. — 2nd ed.
p. cm.
Includes bibliographical references and index.
ISBN 0–582–28993–9
1. National Health Service (Great Britain) 2. Medical care—Political aspects—Great Britain. 3. Medical care—Great Britain—Forecasting. I. Title.
RA412.5.G7R35 1997
362.1′0941—dc21 97–14147
CIP

Set in 10/12pt Times by 35
Produced through Longman Malaysia, PJB

CONTENTS

FIGURES AND TABLES

Figures

Tables

ABBREVIATIONS

ACHEW	Association of Community Health Councils in England and Wales
AMA	American Medical Association
BMA	British Medical Association
BSE	Bovine spongiform encephalopathy
CAP	Common Agricultural Policy
CHC	Community Health Council
CJD	Creutzfeld-Jakob disease
DGH	District General Hospital
DGM	District General Manager
DHA	District Health Authority
DHSS	Department of Health and Social Security
DOH	Department of Health
FHSA	Family Health Services Authority
GDP	Gross domestic product
GP	General Practitioner
GPFH	General Practitioner Fundholders
HCHS	Hospital and Community Health Service
HEA	Health Education Authority
HFA	Health for All
HMO	Health Maintenance Organisation
HoN	Health of the Nation
NACNE	National Advisory Council for Nutrition Education
NAHA	National Association of Health Authorities
NAHAT	National Association of Health Authorities and Trusts
NAO	National Audit Office
NHSE	National Health Service Executive
NHSME	National Health Service Management Executive
OECD	Organisation for Economic Cooperation and Development
OPCS	Office for Population Censuses and Surveys
QALY	Quality-adjusted life year
RAWP	Resource Allocation Working Party
RCGP	Royal College of General Practitioners

RGM	Regional General Manager
SMR	Standardised mortality ratio
TQM	Total quality management
UGM	Unit general manager
UKHFA	UK Health for All
WFP	*Working for Patients*
WHO	World Health Organisation

ACKNOWLEDGEMENTS

Once again my thanks go to Palu for his unfailing patience and support. Thanks as always to librarians Austin McCarthy and Graham Walton at UNN, as well as to my colleagues in the Division of Government and Politics who generously supported a sabbatical term to allow me to finish this second edition.

CHAPTER 1

Introduction

The health care systems of many countries throughout the developed world are being reformed and restructured. The changes taking place are manifested in diverse forms, and have very different starting points, but underlying them are similar sets of questions and pressures.

What needs to be done to best promote the public's health? How relevant are medical definitions of health to current health problems? How can health services be restructured to meet the needs of ageing populations more appropriately? How can the difference between the possible and the affordable in health care be resolved, as medical advance continues to widen the gap? What should the division be between public and private spending on health care, and can publicly funded systems continue to offer a comprehensive range of services? What are the ethics of different ways of rationing health care? How can doctors be made more accountable for the resources they use and what kind of incentives are appropriate? How can health services be made more accountable and responsive to those they serve?

In the current ferment of change and experimentation, the British National Health Service is in the forefront. A pioneering concept in 1948, the NHS remained the prime example of a centrally planned and funded public health service. In 1990 it again pioneered a new model of organising and delivering health services by introducing a 'quasi-market', or managed competition: creating a structure of buyers and sellers by separating responsibility for the purchase of health care from its provision, and allowing limited competition for business between providers – hospitals, community health services, ambulance services, and so on – within strict regulatory guidelines. Several other countries, such as Sweden, the Netherlands, Finland, New Zealand and some of the new democracies of Eastern Europe are experimenting with their own versions of this hybrid development.

In Britain the reforms which were heralded in the White Paper 'Working for Patients' in 1989 were never widely understood nor have they ever commanded public support, but they introduced a maelstrom of change which has transformed the organisation and culture of the NHS in ways which hardly seemed possible a decade ago. Some of those who work in the NHS have found the changes personally and professionally rewarding and exhilarating; others, perhaps the majority, have been left demoralised and exhausted. The 1997 election is now imminent and there will no doubt be further political debate on the benefits and costs of the reforms, six years after they were introduced, but these debates are unlikely to throw much light on the kind of questions raised above, or the pressures which have triggered health sector reform throughout the world.

This book therefore has two main aims. The first is to locate what is happening in the NHS to a broader economic, social, technological, political and ideological context, and the second is to explain in some detail how the reforms have been implemented, the directions they have taken, and what their current status is. Its starting premise is the need for a wider debate among the public on the kinds of questions raised above, which at present is conducted within fairly narrow health circles.

Round and round the mulberry bush

The reorganisation of the NHS which was heralded by the White Paper 'Working for Patients' in 1989, marks another attempt to grapple with basic tensions which arise from its organisational form. Klein (1995) argues that the NHS tries to square two circles. First it tries to reconcile central funding and government accountability for national standards of service with the need for local autonomy to meet local need. The result has been a policy see-saw, with governments alternating between periods of centralisation, the better to gain control, followed by a decentralising reaction against the rigidities which are caused as a consequence.

The second tension results from the compact struck between government and the medical profession in 1948, which balanced central accountability for raising and allocating finance with clinical freedom to spend it. The demand for health care (and the resources it consumes) is shaped not just by patients but by a million clinical decisions by doctors and other professionals. As new treatments and technologies proliferate and new needs are identified, these demands escalate, but even as early as 1954, the then Minister for Health, Enoch Powell, discovered that it became a 'positive ethical duty for (providers) to beseige and bombard the government and force or shame them into providing more money . . . and then more again' (Powell 1966). An irresistible force constantly clashes with an immovable object, leading to periodic political 'crises' on the funding issue, and these reached a peak before the 1987 election. Provider power to shape the service also means that the NHS has been unresponsive to central policy direction and strategic planning. A good illustration of this was the vain attempt to give priority

Figure 1.1 ***Structure of NHS 1948–74***

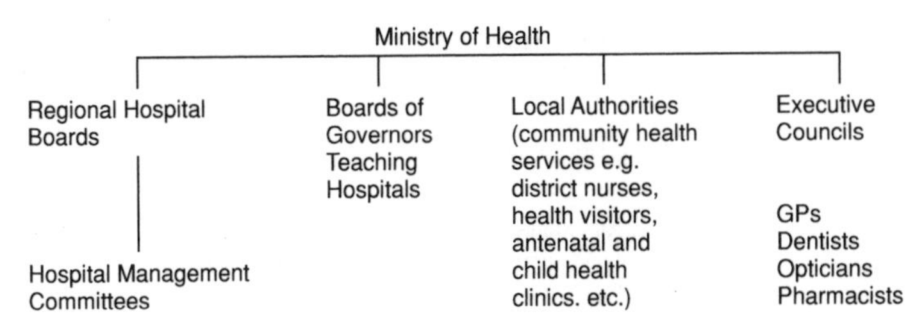

to the 'Cinderella' services such as mental illness and mental handicap throughout the 1960s and 1970s.

There have been four attempts to grapple with these tensions through restructuring or internal reorganisation. The 1974 reorganisation was based on the twin principles of rational planning and efficient management, although what was finally brought into being achieved neither. Rational planning was to be achieved by unifying health services, which were at that time split between local authorities, the boards of governors of teaching hospitals, a regional and local administration responsible for other hospitals and the executive councils who administered the contracts for general practitioners (see Figure 1.1).

When proposals for reorganisation were first mooted by a Labour government in 1968, the future structure of local government was also being considered by the Redcliffe-Maud Commission (1969). Ministers believed the Commission would recommend 40 to 50 local authorities, hence the possibility of creating a matching 40 to 50 area health boards as a single tier of health service administration. Coherent planning and coordination of health and social care would be facilitated by coterminous boundaries between the two authorities.

In the event, the number of local authorities that emerged with social service responsibilities was nearer 90. Keeping the principle of coterminous boundaries meant 90 health authorities, varying widely in population size. But 90 was thought to be too many to be easily controlled from the centre, which meant retaining the existing tier of regional administration as an executive arm of government, while the variation in population size was tackled by creating a third tier of management in large areas: the district. Driven by the original criterion of coterminosity a highly bureaucratic structure was being created.

The original management proposals were also changed out of recognition. In the 1968 (Ministry of Health 1968) proposals, the boards were envisaged as operating as small executive management teams, with the senior administrator acting as managing director and with far less professional and medical input into decision making. The syndicalist nature of the NHS, however, forced a number of compromises: a plethora

Figure 1.2 **Structure of NHS 1974–82**

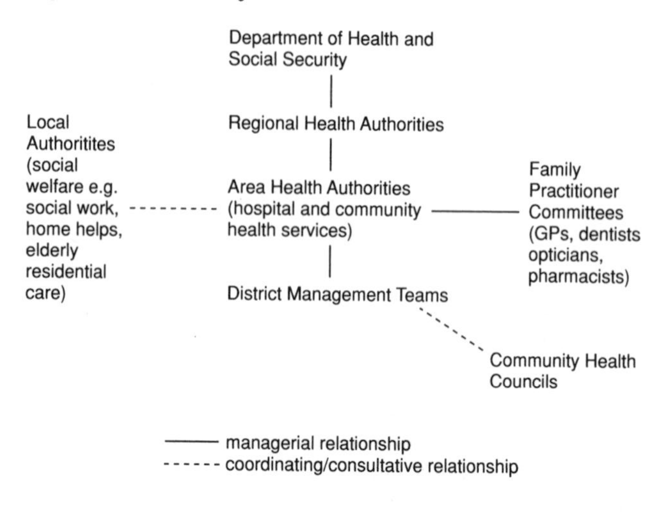

of professional advisory and consultative machinery at every level, and the inclusion of medical and nursing representatives on management teams and health authorities. The end result of this series of political compromises and adjustments, which the Conservatives implemented in 1974, was a seriously flawed structure which certainly could not deliver the government's stated intention of 'maximum accountability upward, maximum delegation downwards' (DHSS 1972) (see Figure 1.2).

Within two years the new Labour government found it necessary to appoint a Royal Commission to investigate the arrangements the Conservatives had put in place, and review the organisation of the NHS once more. Maurice Kogan, whose team at Brunel University undertook a survey of staff attitudes for the Commission found that:

> There was a great deal of anger and frustration at what many regard as a seriously over-elaborate system of government, administration and decision-making. The multiplicity of levels, the over-elaboration of consultative machinery, the inability to get decision-making completed nearer the point of delivery of services and what some describe as unacceptably wasteful use of manpower resources were recurrent themes in most of the areas where we worked.
>
> (Merrison Report 1979: 313)

As a result of the Merrison Report's recommendations, the incoming administration, once again Conservative and headed by Margaret Thatcher, decided on another reorganisation (DHSS 1979), to be carried out in 1982, based on a new set of principles – small is beautiful, with the devolution of decision making as close as possible to the patient. Coterminosity was abandoned and Area Health Authorities were abolished.

Figure 1.3 **Structure of NHS 1982–90**

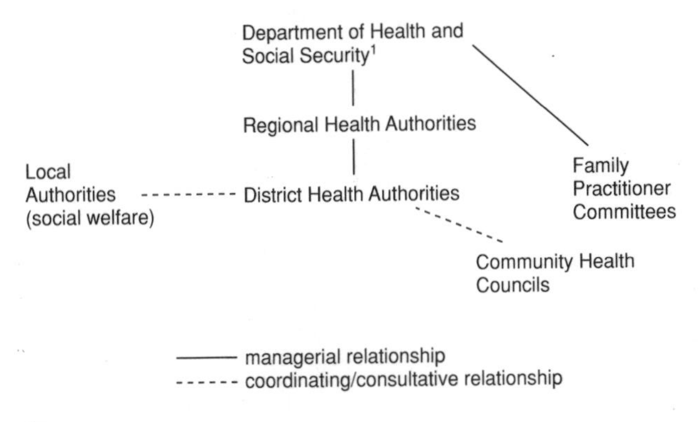

Note:
[1]The Department of Health and Social Security was broken down into two departments again in 1988

Their constituent districts were rearranged into 192 district health authorities, and the 14 regional health authorities retained as a strategic planning tier (see Figure 1.3). The professional advisory machinery was pruned and the planning system simplified, although the composition of health authorities and management stayed intact. The balance had once more swung from centralisation to decentralisation, but the attempt to make doctors and nurses more accountable for resource decisions continued.

Yet the new balance began to be questioned almost as soon as it was put in place, this time by Parliamentary committees. The new planning system adopted in 1981 had moved away from detailed prescriptive national targets to relatively broad outlines of central government priorities, more advisory in intent. Realistically the DHSS had acknowledged the infinite diversity of local circumstances and the reality of local power to shape the implementation of government policy. But this made the DHSS and ministers once again vulnerable to charges of abdicating their responsibilities for financial and policy goals. In response to criticism from both the Public Accounts Committee and Social Services Committee, the DHSS began to develop new ways of trying to achieve the elusive balance between central accountability and local autonomy and bring the management of health care resources under more effective control.

In 1983 the creation of a new general management function was recommended by a business adviser, Sir Roy Griffiths, and almost immediately implemented. This led to further changes in management structures and processes but also represented a significant challenge to professional power to determine priorities. The proposals in Working for Patients (DHSS 1989) were in many ways a logical development and strengthening of the Griffiths management philosophy, but the nub of the reforms – the creation of the quasi-market – was a radical new departure.

Contents

Chapter 2 traces the development of the NHS from the perspective of a changing intellectual climate. The political and ideological ideas which shaped the creation of the NHS came under increasingly fierce attack in the 1970s. In part this reflected the wider 'crisis of legitimacy' affecting the welfare state in Britain and many other Western countries and is part of that critique. But it also reflected more specific arguments about the goals of health policy, the role and function of medicine and the power of the medical profession.

Chapter 3 examines some of the larger trends in society which have major significance for health care in general and the NHS in particular. It begins by looking at the implications of the information revolution and economic restructuring on welfare services, and how these linkages have been theorised within a 'post-Fordist' framework. It goes on to examine the pressures on the health service which derive from demographic change and medical and technological advance.

Chapter 4 looks at the development of Conservative health policy throughout the 1980s, after the 1982 structure was put in place and up to the publication of the White Papers, *Working for Patients* and *Caring for People* in 1989. Chapter 5 discusses the use of market incentives in health care, and the theory and practice of 'quasi-practices' as a prelude to the detailed examination of the NHS reforms. How have they been implemented, what directions have they taken, and with what effects?

Changing the style and responsibilities of health service managers has been an important theme of Conservative health policy. Chapter 6 appraises this development within the context of similar changes throughout the public sector and the challenges facing managers in future. Chapter 7 looks at another important theme of the health service reforms – the search for 'quality' in health care, and the growing realisation of the important role users play in articulating what quality means.

Chapter 8 charts an alternative strategic vision for health policy based on the World Health Organisation's strategy of Health for All 2000. The central aim is the promotion of a holistic model of health according to the core values of equity, solidarity and community and individual empowerment.

Finally, Chapter 9 reviews the strategic context within which health policy choices have to be made in future and the current status of the health service reforms. It looks at some of the most recent policy initiatives of the Conservative government, and critically assesses the Labour Party's proposals for the health service.

References

Department of Health (1989) *Working for Patients*, Cmnd. 555, London: HMSO.
Department of Health and Social Security (DHSS) (1972) *National Health Service Reorganisation: England*, Cmnd. 5055, London: HMSO.
Department of Health and Social Security and Welsh Office (DHSS) (1979) *Patients First: Consultative Paper on the Structure and Management of The National Health Service in England and Wales*, London: HMSO.
Klein, R. (1995) *The New Politics of the NHS*, 3rd edn, London: Longman.
Merrison Report, The (Royal Commission on the National Health Service) (1979) Cmnd 7615, London: HMSO.
Ministry of Health (1968) *National Health Service: The Administrative Structure of the Medical and Related Services in England and Wales*, London: HMSO.
Powell, J.E. (1966) *Medicine in Politics*, London: Pitman Medical.
Royal Commission on Local Government in England (1969) Cmnd. 4040 *The Redcliffe-Maud Report*, London: HMSO.

CHAPTER 2

The ideological context

Health policy can only be understood within the context of the ideas and values which have shaped its development historically. This chapter looks at the main academic and political perspectives on health and health care which have shaped the debate, and revolves around three broad areas of analysis. First, how health and illness are to be defined and what their determinants are; second, the values underpinning the structuring and organisation of health care; and third, the function and power of medicine in modern society and the role of the medical profession within it.

Different perspectives also have a chronological dimension. Historically the Fabian socialist perspective dominated the development of social policy in Britain from the end of the Second World War to the mid-1970s and contributed powerfully to the rationale underpinning a free, comprehensive, universal and state-provided health service. Klein argues that the remarkable political consensus that existed on these principles in 1948 was accompanied by an even more profound consensus about the benefits of medicine and what it could achieve.

> . . . this mirrored the belief that medical science had not only triumphed over disease and illness in the past but would continue to do so in future. On this view, the only problem was how best to create an institutional framework which would bring the benefits of medical science more efficiently and equitably to the people of Britain.
>
> (Klein 1995: 25)

In the 1970s optimism and faith gave way to disillusion and doubt as medical costs soared with little apparent benefit. Even the past successes of medicine were challenged as illusory, and the role and power of the medical profession were subject to a number of influential critiques. While certain of the criticisms made then are now widely accepted even within the medical profession itself, no new consensus has yet emerged on the goals of health policy or the principles which should govern its organisation and distribution.

Inevitably a brief account cannot do justice to individual writers and exaggerates the extent of agreement within each broad perspective, but it does emphasise central points of similarity and difference.

The social-democratic consensus

The founding of the NHS was one of the key acts of the 1945 Attlee government which laid the foundations of the postwar accord on the welfare state, full employment and the managed mixed economy. Built on the economic foundations of Keynesian economics and the social policy prescriptions of the Beveridge Report, the accord bridged the 'reluctant collectivists' in the Conservative Party (George and Wilding 1976), concerned with the survival and prosperity of capitalism, and the Fabian socialists in the Labour Party trying to transform it from within.

Socialist proposals for state-provided health care can be traced back to the Webbs' Minority Report of the Royal Commission on the Poor Law in 1905. The medical profession itself, notably in the Dawson Report of 1920, advocated some kind of comprehensive health care provision for the whole population. The fragmentation and inequities of prewar arrangements were highlighted in 1937 by an influential report from the Department of Political and Economic Planning but it took the Second World War and the Beveridge Report of 1942 to change perceptions sufficiently to legitimise a greatly enhanced role for the state in the provision of health care. Beveridge provided a rationale based on concepts of national efficiency, rationality and the rights of citizenship. As a Liberal, Beveridge falls into the 'reluctant collectivist' camp but his proposals received enthusiastic endorsement from leading Fabians and show the influence of their ideas. In particular, his concern with social benefit and social cost (the costs of ill-health fall on the community, not just the individual), the view that welfare spending should be regarded as a social investment which could increase national productivity and efficiency and his technocratic approach to solving social problems are all typically Fabian.

Klein (1995) argues that the same emphasis on efficiency and administrative rationality characterised internal Labour Party debates on the final shape and form of the service and went hand-in-hand with their commitment to equity and equality. In spite of his radical socialist image and his furious battles with the medical profession over implementation, Bevan's vision of the health service was essentially paternalist. Health knowledge resided with the 'experts', essentially the medical profession, and this won doctors a privileged place in administering the new system, denied to other professional groups. The effect was to 'medicalise' large areas of health policy and define them as off-limits to lay influence.

It also led to the creation of a lopsided system in line with the structure of medical priorities and values. Curative, hospital-based medicine dominated at the expense of prevention, health promotion and community services, and high priority was given to the treatment of short-term episodes of acute illness to the detriment of the care and rehabilitation of the chronically ill. Although both Beveridge and Bevan had acknowledged the superiority of prevention over cure, the design of the new system ensured that it remained underdeveloped. By privileging medicine in the administration of the new service, separating hospitals from local authority responsibilities for prevention and after-care, and leaving the power and independence of the teaching hospitals intact, Bevan created a medical service rather than a health service. Restoring the balance between prevention, cure and care has been a major or minor theme of health policy ever since. It figures prominently as an objective of current policy for the health service, and is a major theme of this book.

The Fabian model of welfare

Fabians continued to dominate the study of social policy throughout the 1950s and 1960s, developing a welfare model which had a powerful influence on policy-makers and contributed to a shared perspective between academics, civil servants and politicians on the role of the state in social policy. Essentially this was based on optimistic views about social progress and economic growth. Welfare spending, it was argued, aided economic development in three main ways. It stabilised demand by income transfers to those who had a high propensity to consume. This in turn contributed to the maintenance of full employment. Finally, welfare spending, particularly on education and health, improved the quality and productivity of labour. If welfare aided economic growth it was also dependent on it. Crosland (1956) argued that economic growth was essential if the Fabian strategy of equality was to succeed. A growing national income would ease the political and social difficulties of redistribution and allow the provision of more generous social benefits which would help to equalise consumption patterns.

Fabians also believed that public welfare had a vital role to play in integrating society, alleviating social conflict and promoting the expression of altruistic sentiments countering, if only partially, the atomism, selfishness and inequalities of capitalist market economies. Integration was a strong theme in the work of Richard Titmuss. In words which betray the influence of functionalist sociology, Titmuss wrote: 'social policy . . . manifests society's will to survive as an organic whole . . . and is centred (on) those institutions which encourage integration and discourage alienation' (Titmuss 1963: 39). The universal and comprehensive nature of the health service enshrined these principles more perfectly than any other social service.

Harris (1987) points out that Fabian academics of this generation were almost unfailingly hostile to market-based welfare systems. Underlying this hostility was a profound belief in the ethical and moral superiority of collective welfare provision. Probably Bevan himself expressed this most eloquently in relation to health care:

> The field in which the claims of individual commercialism come into most immediate conflict with reputable notions of social values is that of health . . . no society can legitimately call itself civilized if a sick person is denied medical aid because of lack of means . . . Society becomes more wholesome, more serene and spiritually healthier, if it knows that its citizens have at the back of their consciousness the knowledge that not only themselves, but all their fellows have access, when ill, to the best that medical skill can provide.
>
> (Bevan 1961: 98–100)

In the next 20 years the NHS did not escape criticism from academic Fabians but it never reached the volume and intensity of the criticism which, for example, social security and income maintenance attracted as they appeared to retreat further and further away from the principles of the Beveridge Report.

Challenging the mystique of medicine

The optimistic consensus on medicine which had helped to sustain high and growing health expenditures in the Western world throughout the 1960s began to dissolve in the 1970s. Medicine's achievements and potential were put under the microscope and re-evaluated more critically. The power and function of the medical profession were subject to a disparate but intense attack.

The roots of disillusion lay in the widening gap between medicine's claims and its achievements. As one set of health problems was eliminated in developed countries (the infectious diseases), another more difficult and intractable set was revealed. Medicine seemed to be able, at best, to alleviate the growing burden of degenerative and chronic illness: arthritis, diabetes, respiratory disease, and mental illnesses like schizophrenia or Alzheimer's disease. Survivors of serious accidents or genetic handicap at birth could be kept alive, but often for a lifetime of expensive treatment and care. Many of the principal modern causes of mortality and morbidity – coronary heart disease, most cancers, stroke, accidents – were difficult and expensive to treat and resistant to cure. Consequently 1940s optimism about a finite amount of ill-health and disease susceptible to a comprehensive health care system was seen to be false, based on erroneous concepts of health and illness. Far from being static these are redefined over time in line with economic and social change.

Wrestling with inequalities

Equally important in undermining the hopes of egalitarians in Britain was growing evidence of persistent inequalities between the classes in health status in spite of 30 years of a free health service. Reviewing the evidence in 1980, the Black Report (DHSS 1980) concluded that at every stage of the life-cycle there was a substantial class gradient in mortality and that class differences had remained comparatively stable since 1930. Self-reported illness, sickness absence rates and a growing number of studies on specific aspects of ill-health all supported the main conclusion: the greatest burden of ill-health and disability was borne by the worst off.

In part this was attributed to inequalities in access and utilisation. The NHS had inherited a gross geographical maldistribution of facilities in 1948 which meant that in practice 'equality of access' was a chimera. Progress was made on certain aspects of the problem (for example, the distribution of general practitioners and underprovided specialities like psychiatry and anaesthesia), but by 1970 Tudor Hart could still proclaim the truth of the 'inverse care law': 'The availability of good medical care tends to vary inversely with the need for it in the population served' (Hart 1971: 405–12).

The evidence on uptake was more mixed although there was a clear class gradient with regard to preventive services. Higher social groups appeared to make more use of health services in relation to need, however (Brotherston 1976; Forster 1976) and research published shortly after the Black Report argued that they also obtained a disproportionate share of NHS resources when ill (Le Grand 1982).

The authors of the Black Report, who included one of the most eminent Fabian academics, Professor Peter Townsend, were clear that such disparities were socially unjust and the NHS needed policies to address them, but they were forced to conclude from the evidence that the major causes of health inequalities lay beyond the NHS and were rooted in the material conditions of life experienced by the different classes. Inequalities in health simply reflected wider structures of economic and social inequality which health care was powerless to redress. The Fabian 'strategy for equality' through redistributing services in kind appeared to have failed. (Although failure is relative: the welfare services may have contained inequalities and prevented them from getting worse.)

The McKeown thesis

Medicine's growing number of critics were given important empirical support by the work of Thomas McKeown, which exposed not only its present limitations but threw doubt on its past successes. McKeown published *The Modern Rise of Population and the Role of Medicine* in 1976 as an accessible summary of two decades of painstaking work, applying the insights of medical and epidemiological knowledge to a historical analysis of Britain's detailed national series of death records, which began in 1847.

McKeown's main purpose was to take away from scientific medicine any credit for the decline in mortality which took place in England and Wales in the nineteenth century. He did so by demonstrating conclusively that many of the most important diseases involved had virtually disappeared before the relevant medical innovations had occurred. He also had an alternative explanation: the major factor responsible was rising standards of living, of which the most significant feature was improved diet (McKeown 1976). Improved public health and hygiene measures – the 'sanitary revolution' from the mid-years of the century – were also important and eliminated up to one-quarter of deaths between then and 1971. McKeown's attack on the 'medical model' of health was shared by critics from radical, feminist and Marxist perspectives.

The radical critique

The radical critique has originated both from within medicine, particularly epidemiology, and from sociology. The first exposes the limitations of modern medical practice, often exposing its claims to scientific status as dubious. Cochrane (1971), for example, argued that medicine has a poor record of evaluative research: fashion, whim and personal preference often dictate the choice of a particular procedure, and many common interventions are unvalidated, of proven in-effectiveness or produce iatrogenic illness (illness caused as a result of medical intervention).

The sociological variant combines similar scepticism with an analysis of medical power and its effects and is based on a wider critique of the professions and professionalism. An early and influential contribution was Eliot Freidson's *Professional Dominance* and *The Profession of Medicine* (1970a; 1970b). Freidson argued that the 'analytical key' to understanding the organisation of health services and their inadequacies was the professional dominance of medicine at the apex of an elaborate division of labour. Other health care professions are subordinate to the organised autonomy of doctors who claim sole rights of diagnosis and treatment. Freidson analyses how medicine has acquired these monopoly legal and political rights from the state, and the consequences of this for patients. Building on this work, John Ehrenreich argues that the cultural practices and values of Western medicine and inequalities of power between doctor and patient lead to the production of a racist, sexist, harmful and ineffective medical system (Ehrenreich 1978).

The most damning and best-known indictment of medicine in the radical tradition is *Limits to Medicine: Medical Nemesis* by Ivan Illich. Centring his discussion on an analysis of present patterns of mortality, Illich argues that medicine is not only ineffective but causes positive damage (iatrogenesis) at three levels. Damage and suffering are inflicted on patients in the course of clinical treatment as a result of 'the undesirable side effects of approved, mistaken, callous or contra-indicated technical contacts with the medical system . . .' (Illich 1976: 26). Second, the 'medicalisation of life' destroys people's capacity for self-care and self-responsibility. Illich claims that doctors have done much to mystify the public about the real causes of ill-health and fostered the illusion of miracle cures for every ill – if enough money is spent looking for them. We are all turned into addicts of medicine as every stage of human life from pregnancy and childbirth to old age and dying becomes colonised and labelled by medicine. 'Life turns from a succession of different stages of health into a series of periods each requiring different therapies' (p. 44). At an even deeper level medicine destroys a people's ability to deal with their own vulnerability and weakness in an autonomous and personal way by attacking traditional cultural values, routines and rituals which allowed individuals to make meaningful the universal human experience of pain, suffering and death.

Radical solutions to the problems outlined differ. Those who, like Ehrenreich, acknowledge the utility of medical science, want to decontaminate its practice by changing the class, sex and racial composition of medical personnel and promoting a cultural revolution in medical institutions to 'purify' them and instil new values. Since Illich sees only harm in the entire medical enterprise, however, he rejects solutions to democratise or control medical practice or equalise the distribution of medical care. Instead he argues that the whole enterprise of scientific medicine needs to be destroyed as part of a wider de-bureaucratisation and de-industrialisation of modern society to enable more autonomous modes of organisation to develop.

Feminist perspectives

The starting point for feminist analyses of health care is the assumption that the practices and institutions of modern medicine control and disempower women both as consumers and producers of health care, and are unresponsive to their needs.

Feminists of all persuasions distrust the medical model of health, with its mechanistic and individualistic bias. Unlike radicals, however, they do not see medical power resting solely on the dominance of an autonomous profession or the control of highly valued science. (On the contrary, feminists would argue that 'value' is accorded to medical science because men control it.) Through an analysis of gender relations in medicine and health care, feminists have related medical power to wider structures of male domination which medicine both reflects and helps to sustain.

In their historical analyses of the development of scientific medicine, feminists have shown how women as the natural (but necessarily unqualified) healers and carers of the sick were displaced by men through a misogynist alliance of Church, state and universities after centuries of struggle (Ehrenreich and English 1979). This ensured that the practice of medicine was based on possession of a university education, from which women were barred. The Church denounced nonprofessional healing as heresy (hence condemning many female midwives to the stake as witches in the fifteenth and sixteenth centuries) and the state was prevailed on to grant a final legal monopoly of practice to the medically qualified by the establishment of the Medical Register in 1858.

The nineteenth and twentieth centuries saw the final triumph of scientific medicine under male control. In the process, earlier holistic concepts of healing associated with women healers were eclipsed by an atomistic approach which reduced patients to no more than their dysfunctioning parts.[1] Women re-entered the healthcare arena in the subordinate role of nurses in Florence Nightingale's reorganised profession for 'respectable' ladies in a relationship with medicine which paralleled the patriarchal structure of the bourgeois family, as a quotation from a nursing journal at the turn of the century makes clear:

> Women are peculiarly fitted for the onerous task of patiently and skilfully caring for the patient in faithful obedience to the physician's orders. Ability to care for the helpless is women's distinctive nature. Grown up folks when very sick are all babies.
>
> (quoted in Garnikov 1978: 110)

Feminist writers have shown how, both historically and today, women's experience of mental and physical ill-health is related to social causes, with its roots in the inequalities of power they experience in marriage, the family and the labour market. They agree with radicals like Illich that modern medical ideologies mask these realities since 'one of the functions of modern medicine is to call unhappiness disease and locate its cause in the unhappy individual not the diseased social system' (Oakley 1983: 106). However, women are the principal victims of this process since embedded in medical ideologies are gender ideologies which label, stereotype and devalue women.

Feminists have paid particular attention to the way in which an ideology which assigns a primary role to women as mothers informs medical control of reproduction. Through a detailed analysis of contraception, abortion, pregnancy and childbirth, infertility treatment and the menopause they have shown how medicine reinforces and sustains wider structures of male domination over women, through the family and the state. Gender ideologies also assign to women a primary role as carers of the sick, disabled and elderly. Feminist analyses have documented the effects of this: the huge if hidden economic contribution made by the unpaid labour of carers and the financial, emotional and physical costs to the individual.

Feminist solutions to the problems they diagnose depend partly on their theoretical perspective, partly on the specific features of the health policy arena they face in different countries. But whatever their theoretical standpoint, in practice British feminists have had to confront the near monopoly position of the NHS as a provider of services and its role as a massive employer of female labour. They have worked for change within it by, for example, the formation of feminist groups of health workers and professionals, campaigns for more woman-centred services, promoting equal opportunity policies for employees and campaigns to protect abortion rights.

The Marxist critique

The Marxist position starts from the premise that modern medicine must be seen as part of the capitalist mode of production. State involvement in health care in capitalist societies stems from capital's need to reproduce both labour power and the existing social relations of production which ensures the continued dominance of the bourgeoisie at an economic, political and ideological level.

State expenditure on health services is directed towards both of these ends. It assists the production of social capital by helping to maintain and reproduce a healthy, productive and pliant labour force. It helps to maintain the legitimacy of existing social relations by relieving suffering and distress, promoting social harmony and caring for nonworking groups. However, the class struggle is played out in medicine as in every other institution of society. The form and organisation of health services in a particular country partly reflects that struggle, hence 'socialised medicine' as in the British health service reflects the organised strength of the working class and their struggle for better health care. As one of the most influential Marxist analysts of health care, Navarro (1986) argues that working-class people have struggled for medical services not because they are 'mystified' by medicine's bogus claims, as Illich argues, but because it has brought genuine benefits which Illich overlooks, particularly in the care and relief of chronic illness. Hence medicine under capitalism has a dual function, both liberating and controlling. The main difference between the radical and Marxist positions revolves around the issue of medical power. Radicals attribute this to the control of an autonomous medical science and knowledge, Marxists to the class position and function of doctors within capitalism. For Marxists, the changing nature of capitalist interests ultimately dictates what happens in medicine even though doctors themselves may oppose the changes. An example of current importance is the growing corporatisation of health care in the United States which, it is argued, has major implications for the status and autonomy of doctors (McKinlay and Stoeckle 1988).

Similarly, the seemingly autonomous development of medical science has been shaped within a capitalist system of values which sees individuals primarily as producers and in which health is defined largely in terms of restoring the individual's 'fitness' to perform his or her social roles as worker, mother or carer. It is therefore hardly surprising to Marxists that Western medicine has been more interested in curative services for the most productive groups and that nonproductive groups like the disabled, mentally ill and handicapped are less well served.

The emphasis on the individual in medical science also camouflages the real causes of ill-health which are rooted in capitalist economic and social structures – poverty, unemployment, pollution, stressful and unsafe working conditions – the costs of which are borne primarily by the working class and help to explain the stability of class inequalities in health status.

As the ineffectiveness of curative medicine is increasingly exposed (and costs soar) Western medicine has paid more attention to prevention, but again within a narrowly individualistic framework. Once again, Marxists claim, medicine performs its camouflage trick for capitalism, masking the extent to which ill-health originates from the exploitation of workers in the production process itself. The possession of good health is increasingly equated with moral virtue: those who continue to 'choose' to smoke, drink or eat the wrong foods are irresponsible and deserving of their fate. This ignores the extent to which individual 'choices' for consumers are structured by powerful corporate interests in the brewing, food, tobacco and pharmaceutical industries. An effective preventive strategy which challenged these interests would seriously disrupt or impose great costs on capitalist producers.

Radical, feminist and Marxist approaches: a comment

Although a detailed critique of these three approaches is beyond the scope of the chapter, it may be helpful to highlight some of their strengths and weaknesses at this point. The radical sociological critique of medicine provides important insights into the sources of professional power, and the way in which self-interest is rationalised in the public good even in the healing professions. The weaknesses are of exaggeration, and in Illich's case a romantic and utopian nostalgia for a past that never existed.

For example, by relying exclusively on mortality data the ineffectiveness of medical science is overstated. Its role in alleviating the pain and distress of non life-threatening illness is ignored. The account also exaggerates the extent to which the 'medicalisation of life' is a modern phenomenon. Strong (1979) argues that historical and anthropological evidence shows that life events like childbirth had long been medicalised, but with much worse outcomes for mothers and babies.

Similarly, radicals overstate the degree of unanimity among the medical profession, which is in fact riven with dissension and competing ideologies. As Strong points out, the treatment of drug abuse, alcoholism and mental illness is marked by serious differences of opinion and some doctors have struggled to de-medicalise these areas in the face of the hostility of their peers.

Finally the sociological critique also exaggerates the credulity of the public about medicine's claims. Although some people may have an unhealthy reliance on doctors to relieve all the ills of this life, several studies show that most people are fairly sceptical about the efficacy of medical treatment and use many sources of advice and help, not just doctors and drugs (Blaxter 1983; Calnan 1988).

The radical attack from within medicine has proved to be more substantial and enduring. Cochrane's (1971) criticisms still seem as relevant and cogent today as they did 20 years ago, and at last seem to be taken seriously by the medical establishment and health policy-makers. Establishing the effectiveness and outcomes of health care in order to allocate resources more rationally has become a key policy issue in many countries. The epidemiological critique has also strengthened. Re-evaluation of McKeown's data shows that, if anything, he underestimated the role of the nineteenth century public health reforms in improving both mortality and morbidity (Sretzer 1988) and today public health medicine is starting to win the argument about how new health gains can be made.

Turning to feminist analyses, their strength lies in exposing the effects of gender relations and ideologies on women as producers and consumers of health care. They have succeeded in raising consciousness (and consciences) on many issues affecting women: the burdens of informal care, the effects of unsafe and unethical practices in contraception (particularly in the Third World), lack of choice and control in childbirth, the damaging effects of stereotyping in biasing doctors' diagnostic and treatment decisions for women patients.

But if issues like these have been put on the public agenda by feminists, the substantive gains they achieved were limited. Under successive Conservative administrations since 1979 traditional images of the family and the roles of women were reasserted. Sex equality slipped far down the political agenda and women had to fight hard to retain the rights they had won in the 1960s and 1970s on abortion, welfare benefits, maternity and employment rights. More significant than feminist campaigns in raising the profile of women in the NHS was the perception of a developing crisis in staff recruitment and retention, particularly in nursing, which is discussed in more detail in Chapter 3.

Finally, Marxist accounts appear to offer an impressively coherent and plausible explanation of the role of the capitalist state in health care, and the function of medicine in capitalist societies at the level of grand theory. But in spite of their strength in accounting for historical continuities and pulling together many diverse elements Marxist analyses cannot adequately account for the differences between capitalist health care systems and the details of their development, and the empirical evidence often contradicts the logic of the argument. For example, the fact that more than half of current spending on acute in-patients in the NHS is devoted to the 'unproductive' over-65s hardly supports the overall thesis. In the end, loading the whole weight of explanation onto the 'changing nature of capitalist interests' is tautological and actually explains very little.

In addition, Marxist prescriptions ultimately depend on the revolutionary overthrow of capitalism by communism, an increasingly unlikely scenario when Marxism as both a political creed and movement has never been weaker. Instead the 1980s has seen neoliberal market philosophies being adopted even by parties of the Left. The retreat of Marxism has been paralleled by the ascendancy of the New Right.[2]

The New Right and the state

A substantial literature has emerged analysing the ideas of the New Right, the distinctions between different schools, and the reasons for their political and intellectual ascendancy in the 1980s. That discussion cannot be replicated here. It is sufficient to sketch in the broad outlines of the New Right critique of the interventionist state, and more specifically, the welfare state (drawing largely on Harris 1987; Clarke *et al.* 1987). Later chapters will try to disentangle in greater detail the effect of New Right ideas on actual Conservative health policies throughout the 1980s as one strand (albeit an important one) of influences in the skein of policy development.

The New Right attack was aimed at the social-democratic consensus of the postwar years, a consensus which, as discussed earlier, was founded on the intellectual ascendancy of Fabian socialism underpinned by values of equality, equity, efficiency and social integration. The managed mixed economy and a highly developed system of collective social provision were the means for achieving these values. Market liberal doctrines and policies were kept alive in these lean years by writers like Hayek and Friedman and right-wing policy institutes like the Institute of Economic Affairs and the Adam Smith Institute. These were tolerated as crankish anachronisms with negligible political influence.

But the economic and social prescriptions of Beveridge and Keynes seemed increasingly unable to reverse either economic decline or deal with the 'crisis of welfare' which in 1981 the Organisation for Economic Cooperation and Development (OECD) forecast for Western nations in the run-up to the next century. The supposed crisis resulted from rapidly growing numbers of elderly people in proportion to the number of wage earners in the population, low economic growth and taxpayer resentment at the 'burdens' of welfare. A yawning gap was forecast between anticipated social expenditures and resources. Particularly alarming were the estimated costs of pension commitments already undertaken, and the projected costs of stubbornly high continuing rates of unemployment (OECD 1981). Keynesian economic management seemed unable to deal with the new phenomenon of stagflation – high inflation coupled with low growth and high unemployment – and market liberals mounted a strong attack on the welfare state as the cause of Britain's economic problems.

The core of the neoliberal argument is the need to free enterprise and initiative from the dead hand of the state. The ill-effects of state interference in the economy take several forms. First, state planning and regulation of the economy inhibit its efficient operation by distorting market forces. Second, the government taxes its citizens excessively to fund public expenditure, and excessive taxation blunts risk-taking and economic effort. Third, a large public sector aids economic decline since it does not create wealth whereas the private sector does.

The interventionist state has political as well as economic ill-effects by inducing unrealistic expectations on the part of voters and electoral trade-offs between parties bargaining for votes. This results in the 'overload' thesis. Excessive demands are placed on governments by sectional interest groups beyond their capacity to meet them. Repeated government 'failure' results not only in a withdrawal of support from specific administrations by the electorate but eventually disillusionment with the institutions and processes of political democracy itself.

These general arguments for 'rolling back the state' underpin a more specific critique of the state's role in welfare which revolves around two themes: economic efficiency and moral values. Regarding the first theme, it is claimed that the provision of welfare by state monopolies leads to waste since they are protected from the efficiency-inducing pressure of market competition. Comprehensive state welfare also induces dependency, reduces incentives to work, and blunts initiative and enterprise. Regarding the second theme, market liberals concur with radical liberals like Illich that professionals and bureaucrats tend to promote their own interests rather than meeting the needs of their clients. Hence far from state welfare being a morally superior form of meeting social needs, as claimed by Fabian socialists, for the New Right state welfare is paternalistic and morally bankrupt, rationing resources in a biased and potentially discriminatory way. Individuals are coerced in two ways: as taxpayers they are forced to pay for wasteful services and as consumers they are denied any choice over the level or type of services they wish to consume.

The New Right also deny the role of welfare in promoting social integration. Titmuss's concept of society as an organic entity is, for market liberals, simply metaphysics: society is no more than the individuals and families who make it up. Integration is achieved through the impersonal (and nondiscriminatory) mechanisms of the market. But families owe responsibilities to each other, and for humanitarian and religious reasons the duty of charity to others. State welfare, it is claimed, undermines both kinds of obligation.

The National Health Service as a public sector monopoly was an exemplar of everything the New Right most criticized. It appeared to have an irresistible momentum for growth demanded by its one million employees and supported by public opinion. The major resource users, doctors, were not held accountable for spending taxpayers' money. There were no fiscal incentives for the spenders to economise or for consumers to limit their demands. In addition to lack of choice, the public tolerated standards of service which they would never dream of tolerating in the private sector.

The solutions offered by New Right commentators and their fate is the subject of later chapters. It is worth pointing out, however, that the neoliberal perspective concentrates on the efficient delivery and financing of services and on issues of consumer choice. There is no explicit critique of prevailing medical definitions of health and illness, and no vision about what the goals of health policy should be (since by definition consumer choice in the market determines priorities). In this respect it differs from the four perspectives discussed earlier in the chapter, which converge in adopting a social model of health for a restructuring of priorities and goals. In contrast, neoliberals' emphasis on individual choice and personal responsibility for health makes them underestimate the importance of environmental factors. Policy strategies which attack the social and economic determinants of ill-health are dismissed as futile attempts at social engineering.

Conclusions

This chapter has looked at the main academic and political perspectives which have shaped thinking on health and health care. Many of the themes and issues raised will re-emerge in later chapters. In terms of policy influence, the New Right captured the intellectual and political high ground in Britain and many other countries throughout the 1980s. In the post-Thatcher era, and as both Labour and Conservative parties return to the centre ground, it is tempting to see those years as an aberration, tempting but false since the parameters of the debate have fundamentally shifted.

Notes

1 From a post-structuralist perspective, Foucault's (1973) account of the history of medicine shows how the development of hospitals from the end of the eighteenth century crucially affected these developments, framing both the organisation of medical ideas and the language in which they were embodied.
2 For an example of Marxist analysis used as a partial explanation for British health policies in the 1980s, see Harrison *et al.* 1990.

References

Bevan, A. (1961) *In Place of Fear*, London: E P Publishing.
Blaxter, M. (1983) 'The causes of disease: women talking', *Social Science and Medicine*, 17(2): 59–69.
Brotherston, J. (1976) 'Inequality: is it inevitable?', in C.O. Carter and J. Peel (eds) *Equalities and Inequalities in Health*, London: Academic Press.
Calnan, M. (1988) 'Lay evaluation of medicine and medical practice: Report of a pilot study', *International Journal of Health Services*, 18(2): 311–22.
Clarke, J., Cochrane, A. and Smart, C. (1987) *Ideologies of Welfare: From Dreams to Disillusion*, London: Hutchinson Education.
Cochrane, A. (1971) *Effectiveness and Efficiency: Random Reflections on Health Services*, London: Nuffield Provincial Hospitals Trust.
Crosland, A. (1956) *The Future of Socialism*, London: Cape.
Department of Health and Social Security (DHSS) (1980) *Inequalities in Health* (The Black Report), London: HMSO.
Ehrenreich, J. (1978) *The Cultural Crisis of Modern Medicine*, New York: Monthly Review Press.
Ehrenreich, B. and English, D. (1979) *For Her Own Good: 100 Years of the Experts' Advice to Women*, London: Pluto Press.
Forster, D.P. (1976) 'Social class differences in sickness and general practitioner consultations', *Health Trends*, 8: 29–32.

Foucault, M. (1973) *The Birth of the Clinic: An Archaeology of Perception*, London: Tavistock.

Freidson, (1970a) *Professional Dominance: The Social Structure of Medical Care*, New York: P. Atherton.

—— (1970b) *The Profession of Medicine: A Study of the Sociology of Applied Knowledge*, New York: Harper Row.

Garnikov, E. (1978) 'Sexual division of labour: the case of nursing', in A. Kuhn and A.M. Wolpe (eds) *Feminism and Materialism*, London: Routledge.

George, V. and Wilding, P. (1976) *Ideology and Social Welfare*, London: Routledge and Kegan Paul.

Harris, D. (1987) *Justifying State Welfare*, Oxford: Blackwell.

Harrison, S., Hunter, D. and Pollitt, C. (1990) *The Dynamics of British Health Policy*, London: Unwin Hyman.

Hart, T. (1971) 'The inverse care law', *The Lancet*, 1: 405–12.

Illich, I. (1976) *Limits to Medicine: Medical Nemesis*, 2nd edn, London: Marion Boyars.

Klein, R. (1995) *The New Politics of the NHS*, 3rd edn, London: Longman.

Le Grand, J. (1982) *The Strategy of Equality: Redistribution and the Social Services*, London: Allen and Unwin.

McKeown, T. (1976) *The Modern Rise of Population and the Role of Medicine: Dream, Mirage or Nemesis?*, Rock Carling Monograph, London: Nuffield Provincial Hospitals Trust.

McKinlay, J.B. and Stoeckle, J. (1988) 'Corporatization and the social transformation of doctoring' *International Journal of Health Services*, 18(2): 191–203.

Navarro, V. (1986) *Crisis, Health and Medicine*, London: Tavistock.

Oakley, A. (1983) 'Women and health care', in J. Lewis (ed) *Women's Welfare, Women's Rights*, London: Croom Helm.

Organisation for Economic Cooperation and Development (OECD) (1981) *The Welfare State in Crisis*, Paris: OECD.

Sretzer, S. (1988) 'The importance of social intervention in Britain's mortality decline 1850–1914: a reinterpretation of the role of public health', *Social History of Medicine*, 1: 1–37.

Strong, P.M. (1979) 'Sociological imperialism and the profession of medicine' *Social Science and Medicine*, 13a: 199–215.

Titmuss, R. (1963) *Essays on the Welfare State*, 2nd edn, London: Allen and Unwin.

CHAPTER 3

Scanning the future: the environmental context

'Change is not what it used to be' (Handy 1989).

The ideological debates which surround the NHS often seem to take place in a vacuum, oblivious to the massive social, economic and technological changes which are taking place in postindustrial societies. Like any other major social institution, the NHS is profoundly affected by these developments and will continue to be so.

This chapter looks at change in three major areas. First, the effects of economic restructuring, the debates surrounding 'post-Fordist' developments, and their significance for the delivery of welfare. Second, the questions posed by demographic change and how the NHS is affected, both as an employer and provider of services. Finally, some of the new dilemmas and opportunities posed by developments in medical technology and the related sciences and the need to subject these to rigorous assessment and evaluation. The conclusion draws the three parts of the chapter together and discusses their inter-relationships.

Part 1 – Facing up to the information age

Handy (1989) argues that while most people would accept that the pace of change has speeded up, few realise its scale and ferocity. Profound technological developments have already critically restructured the economies of developed societies from the production of things to the production of information. The evidence lies in the changing occupational structure, in particular the shift away from manufacturing to service industry. Manufacturing employment fell in Britain by over one-third from 1971 to 1990, to barely 23 per cent of all employees, with a corresponding one-third increase in the service sector. The main growth in the service sector, however, has been in jobs which are connected in some way with information (Dept. of Employment 1993), a trend which is projected to continue (Lindley and Wilson 1994).

Some of the 'megatrends' of the information age could reverse those associated with industrial society (Naisbitt 1990, Handy 1989). First, the falling real cost of information technology permits considerable decentralisation of production to take place, without loss of administrative control. Advances in computer networking, satellite communications and fibre-optics permit easy communication not only nationally but internationally between the component parts of an organisation, and between networks of suppliers, producers and distributors.

Second, the information society leads to a flattening of hierarchies, the creation of slimmer, flatter organisational structures. The communication and control function of middle management becomes redundant when everyone has their own computer terminal. In addition, the information society substitutes brain for brawn: 70 per cent of its jobs require intellectual skills and at least half of them require a professional qualification or education to degree standard. Such workers are expensive and in short supply, cannot be managed by the old 'command and control' hierarchies, and expect more scope for creativity and autonomy in their work. Hierarchy is under attack for another reason as well. Information is by its nature a shared resource. Once produced it is hard to control. If knowledge is power, then power is going to be dispersed.

Developments in the world economy

The development of powerful information technologies has been accompanied by dramatic transformations in the global economy and the organisation of production. National economies have become relatively less self-contained, more opened up to global processes of production and competition. Multinational corporations 'source' their finished products from factories or workshops around the world, networked into complex production and distribution chains. To support these endeavours, capital markets have also internationalised, generating large flows of direct investment to finance corporate expansion in different countries. The growth of internationalisation has been accompanied by the expansion of trade and investment between states, the deregulation of previously protected economies and the opening up of established trading blocs to foreign competition.

These combined sets of forces have had a dramatic effect on Britain's economy, shifting her patterns of trade and exposing her industry to much fiercer competition. In addition the pace of technological development means that the advantages to companies from new products or improvements are short-lived and soon overtaken by others. Markets have also become increasingly fragmented and complex as rising affluence leads to demands by discriminating consumers for differentiated products.

How have companies coped with these pressures? A major survey by the Henley Centre for Forecasting (1991) found that they had done so in ways which reduced their fixed overheads, increased their market responsiveness and enhanced their capacity to adapt and deal with change. *Flexibility* and *decentralisation* have become the new key words. Many companies have considerably slimmed down and changed their corporate structures. Much more autonomy is given to subsidiary companies although they must still meet key financial and policy targets. IT provides the 'organisational glue' for corporate objectives to be maintained within looser federal structures of inter-dependent companies.

Internal structures modelled on the 'organismic' organisation (Burns and Stalker 1961) with flexible project-based teams, are better placed to respond rapidly to change than fixed hierarchies. IT also allows greater devolution of decision making to the lowest practical level and allows operational staff to take responsibility for ever-widening aspects of their total work: accessing information, planning, budgeting, delivery and quality control. In theory this should make the content of jobs more satisfying and skilled, and allow more scope for innovation.

Flexibility is also enhanced by contracting out peripheral or non-core functions. (Atkinson 1985, Atkinson and Meager 1986). Handy argues that an efficient organisational design for the future is the 'shamrock' organisation: one leaf of the shamrock contains the 'core' professional staff, those with the crucial knowledge on which the organisation depends, from whom much is expected and to whom much is given. The expense of this 'core' group forces organisations to shed all non-core activities and staff to specialist contractors who in theory do the work better and at less cost. This is the second leaf of the shamrock. Finally there is the flexible workforce of part-timers and temporary workers which has seen the biggest employment growth since the early 1980s, particularly in the service sector, and which accounts for the majority of the growth in female employment. By this means the organisation tries to adapt to peaks and troughs in demand without taking on the burden of high fixed labour costs. The workforce therefore becomes increasingly polarised and fragmented, between the skilled and unskilled, core and periphery, and between the knowledge workers and those who lack the qualifications to join their ranks.

Fordism, post-Fordism and the welfare state

How are we to theorise and explain these changes? In this section we examine the increasingly influential notion that advanced capitalist economies are experiencing a transition from 'Fordist' forms of mass production and mass consumption of standardised products to 'post-Fordist' forms of flexible production to meet a growing diversity of consumer tastes. The origins of these concepts derive from Marxist regulation theory (Aglietta 1979), theories of 'flexible specialisation' (Hirst and Zeitlin 1991) and the concept of the 'flexible firm' of core and periphery workers (Atkinson 1984; Atkinson and Meager 1986). A detailed examination of this broad and contentious body of theory is beyond the scope of the chapter, but a brief outline of the main arguments is given below, in order to focus on what is our main interest, the role and restructuring of the welfare state.

Central to the change from Fordism to post-Fordism, it is argued, are changes in the structure of production (embracing production technologies, the organisation of the labour process and strategies of management). Fordism was based on the mass production of goods manufactured in long runs on assembly lines, requiring massive capital investment in fixed and inflexible plant. These methods of production were pioneered and typified by Henry Ford's first car plant in Detroit, just before the First World War, where Ford's technical innovations were supported and underpinned by the organisational innovations of F.W. Taylor and the principles of 'scientific management'. In effect these methods fragmented and deskilled work tasks to an extraordinary degree, and subjected labour to rigid discipline and strong management control. (For further discussion on scientific management see pages 122–23.) The concentration of large numbers of semi-skilled workers in large plants, however, facilitated the emergence of strong trade unions and collective wage bargaining, often conducted at national level through corporatist arrangements between government, employers and unions.

Central to post-Fordism are the technological developments we have discussed above, which permit the development of flexible specialisation and decentralised production methods in response to the market pressures of global competition. At the same time 'flexible' employment practices and the growth of the periphery workforce tend to weaken trade union negotiating strength and collective wage bargaining, substituting more localised and individualised arrangements.

The application of the concepts of Fordism and post-Fordism to welfare has occurred in two ways. The first uses the framework to analyse changes in the development of the welfare state, and in particular the restructuring which has occurred in the 1980s and 1990s in Britain and other industrialised countries. This 'neo-marxist' approach, draws explicitly on regulation theory (Aglietta 1979) and is exemplified by the work of Jessop (1990, 1991a, 1991b), also Hirsch (1991). The second approach, which Williams (1994) calls the 'radical technological' approach, examines the way key aspects of post-Fordism are being introduced into welfare, and speculates on alternative future scenarios. This approach is exemplified by the work of Hoggett (1987, 1991) and Murray (1991). An overview of both approaches is given below.

Neo-Marxists go beyond the analysis of changes in the structure of production to specify the state mechanisms (political, ideological, social and economic) which are congruent with and regulate a particular regime of capitalist accumulation and show how these are changing in the transition from Fordism to post-Fordism. In particular, the Keynesian welfare state serves as one of the crucial internal regulatory mechanisms under Fordism. By its commitment to full employment and macro demand management it maintains high and stable levels of demand for industry's products; facilitates the appropriate cultural and behavioural attributes (including norms of mass consumption), and manages the dysfunctions and conflicts emerging from the production system by the provision of welfare services and benefits.

Yet the very institutions which underpinned and stabilised a Fordist regime of accumulation, helping to engineer the long boom from the end of the war to the early 1970s, were also seen to be the cause of its inability to adapt to changing international conditions in the world economy and technological developments in the late 1970s. The Keynesian welfare state was seen as a major cause of the 'rigidities' faced by capital in its attempts to restructure along 'post-Fordist' lines. In the British case, the organised strength of trade unionism posed particular difficulties for capital's attempts to modernise in the face of intensified competition and declining levels of profit. The Keynesian welfare state was deeply implicated in this since it strengthened the negotiating power of labour in the market place by the provision of generous social benefits and the commitment to full employment 'driving up wage costs beyond corresponding rises in productivity, hampering the process of structural adjustment and consolidating the veto powers of organised labour' (Pierson 1994: 98). The costs of welfare continued to grow even as revenues declined, leading to the 'crisis of welfare' discussed in Chapter 2.

So far the argument has been conducted at a high level of abstraction. In practice there was considerable variety in the forms and effectiveness of regulatory regimes under Fordism in different states, and the restructuring of welfare, in the transition from Fordism to post-Fordism, is equally subject to different approaches and constraints. The UK under Thatcherism was marked by an aggressibly neoliberal response in which '. . . social policy [was] made much more explicitly subservient to the interests of the economy and wherever possible subject to the rigours of market-based competition' (Pierson 1994: 102). The balance of power between employers and labour has been 'redressed' through abandoning the commitment to full employment and through legislation to curb union rights. In addition an attack on the power of professional groups (particularly in health and education) has been accompanied by a remodelled and assertive managerialism, based on private sector principles and practices (Pollitt 1990; Newman and Clark 1994). A massive programme of privatisation has transferred much of the public sector back to private ownership and what was left has been subjected to competition through the introduction of quasi-markets and programmes of compulsory competitive tendering.

In parallel with these changes and the introduction of a 'business' discourse into public agencies has been an allied stress on the recipients of services as 'consumers' and 'customers'. The private and voluntary sectors have been encouraged to take a greater role in the provision of welfare in the name of 'consumer choice' and the rhetoric of 'consumerism' underlays such things as the Citizen's Charter and the publication of league tables of performance for schools and hospitals. While business has been given a more important role in running the 'local state' (Cochrane 1991) – as appointees on quangos, for example – the role of the traditional local power centre, local authorities, has been weakened. At the same time, reforms in education, training and the social security system have been geared towards vocational training and the promotion of 'enterprise'; improving work incentives and the stigmatisation of the non-working poor. The aim of this emergent post-Fordist welfare state has been:

> to strengthen . . . structural competitiveness of the national economy by intervening on the supply side and to subordinate social policy to the needs of labour market flexibility and/or to the constraints of international competition.
> (Jessop 1994: 24)

Yet the success of the neoliberal project in achieving its aims seems doubtful. Many of the changes introduced by the Conservatives have had perverse and contradictory consequences. For example, the flexibility of the labour force has not been enhanced by Conservative housing policies which erected new barriers to labour mobility (Pierson 1994: 105) Constant policy change in education and training does not seem to have notably increased the skill levels of British young people, as assessed by international comparisons (Guardian 1996a, 1996b). The fragmentation of the 'local state' has made strategic planning and policy coordination increasingly difficult to achieve. Jessop speculates that:

> Rather than moving towards an efficient and competitive post-Fordist regime, we seem to be moving further down the international economic hierarchy as flawed post-Fordism replaces flawed Fordism.
> (1994: 35)

The **radical technological** approach comes to a similar conclusion but by a different route. Here the main focus is to trace the way post-Fordist developments in the structure of industrial production are paralleled by similar developments in welfare and the public services, and their potential for creating either a more 'socially valued, decentralised and equitable, democratic and user-led public service' (Williams 1994:

54) or for imposing different forms of political and social control. Both Hoggett and Murray argue that in the Keynesian welfare state many of the features of Fordist/Taylorist industry were replicated by standardised forms of service which allowed little scope for choice or diversity. Delivered by inflexible and remote bureaucracies, they were managed by Taylorist methods, with staff who were deskilled and closely controlled.

Today the same patterns of organisation and management which IT has recently made possible in the industrial sector are seen to be emerging in welfare: more decentralised patterns of service provision, devolved management, more pluralistic sources of provision to meet more diverse needs. However, the political purposes to which these technological capacities are used are still uncertain: will they be used to empower users and providers in new ways or to exert new, perhaps more 'remote' forms of control? (Hoggett 1994: 46)

There are difficulties, however, in applying models derived from industry and manufacturing to the welfare sector, or in characterising the changes taking place there as a qualitatively different shift between Fordism and post-Fordism (Hood 1990). Indeed in regulation theory the difficulty of subjecting 'human' services in the public sector like health and education to Fordist labour processes was a main cause of the 'crisis of Fordism' in the 1970s. It was difficult to increase productivity, and hence to control costs, because of their labour-intensive and professionalised nature.

The links between changes in technology and organisational change in the public sector are also unclear in Hoggett's version of 'post-Fordism' (Held 1996: 580–81) and the developments taking place there reflect contradictory tendencies, producing new rigidities as well as flexibilities for employers and employees alike (Cochrane 1991). Critics have also argued that the dominant paradigm of the 'new' public management is an updated version of Taylorism, which springs out of Fordist labour disciplines and controls (Hood 1991; Pollitt 1993).

A flexible labour force?

The difficulties of applying the theory in the public sector become clearer if we look more closely at the concept of a flexible labour force, and the ways in which 'flexible' strategies have been pursued in health and social care.

Flexibility could mean:

- Functional flexibility – reskilling or multi-skilling workers to take on a larger number of tasks and break down demarcation lines between jobs;
- Numerical flexibility – which enables employers to match labour inputs to peaks and troughs in demand. This embraces a number of

strategies – part-time and temporary working; subcontracting or 'outsourcing'; shiftworking and overtime;

- Working hours flexibility – is a special category of numerical flexibility, and refers to changes in the number and timing of hours worked either weekly or annually;
- Flexibility in place of work – refers to traditional homeworking and also 'teleworking' – working at home using computer and telecommunications equipment.

The *Employment in Britain* survey has provided general evidence of increasing *functional flexibility* across all occupational levels which is strongly associated with the use of computerised or automated equipment (Dept. Employment 1994). However, increases in skill demands also cover a wide range of general work skills, related to job enlargement (taking on a larger number of roles at a similar level in the production process) and job enrichment (the merging of tasks at different levels).

Systematic survey evidence specifically for health and social care is lacking, but many aspects of implementing the NHS and Community Care Act 1990 as well as developments like clinical management, expansion of nursing roles and responsibilities, and accelerated introduction of computerised information and management systems have all exerted similar pressures there. Developments like the 'generic hotel worker', who can be flexibly deployed between cleaning, catering and laundry functions, 'integrated care teams' in community care, in which professional demarcations are broken down, and 'patient-centred care' initiatives in hospitals, are other instances (Pinch 1994: 210). 'Re-engineering' whole hospitals, pioneered by the Leicester Royal Infirmary and King's Healthcare Trust, London, which involves starting with a blank sheet and plotting how a patient would best be treated if existing procedures did not exist, produces even more radical change in job descriptions and skills (Brindle 1996).

When we turn to numerical flexibility, however, the evidence is more equivocal. The NHS has always made extensive use of part-time and temporary employment contracts, shiftworking and contracting out, so there is nothing particularly novel or distinctively 'post-Fordist' about them. However, there has undoubtedly been an intensification of these trends since the NHS and Community Care Act was passed in 1990. NHS trusts are using their new personnel freedoms to adopt 'core-periphery' employment strategies to reduce their fixed overheads, and making greater use of temporary contracts, particularly for nurses. 'Management by contract' has been institutionalised for clinical as well as support services, and 'outsourcing' and contracting out is common. But these trends reflect a relentless and politically willed drive to force down unit costs which often imposes new forms of *inflexibility* on managers as well as employees. Competitive tendering procedures may mean that inhouse staff have to accept more rigid discipline and hierarchical control to win the contract, not less. Highly specific contracts may be difficult to renegotiate easily and subcontracted staff will do just what they are contracted to do, no more and no less.

Finally, turning to the last two categories of flexible labour market strategies, the Department of Employment argues that changing the patterns of hours worked can be a means by which the permanent full-time workforce can 'compete' in terms of flexibility with part-time staff but is also the means by which 'family friendly' policies can be introduced. Flexitime, job-sharing, teleworking, term time or annualised hours contracts can all be ways of ensuring employees can strike a better balance between work and family commitments. Yet the Department's own evidence suggests that these practices are still not common in Britain (Department of Employment 1993), indeed the evidence we have suggests an *intensification* of working hours and practices. Full-time employees in Britain work a longer week than in any other EU country; 44 per cent of British workers say they come home exhausted and 41 per cent of managers work over 50 hours a week (Demos 1995). The 'long hours' culture has affected the NHS as well. 60 per cent of health service managers reported working over 45 hours per week, with top managers reporting an average of 56 hours in a recent survey by the Institute of Health Service Managers (Moore 1995).

In conclusion, even this brief empirical excursion demonstrates the complexity of the evidence and the difficulties of interpreting it within the Fordist/post-Fordist framework. Some sceptics believe that theories of post-Fordism are either tautological or of little utility in explaining the specifics of social and economic change (see for instance, Byrne 1994; Cochrane 1991; 1993; Rustin 1989). However, we can salvage something of utility from this debate. In particular the neo-Marxist variant provides a framework linking what is happening in welfare to broader changes in the economy and society at a national and inter-national level, admittedly at a high level of abstraction. In addition, although there is still an uneasily functionalist ring to the explanation of change in terms of the onward march of capitalist restructuring, the open-ended, indeterminate nature of this process in the postmodern era is also stressed, leaving room for political and social choices about the form a new welfare settlement will take in future.

Part 2 – Facing up to demography

Post-Fordists place a heavy emphasis on changes in production and consumption in explanations of the restructuring of welfare and tend to ignore or confound the influence of other important factors, such as a changing demography. Yet demographic predictions were an important component of the financial crisis of welfare predicted for Western states by the OECD in the late 1970s. Since then much has been written about the ageing of Western populations and its economic consequences. The facts for this country are as follows.

Declining fertility

Britain faced a 35 per cent reduction in the number of 18-year olds in the decade 1984–94, with most of the reduction taking place after 1990. This marks a long-term trend of declining fertility which appears to have stabilised at 1.8 births per woman, below population replacement rate.

An ageing workforce

Between 1993 and 2000 the civilian labour force will grow from 27.9 million to 28.7 million (Dept. of Employment 1995: 28) but due to the precipitate drop in the younger age groups a sustained period of ageing within the working population has begun.

The feminisation of the workforce

Since 1970 the number of men in the workforce has fallen by 0.7 million while the number of women has risen by 2.8 million. By the end of the century women will make up 45 per cent of the total civilian labour force. This will reinforce the trend to lower fertility. Once women can control unexpected births through contraception they spend longer in the labour force and invest more in education and qualifications which in turn increases their earning potential and increases the economic incentives against starting a family. This is borne out by research on birth rates since 1952: higher earnings for women depress the birth rate, higher earnings for men raise it (Ermisch 1990). Additionally Britain's high divorce rate (nearly 40 per cent in 1993) and the economic insecurity experienced by lone mothers is another incentive for women to stay in the workforce and increase their skills.

Growing numbers of elderly people

The proportion of the population aged over 65 is currently stable (at 16 per cent since 1984). This is predicted to increase to 17 per cent by 2011, and then more rapidly as the postwar 'baby boomers' reach retirement. The number of people over 65 will increase by 50 per cent to over 14 million between 2001 and 2131, from one in six to one in four of the population if current fertility trends hold constant (a heroic assumption to make over a thirty-year period). Within the overall age group a further significant ageing is taking place, which has been termed the 'ageing of the aged' (OECD 1994) due to increases in life expectancy, currently standing at 74 for men and 79 for women. Only 4 per cent of the population are currently over 80, but this is predicted to rise to 5 per cent by the year 2021 (CSO 1996).

Demographic trends and the labour market: the case of nursing

The NHS is the biggest civilian employer in Europe and the largest employer of women. The health care sector accounts for 5 per cent of the UK workforce, employing 1.5 million people in 1990 of which one million were NHS staff. 78 per cent of those workers were female, and the largest group are nurses, accounting for 50 per cent of the total (NHS Executive 1995). The NHS is therefore a key player in the labour market, particularly for female labour.

With declining numbers of young entrants to the labour market and growing demands for skilled and educated staff (IMS 1987) skill shortages seriously affected many sectors of the economy in the late 1980s. Many analysts predicted a 'demographic timebomb' for the NHS which had traditionally been a major recruiter of young women with five or more qualifications at GCSE level. Some projections showed that the NHS would need to increase its recruitment from one in three of the available pool to nearly one in two (Callender and Pearson 1989; Committee of Public Accounts 1987; Reid 1986). There was a number of ways of tackling the problem:

- reduce the demand for qualified nurses by more efficient management of the existing labour force to reduce wastage rates and use professional nursing skills more appropriately (Beardshaw and Davies 1990; DHSS 1986; Mersey RHA 1989, National Audit Office 1985, 1987).
- refocus and widen recruitment to nursing by attracting 'non-traditional' groups – mature women, men, less-qualified entrants.
- measures to improve the attractiveness of nursing as a career in competition with others, which might mean focusing both on pay and non-pay factors.

There were four main ways in which these strategies were put into practice. First, new management systems for assessing nursing workload related to patient dependency levels, and sometimes including quality of care indicators, have been widely implemented (Harrison and Pollitt 1994: 68). Skill-mix exercises, designed to substitute unqualified for qualified labour, have substantially reduced aggregate demand for qualified nurses. For example, between September 1990 and 1991 alone the

NHS lost 15,400 qualified nurses – a drop of 5.2 per cent – but the number of unqualified staff rose by 137,400, a rise of 17 per cent.

Secondly, the education and training of nurses and associated workers is being radically restructured in line with the Project 2000 proposals of the United Kingdom Central Council for Nursing, Midwifery and Health Visiting (UKCC), published in 1986. Project 2000 argued the necessity for change as much in terms of keeping pace with service needs and professional nursing developments as tackling the deficiencies of existing nurse training and the challenges posed to recruitment by demographic trends. The main proposal was the creation of a single level of registered nurse through a three-year education and training programme, comprising a general foundation followed by specialist branch programmes. Student nurses should be supernumary for their whole training, not used as exploited 'pairs of hands' on the wards, and the privileging of academic, educational needs over service needs was reflected in a change of location: out of Colleges of Nursing located within hospitals, and into institutions of higher education.

The authors expected more specialist practitioners to develop in all aspects of hospital and community nursing, acting as team leaders in many cases. The 'new nurse' would have a higher and broader level of competencies: 'a knowledgeable doer, able to marshall information to make an assessment of need, devise a plan of care and implement, monitor and evaluate it' (UKCC 1987: 2). Complementing the role of the 'new nurse' is the new health care support worker. The role has evolved as a basic but flexible care worker, with a minimum of three months skill-based training, who can gain a qualification validated by the National Council for Vocational Qualifications. This will be a flexible qualification which can be used in other sectors of the caring industry, or be traded up to enable access to nursing, social work or other occupations. Through this system of flexible 'bridges and ladders', the NHS hoped to tap new sources of labour into nursing itself, from unqualified school leavers, previously unemployed middle-aged women, and men.

Thirdly, in a move designed to make more explicit links between qualifications, experience and pay, the nursing career structure was regraded into nine main clinical grades in 1988. This was matched by substantial pay rises, particularly for more senior grades, and bursaries for Project 2000 student learners.

Finally, under the impetus of major criticisms about the failure of the NHS to be aware of the needs of its overwhelmingly female workforce, the service showed interest in a range of equal opportunity measures and began to experiment with crèches, job sharing, flexible working, stay-in-touch schemes for staff taking career breaks, and so on. Wilson and Stilwell (1992: 123) conclude from their short survey of these developments that although much more awareness was shown about the issues by health authorities, this was not matched by the scale of their response, although one area of real success was improving the representation of women at senior managerial and board level, through the initiatives of the Women's Unit within the NHS Executive.

In the event, the crisis of recruitment was averted, at least temporarily (for the re-emergence of nursing shortages, see Mark 1996; British Medical Journal 1996). The length and depth of the recession and high levels of unemployment were partly responsible for this but rapid changes in the structure and organisation of nursing, particularly the replacement of qualified by unqualified staff, played an important part, as discussed above. Taken together, the different strands of the nursing 'package' appear to represent a major attempt to meet future demographic challenges, but they can also be analysed within a post-Fordist framework. For example, there is explicit acknowledgement in Project 2000 of the trends towards decentralised work patterns. Increasingly nurses and their assistants will work in many different health care settings in the community, often in multidisciplinary teams, aided by information technology to relay essential information for planning and resource management purposes to small 'head office' staffs. The split between the highly trained Project 2000 Diplomate and the health care support workers who do most of the basic physical tasks of care has similarities to Atkinson's model of the flexible firm, with a re-skilled elite whose jobs encompass an increasingly wide range of tasks, and a larger number of numerically flexible, less skilled workers (Atkinson 1985).

However, the *content* of those skills and the roles of the core and periphery workforce reflect a continuing (and gendered) struggle for professional autonomy and occupational control by nurses. Project 2000 embodies new philosophies of care and a new approach to the nursing process, which aims to replace routinised, task-centred nursing with a more holistic, patient-centred approach, and replace an intuitive approach to nursing with a more analytical one. Witz (1995: 30) argues that this strategy reflected the concern of nursing leaders that postwar nursing had developed as an extension of the doctor's diagnostic and curative role, emphasising technical, medically derived curative tasks with caring increasingly left to nursing auxiliaries. The 'new nursing' is an attempt to redefine a professional role based on the carative kernel of nursing which could, at the same time, 'establish the centrality of clinical nursing for qualified nurses, assert the independence of nursing from medicine and distinguish the trained nurse from the untrained auxilliary' (Dickinson 1982: 62, quoted in Witz 1995).

Witz argues that this strategy is based on an *enhanced* nursing role, in which the nurse establishes a unique sphere of competence and autonomous practice, a role which is complementary to the patient, rather than subservient to the doctor. An alternative model would be *extending* the role of the nurse: enlarging their sphere of competence to allow them to take over some specialist medical tasks and functions, devolved to them by doctors. The enhanced role may be seen as reflecting broader, holistic models of health and patients' needs, the second capitalises on the need for cheaper ways of delivering health care and new modes of delivery (the growing importance of primary care for example). Moves to reduce junior doctor's hours and difficulties in medical recruitment in some specialities also support this development (Witz 1995: 31). The carative strategy is therefore a way forward paved by nurses themselves to establish a sphere of autonomous practice; the second reflects the pragmatic concerns of doctors about overload and the desire to devolve routinised technical tasks to nurses, still under their control. Consequently the first model appears to have provoked more medical opposition than the second (Witz 1995: 34–36).

Whether nurses will succeed in establishing themselves as 'professionals of care' rather than 'handmaidens of cure' (Pashley and Henry 1990) will also be affected by the responses of another powerful occupational group, managers. At first sight it appears to be a costly strategy which managers, trying to hold down costs in a competitive, market environment, would be expected to oppose. Yet there may be a convergence of interests between the two groups, around the concept of the health care support worker. The cost-cutting attractions to managers of a flexible, cheap care worker balance the higher educational and salary costs of the new nursing elite, although there are dangers for nurses if this trend goes too far (see, for instance, Hancock 1996).

It is clear that what happens to nursing as a profession in the 21st century will depend on a complex mixture of forces which cannot be analysed simply within a post-Fordist framework, or seen as a straightforward response to demographic and labour market trends. Changes in the organisation and delivery of health care; models of care which reflect enhanced conceptions of patient need; changing interests and power struggles between gendered occupational and professional groups: all intertwine to leave the final outcome of nursing's professional project uncertain.

Demographic change and the costs of care

We turn now to another aspect of demographic change which has attracted much alarmist attention, the projected burdens and costs of caring for growing numbers of elderly people. These projections are also based on assumptions which need re-examining.

Growth in the number of elderly people in the population is one important source of growing demands on health and social services. People over 65 comprised 16 per cent of the population in 1990–91, but

40 per cent of total Hospital and Community Health Service spending was directed at this group. Similarly 40 per cent of local authority social services expenditure goes on the elderly. The health and social service needs of the elderly rise exponentially with age. Current estimates suggest that those over 85 cost on average £4,000 per year, or 15 times the cost of a person of working age.

Bleak scenarios of the 'economic burden' that elderly people impose on the working population drive current policies. They underlay the 1988 Social Security Act and the impetus given to private pensions. They also drove the response of early Thatcher governments to health and social care for the elderly. For example, the Health Advisory Service (1983) warned of a 'rising tide' of senile dementia which could 'overwhelm the entire health care system' and a consultative paper in 1981 argued that the informal, voluntary and private sectors must play a bigger role in the provision of care. This 'mixed economy of care' was given statutory force by the 1990 NHS and Community Care Act nine years later. Assumptions about the ageing process and the costs of care are being used to legitimate major changes in the scope, scale and mode of welfare funding and provision for the elderly.

Yet the problems that Britain's ageing population pose for the cost of welfare in future are, in a comparative context, not pressing. The process of ageing in Britain is relatively well advanced and it has the oldest population of the seven leading industrial nations (known as the G7). It is true that the ratio between the numbers in the population of working age and the number of pensioners will worsen, but not as dramatically or as adversely as in the majority of first world states (see Table 3.1 below).

Table 3.1 **Ratio of persons aged 15–64 to persons aged 65 and over in the EU countries.**

	1960	*1980*	*2000*	*2025*
Ireland	5.15	5.46	6.85	5.08
Portugal	7.87	6.10	4.63	3.64
Spain	7.81	5.88	4.39	3.38
United Kingdom	**5.56**	**4.26**	**4.24**	**3.12**
France	5.32	4.57	4.24	3.01
Greece	7.94	4.88	3.89	3.01
Belgium	5.41	4.57	4.05	2.95
Italy	7.04	4.90	4.02	2.90
Denmark	6.06	4.48	4.37	2.73
Luxembourg	6.25	5.00	4.33	2.66
West Germany	6.25	4.27	4.00	2.59

(*Source*: Adapted from Ermisch, 1990: 45)

From having the lowest ratio in Europe in 1980, only Ireland, Portugal and Spain will have a more advantageous position than the UK in 2040. In addition the share of national resources devoted to welfare in Britain is smaller than most industrial nations, and we rank 17th out of 21 countries in the OECD in the proportion of national income devoted to social expenditure (Hills 1993: 10). It should not be beyond the economy's capacity to meet present modest service standards for elderly people in the next century.

To put this into perspective and demonstrate what it would mean to the taxpayer, Hills shows that the costs of unemployment to the public finances over *three* years during the recession of 1990–93 outweigh the higher demands expected from an ageing population over the next *fifty*. This is to assume, however, that present policies and the models of ageing they are based on remain the same.

'Downhill all the way'

Current policy assumptions about the economic costs of the elderly in future are premised on bleak models of ageing and the ageing process, which Gail Wilson summarises as 'downhill all the way' (Wilson 1991). Western attitudes to old people have historically been negative, portraying the 'seventh age of man' as one of helplessness and decline. Policy statements on the elderly have similarly reflected the view that old age is associated with an irreversible decline into disability and dependency regardless of differences in income, class, gender and race which significantly affect the experience of ageing. Means (1988) argues that some authors treat the total group of 'pensioners' (a group which may cover 40 years given the trend to early retirement) as a 'special needs' category.

Increasingly this model of ageing is being challenged by a growing body of work. Walker (1980, 1987), Townsend (1981) and Bosanquet (1987) have argued that old people are forced into dependency by the rest of society through early retirement policies, stigmatising social security, and welfare services which undermine independence. Arber (1996) argues that current attitudes are both ageist and sexist, given that there are 50 per cent more women than men over 65, and three women to every man over 85. Far from being an unproductive burden on the working population, the contributions made by older people are considerable. Over one-third of all informal care for older people is provided by those who are over 65 themselves. They are a major source of child care for their working children and their partners and form the backbone of the voluntary sector.

The view that growing longevity inevitably means a growing and costly burden of disability in future has also been challenged. For instance about one-fifth of health care costs are devoted to people in their last year of life, and represent the costs of dying. US studies (reported in Hunter 1996) suggest that the most long-lived, who die over the age of 80, incur only 80 per cent of the costs of those who die between the ages of 65 and 79, and that these are concentrated mainly on nursing home and domiciliary care. The higher costs associated with deaths at younger ages are almost wholly related to the use of high technology procedures and other 'medical practices of dubious efficicacy' (p. 21). The problem relates to the inappropriate use of 'rescue medicine', (see p. 44 below), not ageing per se.

Related to this is the question of whether longer life means worsening health, or whether there has been a 'compression of morbidity' with the onset of disability pushed back into fewer years before death. In this 'terminal drop' model of ageing (Wilson 1991) old people stay reasonably healthy and independent till some final trauma takes them off. Recent research in this area is summarised by Arber who concludes that 'older people now have lower levels of disability and fewer chronic disabling conditions than in the past', and that marked improvements continue to be made in relatively short time periods (Arber 1996: 31). The improving health status of people in old age reflects improving conditions of life experienced in youth and middle age, but the research evidence also suggests that health promotion strategies aimed at the middle-aged and elderly could be a highly cost-effective policy option. Fries demonstrated this in his research with 6,000 retirees in California. Those who received a low-cost health promotion package recorded 20 per cent lower medical claims than those who did not, and the savings amounted to six times the cost of the package (cited in Maynard 1990).

Nevertheless, for the foreseeable future a considerable proportion of elderly people *will* require care at specific periods of their lives. The proportion of those over 85 unable to bathe, shower or wash all over is seven times higher than those in the 65–69 age group (Walker 1987) and the percentage of people receiving a 'personalised social service' (home help, meals, day centre, district nurse, health visitor or chiropodist) increases six-fold between those two age groups (Hills 1994). The current direction, implementation and financing of community and long-stay care after the 1990 legislation has caused much public concern, and is discussed in the following chapters. Here we should point out that the demographic evidence suggests that cost may not be as difficult a problem for society to solve as the employment of paid carers, as dependency ratios shift and the supply of informal female carers is further shrunk by their engagement in the labour force. In 1900, for every individual over the age of 85 (the group with the most pressing care needs), there were 24 women in their fifties (the group which traditionally provided the care). By the year 2000 the ratio will be one to three.

In conclusion the challenges posed by an ageing population need radical rethinking and immense cultural changes in attitudes. The resources, powers and energies of older people need to be positively harnessed and policies should be geared to sustaining their independence for as long as possible. The growing consumer power of older people and the fact that already one in four voters is retired may help to bring this about. From the perspective of the NHS, considerable health gains and reductions in expenditure over the longer term could be achieved by expanding health promotion work with older people, a previously neglected group.

Part 3 – Pushing back the boundaries: developments in medical technology

If demography acts as a constraining context on health care provision, future developments in medical technology open up a bewildering scenario of choice. Medical advance not only enhances clinical capability, it carries with it profound ethical, legal, social and economic implications. Recent developments in the sale of organs for transplants, life support for profoundly handicapped or brain-damaged patients, or the treatment of infertility have rehearsed some of the dilemmas and controversies. These will multiply in future with the development of new technologies and new branches of science such as molecular biology (and its application, biotechnology) which is pushing medicine into a new age, from the pharmacologic to the molecular. The progress of transplant surgery illustrates how this is happening. Organ transplants have now become relatively common, with lungs, liver, kidneys, pancreas and cornea joining hearts. Survival rates and quality of life afterwards have improved, as new drugs have been developed to combat tissue rejection. Growing success rates have lead to long waiting lists for donor organs, and hence surgical experiments with animal organs. A remarkable step forward occurred with the 'transgenic pig', a pig whose genes have been altered to facilitate transplants and make its genetic material compatible with humans. The next step may involve the 'transplant' of genes themselves, reproduced in the laboratory or derived from animals, to prevent heart disease and the illnesses which affect other organs, so obviating the need for organ transplants at all (Appleby 1995a). The issues surrounding genetic engineering of this sort are profound and take society into uncharted moral, ethical and legal territory. Already genetic screening for inherited disorders or susceptibilities has raised issues about confidentiality of information, and its use by insurers and employers.

Turning to other developments, improvements in medical technologies in current use signify a trend to safer, non-invasive and more efficient procedures, enabling shorter inpatient stays, more day case and outpatient treatment. Lasers, endoscopes and catheters have had a profound effect on many specialities and hence on the way services are organised. For example, the NHS Executive have urged purchasers to achieve a target of 60 per cent of all elective surgery to be carried out on a day case basis by 1997–98. Further advances in 'keyhole' surgical techniques are predicted using robotics, virtual reality and operations by remote control (Bloor and Maynard 1994). Imaging techniques continue to improve the safety and accuracy of diagnosis as magnetic resonance imaging (MRI) and positron emission tomography are added to computerised tomography (CT scanners). Developments in biotechnology, in particular monoclonal antibodies, have made possible over-the-counter pregnancy and ovulation testing, and in future will enable many more diagnostic tests to be carried out simply in GPs' surgeries and patients' homes.

One clear implication of many current advances is growing decentralisation of health care. For example, the miniaturization of machinery and equipment based on electronics allow for greater portability of equipment which has implications for the location of diagnostic and treatment services, allowing much more to be done out of hospital, in the patient's home or GP's surgery. Another development is telemedicine, in which images can be conveyed digitally throughout the world, allowing a doctor in one area or country to help another thousands of miles away diagnose a problem, or guide them through a particular surgical technique. Developments such as these have major implications for the planning of different types of hospital in future.

This brief survey of medical developments demonstrates that once again information technology is at the heart of them, both in terms of diagnostic and therapeutic techniques and in linking patient data across hospital, community and primary care settings. This in turn underpins the move to decentralised care and the stripping away of much that is done in acute hospitals today. It also adds considerably to the quantity and quality of information to aid clinical and patient decision making, as specialist knowledge and the latest medical practice become more accessible through global databases and networks.

Evaluating medical technologies: dilemmas of choice

Sometimes new health care technologies, whether they be drugs, devices or clinical procedures, produce savings compared to the ones they replace or allow more cost-effective patterns of care. Often they promise improvements at much greater cost, widening the gap between the possible and the affordable. Just one example will illustrate the dilemmas. Taxol is a new anti-cancer drug which appears to extend survival rates from ovarian cancer from one to three years in US trials. The drug costs £9,000 per patient and there are 5,500 cases in Britain a year, but research studies have also demonstrated its promise as a first-line treatment for breast cancer, the most common cause of female cancer in Britain. With 24,000 cases a year the potential bill would be over £200 million pounds annually (Pallot 1996). Hence criteria to regulate and deploy the use of new and existing technologies have become increasingly urgent. Up to 50 per cent of the rise in health spending in the United States has been attributed not only to the introduction of new technologies but to the inappropriate overuse of existing ones (Banta and Thacker 1990).

As we saw in Chapter 2 this 'misappropriation' of resources draws the sharpest attacks from medicine's critics who would divert more resources into the 'low technology' care of the elderly and handicapped and effective illness prevention strategies. Lay opinion is ambivalent. Media publicity on the high-technology marvels of medicine fuel exaggerated expectations of what new 'breakthroughs' can achieve. Expensive technology like CT scanners can attract charitable funding on a large scale. In addition the public reacts strongly to media publicity of patients denied access to treatments, a recent high profile case being that of Jaymee Bowen whose father took Cambridge and Huntingdon Health Authority to court when they refused to fund a second bone marrow transplant for leukaemia (Guardian 1996). But many people are also aware from personal experience that high technology medicine is used inappropriately and ineffectively, prolonging or inflicting unnecessary suffering.

Jennett's (1986) admirably dispassionate analysis of the issues throws much needed light into this confused debate. Jennett argues that technological development in health care is a continuous process: today's 'high tech' is tomorrow's 'low tech'. In addition the costs and benefits of new procedures change over time as they become diffused more widely and in comparison to available alternatives. New technology may represent a cost saving on older forms of treatment but still represent a cost push in overall terms by extending the boundaries of those who could potentially benefit.

Arguments about the pros and cons of high-technology medicine are bedevilled by many false assumptions. One of these concerns the dichotomy between 'cure' versus 'care'. In practice much hospital medicine is neither. Jennett argues that 'most patients who now reach hospitals have progressive disease, the ultimate outcome of which cannot be influenced' (Jennett 1986: 4). This may be life-threatening like cancer, or nonlife-threatening but disabling like arthritis. Much high-technology medicine is therefore palliative, alleviating the effects of the disease by relieving pain or restoring mobility. It is part of the panoply of measures available to the clinician in the total care and management of the patient, perhaps over many years.

Another false assumption is that diagnosis leads to therapy and therapy to cure. Campaigns for diagnostic technology like CT whole-body scanners or magnetic resonance imaging are often premised on the assumption that earlier diagnosis will lead to an improved outcome for patients. The evidence to substantiate this is is limited to very few conditions. More often diagnosis reveals untreatable disease or leads to misplaced attempts at therapy. Jennett argues:

> Much of the debate about therapeutic technology is about its failures. These result largely from its use in patients who either do not benefit at all or who derive only temporary improvement or whose rescue leaves them more severely disabled than they were.
>
> (Jennett 1986: 13)

Much intensive care and cancer treatment falls into this category. The key message emerging from the discussion is that the deployment of medical technology must rest on rigorous and continuous assessments of effectiveness, cost and safety, and the appropriate selection of patients who can benefit.

An imperfect science, an uncertain art

> 'Few decisions in health care are made with good evidence'
>
> (Smith 1994: 217)

Many medical technologies in current use have not been evaluated and the standards of evaluation for many more do not meet the highest standards of scientific rigour (Smith 1991, 1993). Where good evidence is available it is often not widely disseminated or readily available (Antman *et al.* 1992) hence much medical practice is based on ignorance, confusion, whim and guesswork.

Many procedures are carried out which are ineffective. Of the top ten most common procedures in the NHS, only two – cataract removal and hernia repair – are known to be technically successful and beneficial (Appleby 1995b: 26). Conversely, known cost-effective treatments are not routinely provided. Breast cancer is a good example, where thousands of lives could be saved if known beneficial therapies in current use were universally applied (Health Service Journal 1995).

Some therapies are adopted with undue haste and enthusiasm. Szczepura (1992) argues that part of the explanation for the rapid adoption of technologies like magnetic resonance imaging lies in the prestige of possessing 'high-tech' equipment and the comparative ease with which MRI can be added to the existing diagnostic armoury. Technologies which require a major change in work patterns or practices (day surgery, for example) may be adopted much more slowly (Stocking 1992). However, often the reason for differential uptake is due to the fact that the evidence itself is confusing and difficult to interpret.

As the evidence of the overuse and misuse of medical technologies accumulates, most Western governments have responded by more formal systems of evaluation and assessment and growing interest in what has been termed the 'outcomes movement' (Epstein 1990).

Figure 3.1 ***Types of assessment***

Safety	⟹	Does the technology pose an unacceptable level of risk to patients?
Efficacy status	⟹	Does the technology improve patient's health when delivered under ideal conditions?
Effectiveness status	⟹	Does the technology improve patient's health when used in regular practice?
Efficiency	⟹	Do the benefits of using the technology justify the cost?

Source: Drummond (1992)

The 'gold standard' for assessing clinical efficacy and safety is the randomised control trial (RCT), where the outcomes of alternative forms of treatment are compared experimentally. The results of RCTs, however, relate to well-controlled, essentially ideal conditions but may reveal little about the effectiveness or safety of a procedure in widespread use in ordinary clinical practice. This may require much more work (see St. Leger *et al.* 1992 for a description of the different forms of clinical evaluation, and their strengths and weaknesses). Evidence of safety, efficacy and effectiveness must be complemented by evidence of efficiency and value for money. Such evidence is provided by economic evaluations which relate outcomes to the costs of achieving them, and can be built into clinical trials. The main types of economic evaluation are outlined below.

Economic evaluation in health care

Cost-effectiveness analysis – can be used to compare the different costs of achieving a given outcome by alternative means. For example, there are different ways to reach a given immunisation target for children. Parents can be sent appointments, immunisations can be arranged at school, health visitors can make home visits, etc. The outcome may be the same, only the costs differ. Cost-effectiveness analysis only allows the choice of the cheapest and/or most effective

continued

way of delivering a particular service but doesn't allow comparison of benefits and costs across treatments or services.

Cost-utility analysis – this is a concept in economic theory which attempts to provide a common measure of utility or satisfaction for such comparisons to take place. One such measure is the QALY – quality adjusted life years. It consists of the average expectation of life following treatment, multiplied by an index of quality of life. This consists of a set of scores measuring four aspects of life-quality: physical mobility, capacity for self-care, freedom from pain and distress, and social adjustment. Thus survival in a comatose condition for five years would score considerably less than survival in a normal condition for three years. Division of the average total cost of treatment and care by the QALY measure gives rise to the cost per quality-adjusted life year. It then becomes possible to compare treatments for the same disease in terms of cost per QALY gained by one treatment over another, or compare the comparative advantages of treatments for diverse conditions. Hence, the cost of achieving one QALY for renal dialysis might be equal to 19 hip replacements or 190 preventive advice sessions on smoking by a GP.

Cost-benefit analysis – attempts to measure all the inputs and outputs of treatment and care in common units, usually money. The 'cost' element encompasses the obvious financial costs of treatment and care and also wider costs to the patient, his family and society at large. These may include loss of earnings, state benefits, disruption of family life and loss of function through side-effects of treatment and sequelae of disease. 'Benefits' include restoration of function to the patient and any consequent ability of the patient or his or her family to contribute to the common good, e.g. by being in employment. Some costs and benefits are naturally measurable on a money scale, but for others the translation to money-equivalents may be controversial, e.g. the value of informal care by a relative.

The drive towards a knowledge-based health service has become a central aim of the NHS. After 40 years of comparative neglect of research and development (R&D) the Department of Health (DOH) produced a national strategy in 1991 under the leadership of their first R&D director, Michael Peckham, which represented 'probably the first systematic attempt to establish a comprehensive, pervasive R&D initiative for a national health system' (HSJ 1991). This was matched by a commitment to spend 1.5 per cent of the health service budget on R&D within five years, an increase from a base level of 0.8 per cent. The co-ordination and funding of R&D at central and regional levels is being reorganised following the report of the Culyer Task Force (Culyer 1994). A central aim of the R&D strategy has been the need to improve effectiveness and cost-effectiveness in health care (DOH 1993, 1994), and towards this aim a number of important initiatives have been taken:

- National priorities for R&D are being established through the Central Research and Development Committee, its Priorities Working Group and the expert review groups convened to look at key areas;
- The Clinical Outcomes Group coordinates work on clinical guidelines and has appraised and recommended a small number of those which are supported by high-quality research and professional consensus;
- The NHS Standing Group on Health Technology Assessment determines priorities for health technology assessment and commissions research;
- The NHS Centre for Reviews and Dissemination was established at the Nuffield Centre in Leeds to commission reviews of the effectiveness and cost-effectiveness of new and existing health technologies. Dissemination is taken forward in a number of ways including the distribution of the Effectiveness Bulletins, accessible overviews of findings in key areas;
- The establishment of the Cochrane Centre in Oxford in 1992, which is now the focal point of a worldwide collaboration to perform systematic reviews of randomised controlled trials of health care.

This list demonstrates impressive progress in the first four years of the strategy, but will the results of research be taken up in practice, informing the day-to-day decisions of clinicians and managers on the ground? There is good evidence that the provision of information by itself is insufficient to change practice for a variety of reasons, ranging from lack of time to read and digest it to cultural resistance to actual organisational barriers. The DOH is putting responsibility for effecting change firmly on purchasers (DOH 1995) who can insist through their contract negotiations that evidence-based protocols and guidelines for the prevention, treatment and management of particular diseases be followed. Analysing, assessing and prioritising the results of research within a local context is not easy, however, and acting on it may involve conflictual negotiations with clinicians, who fear that such developments will be used to regulate and control them in ways already familiar in the US. There insurers will not pay for medical procedures or tests which are no longer justifiable in routine practice, and the use of disease management protocols is widespread. Clearly there are many problems to resolve, yet moving towards a 'knowledge-based health service' may be the only way in which we can steer a course through the complexities of modern medicine in future, however difficult the progress may be.

Conclusions

In conclusion let us try to pull together the three parts of this chapter and draw the links between what at first appear disparate issues. In Part 1 we saw how the intensification of global competition and other national and supra-national economic forces combined with the transformative power of new computerised technologies are changing the organisation of production and the labour process. In addition, they are causing a major re-think about the scope and role of welfare in advanced industrial societies and a restructuring of the welfare state which, in this country, has been driven by the ideological and political hegemony of the New Right in the Thatcher/Major years.

The neoliberal orthodoxy argues that generous welfare benefits are a burden on the productive economy, not the social investment that social democrats believed them to be during the postwar consensus, and that they fetter Britain in her global economic battle to win markets and inward capital investment. Social policy must be made firmly subordinate to the needs of the economy, and to that end a major restructuring of the welfare state has been undertaken. At the same time, information technology provides new opportunities to restructure the public sector labour force in the name of improved efficiency and flexibility.

Yet while economic developments and political preferences appear to converge in seeking to reduce the costs of welfare, within health care, opposing expansionary forces are at work Demands are increasing under the twin pressures of an ageing population and exploding medical technologies. It was argued that to some extent the impact of demographic change had been exaggerated in order to legitimate New Right attacks on welfare, but the cost implications of medical developments have caused all Western governments to subject the content and organisation of health care to much greater critical scrutiny.

Within this environment different occupational groups like doctors, nurses and managers struggle to make sense of their situation, fend off threats and determine a future strategy which guarantees or improves their current status. Core-periphery strategies within nursing, discussed in detail in Part 2, can be analysed both as a response to demographic and labour market trends, and within post-Fordist concepts of the 'flexible firm'; but they are also a continuation of the professional project of nursing. The 'new nursing' embodies two possibly contradictory ways forward: one based on *enhancing* the carative aspects of the nursing process, the other *extending* the nurse's role to practice some tasks previously defined within the medical domain. It was argued that the first route is more likely to provoke medical opposition, because it defines a unique sphere of autonomous professional practice for nurses, whereas the second still subjects nursing work to medical control. It also relieves doctors of many routine technical tasks leaving the creative heart of medicine – diagnosis – to them (just as nurses seek to redefine their professional core, leaving many of the routine tasks of caring to the health support worker). Yet as we have seen, even diagnostic autonomy is under challenge by the 'outcomes movement' discussed in Part 3, and the requirement, in the name of efficiency and effectiveness, that doctors practice evidence-based medicine. This means being bound by a flood of guidelines and protocols which seek to contain medical practice within much stricter boundaries. Questions of gender and of labour supply provide additional complications, as both affect the bargaining strength of different groups.

In conclusion, in this chapter we have sought to show how macro-level trends and developments in economics, technology and demography, which may appear at first sight remote, are significantly affecting health care workers and users in direct and indirect ways. Revolutionary changes in the policy environment of health care are already having a major impact on the NHS and its future development.

References

Aglietta, M. (1979) *A Theory of Capitalist Regulation*, London: New Left Books.

Antman, E., Lau, J., Kupelnick, B., Mosteller, F. and Chalmers, I. (1992) 'A comparison of the results of meta-analysis of randomised controlled trials and recommendations of clinical experts' *J. of American Medical Association*, 268: 240–8.

Appleby, J. (1995a) 'The heart of the matter' *Health Service Journal*, 105(5474): 34–5.

—— (1995b) 'The top ten' *Health Service Journal*, 105(5443): 34–5.

Arber, S. (1996) 'Is living longer cause for celebration', *Health Service Journal*, 106(5512): 28–31.

Atkinson, J. (1985) 'The Changing Corporation' in D. Clutterbuck (ed.) *New Patterns of Work*, Aldershot: Gower.

Atkinson, J. and Meager, N. (1986) *Changing Working Patterns: How Companies Achieve Flexibility to Meet New Needs*, London: NEDO.

Banta, D.H. and Thacker, S.B. (1990) 'The case for reassessment of health care technology', *Journal of the American Medical Association*, 264(2): 235–40.

Beardshaw, V. and Davies, C. (1990) *New for Old? Prospects for Nursing in the 1990s*, Research Report 8, London: King's Fund Institute.

Bosanquet, N. (1987) *A Generation in Limbo: Government, the Economy and the 55–64 Age Group*, London: Public Policy Centre.

Bloor, K. and Maynard, A. (1994) 'Through the keyhole', *Health Service Journal*, 104(5429): 24–6.

Brindle, D. (1996) 'Back to basics of the bar' *The Guardian*, 24th July, p. 11.

British Medical Journal (1996) 'Nursing shortfall hits Britain' *BMJ*, 312: 13.

Burrows, R. and Loader, B. (1994) *Towards a Post-Fordist Welfare State?* London: Routledge.

Burns, T. and Stalker, G.M. (1961) *The Management of Innovation*, London: Tavistock.

Byrne, D. (1994) 'Planning for and against the divided city' in Burrows and Loader (1994).

Callender, C. and Pearson, R. (1989) 'Managing in the 1990s: the challenge of demographic change', *Public Money and Management*, Autumn, 9(3): 11–19.

Central Statistical Office (1996) *Social Trends 1996*, London: HMSO.

Cochrane, A. (1991) 'The Changing State of Local Government: Restructuring for the 1990s', *Public Administration*, 69: 281–302.

Committee of Public Accounts (1987) *Control of NHS Manpower*, 11th Report of Session 86/87, HC Paper 213.

Culyer, A. (1994) *Supporting Research and Development in the NHS: a Report to the Minister for Health by a Research Development Task Force*, London: HMSO.

Demos (1995) *The Time Squeeze*, London: Demos.

Department of Education and Employment (DEE) (1996) Competitiveness White Paper.

Department of Employment (1994) 'The flexible workforce and patterns of working hours in the UK', *Employment Gazette*, July 1994: 239–46.

—— (1995) *Labour Market and Skill Trends 1995/6*, London: Dept. of Employment Skills and Enterprise Network.

Department of Health and Social Security (DHSS) (1983) Circular HC (83) 13 Health Services Management *Competitive Tendering in the Provision of Domestic, Catering and Laundry Services*, London: DHSS.

—— (1986) *Mix and Match: A Review of Nursing Skill Mix*, London: HMSO.

Department of Health (DOH) (1993) *Improving Clinical Effectiveness*, EL (93) 115.

—— (1994) *Improving the Effectiveness of the NHS*, EL (94) 74.

—— (1995) *Priorities and Planning Guidance for 1995–96*, EL (94) 55.

Dickinson, S. (1982) 'The nursing process and the professional status of nursing' *Nursing Times* 78: 61–4.

Drummond, M. (1992) 'Test drive', *Health Service Journal*, 102(5325): 26–7.

Epstein, A.M. (1990) 'The outcomes movement: will it get us where we want to go?', *New England Journal of Medicine*, 26 July: 266–9.

Ermisch, J. (1990) *Fewer Babies, Longer Lives*, York: Joseph Rowntree Foundation.

Fries, J. (1989) 'The compression of morbidity: near or far?', *The Milbank Quarterly*, 667(2): 208–33.

Guardian (1996a) 'UK lags on education', 19th October, p. 10.

Guardian (1996b) 'UK scores low on education', 6th May, p. 7.

Guardian (1996c) 'When rights collide: Jaymee's to fight, the NHS's to resist' Editorial, 23rd May, p. 18.

Hancock, C. (1995) 'With the benefit of foresight', *Health Services Journal*, 105(5459): 27.

Handy, C. (1989) *The Age of Unreason*, London: Business Books.

Harrison, S. and Pollitt, C. (1994) *Controlling Health Professionals*, Buckingham: Open University Press.

Health Advisory Service (1983) *The Rising Tide: Developing Services for Mental Illness in Old Age*, London: HMSO.
Health Service Journal (1991) 'Making the most of a reversal of misfortune', 2nd May, p. 14.
—— (1995) 'Breast cancer study highlights survival rates' 18th May: 6.
Hills, J. (1993) *The Future of Welfare: a Guide to the Debate*, London: Joseph Rowntree Foundation.
Hills, J. (ed) (1990) *The State of Welfare: the Welfare State in Britain since 1974*, Oxford: Clarendon Press.
Held, D. (1996) *Democracy and the Global Order*, London: Polity Press.
Henley Centre for Forecasting (1991) 'Why companies will change', *Director*, 44(8): 63–73.
Hirsch, J. (1991) 'From the Fordist to the Post-Fordist State' in B. Jessop, H. Kastendiek, K. Nielsen and O. Pedersen (eds) *The Politics of Flexibility*, London: Edward Elgar.
Hirst, P. and Zeitlin, J. (1991) 'Flexible Specialisation versus Post-Fordism: Theory, Evidence and Policy Implications' *Economy and Society*, 20: 1–56.
Hogg, C. (1988) 'New medical techniques and the NHS', *Radical Community Medicine*, Summer: 35–41.
Hoggett, P. (1987) 'A farewell to mass production? Decentralisation as an emergent private and public paradigm', in P. Hoggett and R. Hambleton (eds) *Decentralisation and Democracy*, Occasional Paper 28, Bristol: School of Advanced Urban Studies, University of Bristol.
—— (1991) 'A New management in the public sector? *Policy and Politics*, 19: 243–56.
—— (1994) 'The politics of the modernisation of the UK welfare state', in Burrows and Loader (1994).
Hood, C. (1990) 'De-Sir Humphreying the Westminster model of bureaucracy: a new style of governance', *Governance*, 2: 205–14.
—— (1991) 'A public management for all seasons?', *Public Administration*, 69(4): 3–19.
Hunter, D. (1996) 'New line on age-old problems', *Health Service Journal*, 106(5508): 21.
Institute of Manpower Studies (IMS) (1987) *How Many Graduates in the 21st Century?* Brighton: University of Sussex.
Jennett, B. (1986) *High Technology Medicine: Benefits and Burdens*, Oxford: Oxford University Press.
Jessop, B. (1990) 'Regulation theories in retrospect and prospect' *Economy and Society*, 19: 153–216.
—— (1991a) 'The Welfare State in the transition from Fordism to Post-Fordism' in B. Jessop, H. Kastendiek, K. Nielsen and O.K. Pedersen *The Politics of Flexibility: Restructuring State and Industry in Britain, German and Scandinavia*, London: Edward Elgar.
—— (1991b) 'Thatcherism and Flexibility: the White Heat of a Post-Fordist Revolution', in Jessop *et al.* (1991a).
—— (1994) 'The Transition to Post-Fordism and the Schumpeterian Workfare State', in Burrows and Loader (1994).
Lindley, R. and Wilson, R. (eds) (1994) *Review of the Economy and*

Employment 1994: Occupational Assessment, Warwick: Institute of Employment Research.

Mark, A. (1996) 'Ill-staffed by moonlight', *Health Service Journal*, 23rd May: 17.

Maynard, A. (1990) 'Down with morbidity', *Health Service Journal*, 20 Sept.: 1393.

Means, R. (1988) 'Council housing, tenure polarisation and older people in two contrasting localities', *Ageing and Society*, 8(4): 395–421.

Mersey RHA/Nuffield Institute for Health Services (1989) *But Who Will Make the Beds?: A Research-based Strategy for Ward Nursing Skills in the 1990s*, Leeds: Nuffield Institute for Health Services, University of Leeds.

Moore, W. (1995) 'Is the 56-hour week good for you, your family, or the NHS?' *Health Service Journal*, 105(5461): 24–7.

Murray, R. (1991) 'The State after Henry', in *Marxism Today*, May: 22–7.

Naisbitt, J. (1990) *Megatrends 2000: the next ten years*, London: Sidgwick and Jackson.

National Audit Office (NAO) (1985) *NHS: Control of Nursing Manpower*, Session 1984/85, HC Paper 558.

—— (1987) *Control over Professional and Technical Manpower*, Session 86/87, HC Paper 95.

Newman, J. and Clarke, J. (1994) 'Going about our business? The managerialization of public services', in J. Clarke, A. Cochrane and E. McLaughlin (eds) *Managing Social Policy*, London: Sage.

NHS Executive (1995) *Opportunity 2000 – Women in the NHS*, EL (95) 126.

OECD (1994) 'Who looks after the elderly?' *OECD Observer*, No.188 June/July: 15–18.

Pashley, G. and Henry, C. (1990) 'Carving out the nursing nineties', *Nursing Times*, 12: 405–12.

Pallot, P. (1996) 'The cost of living', *Health Services Journal*, 106(5505): 11.

Pierson, C. (1994) 'Continuity and discontinuity in the emergence of the "post-Fordist" welfare state' in Burrows and Loader (1994).

Pinch, S. (1994) 'Labour flexibility and the changing welfare state: Is there a post-Fordist model?' in Burrows and Loader (1994).

Pollitt, C. (1990) *Managerialism and the Public Services: the Anglo-American Experience*, Oxford: Blackwell.

Reid, N.G. (1986) 'Nursing Manpower: the problems ahead' *International Journal of Nursing Studies*, 23(3): 187–97.

Rustin, M.J. (1989) 'The politics of Post-Fordism: or, the trouble with New Times', *New Left Review*, 175: 54–77.

Smith, R. (1991) 'Where is the wisdom?' *British Medical Journal*, 303: 798–9.

—— (1993) 'Filling the lacuna between research and practice: an interview with Michael Peckham', *British Medical Journal*, 307: 1403–7.

—— (1994) 'Towards a knowledge based health service', *British Medical Journal*, 309: 217–8.

St. Leger, A.S., Schnieden, H. and Walsworth-Bell, J.P. (1992) *Evaluating Health Services' Effectiveness*, Milton Keynes: Open University Press.

Stocking, B. (1992) 'The future starts here', *Health Service Journal*, 102(5322): 26–8.

Szczepura, A. (1992) 'Rush to arms', *Health Service Journal*, 102(5286): 20–2.

Townsend, P. (1981) 'The structured dependency of the elderly: the creation of social policy in the twentieth century', *Ageing and Society*, 1(1): 5–28.

United Kingdom Central Council for Nursing, Midwifery and Health Visiting (1986) *Project 2000: A New Preparation for Practice*, London: UKCC.

UKCC (1987) *Project 2000: The Final Proposals*, London: UKCC.

Walker, A. (1980) 'The social creation of poverty and dependency in old age', *Journal of Social Policy*, 9(1): 45–75.

—— (1987) 'Enlarging the caring capacity of the community: informal support networks and the Welfare State', *International Journal of Health Service*, 17(3): 369–86.

Williams, F. (1994) 'Social relations, welfare and the Post-Fordism debate', in Burrows and Loader (1994).

Wilson, G. (1991) 'Models of ageing and their relation to policy formation and service provision', *Policy and Politics*, 19(1): 37–47.

Wilson, R.A. and Stillwell, J.A. (1992) *The National Health Service and the Labour Market*, Hants: Avebury.

Witz, J. (1995) 'The challenge of nursing' in Gabe, J., Kelleher, D. and Williams, G. (eds) *Challenging Medicine*, London: Routledge.

CHAPTER 4

Reforming the NHS: the conservative record

In the 1980s the policy prescriptions of the New Right gained intellectual ascendancy not only in Western Europe and North America but throughout the world. From India to Brazil, to the new democracies of Eastern Europe, governments espoused free market principles, privatised their state industries and began to restructure their welfare systems.

Health policy did not escape this intellectual challenge, but policy prescription cannot be assumed to lead to policy change. Governments attempting to implement change in this area often encounter entrenched organisational resistance from powerful providers and from recipients of services who benefit from the status quo. The extent to which ideas and values actually shape policy change requires careful empirical enquiry. Radical rhetoric can disguise essential continuities in policy or simply provide a post-hoc gloss to changes which were happening anyway.

In Britain the election of the first Thatcher government in 1979 heralded the beginning of an ambitious attempt to 'roll back the state' by a true believer in private enterprise and market values. What effect did this have on the NHS? This chapter examines the Conservative record throughout the 1980s up to the passing of the 1990 NHS and Community Care Act.

Creeping privatisation?

One way of assessing the government's radical intent is to examine its policies towards the provision of private health care. The new government quickly showed its enthusiasm for the private medical sector which was growing rapidly in 1979, and in 1980 Gerard Vaughan, Minister of Health, expressed the belief that it might grow to around one-quarter the size of the NHS. But the expansion which took place throughout the 1980s did so largely without direct government help. Intervention was confined to abolishing the Health Services Board set up by Labour to regulate private-sector growth, stopping the phasing out of pay beds and allowing consultants on full-time health service contracts to earn up to 10 per cent of their NHS salaries from private practice without any

Figure 4.1 ***Total UK private acute care expenditure: cash and real spending (1972 prices)***

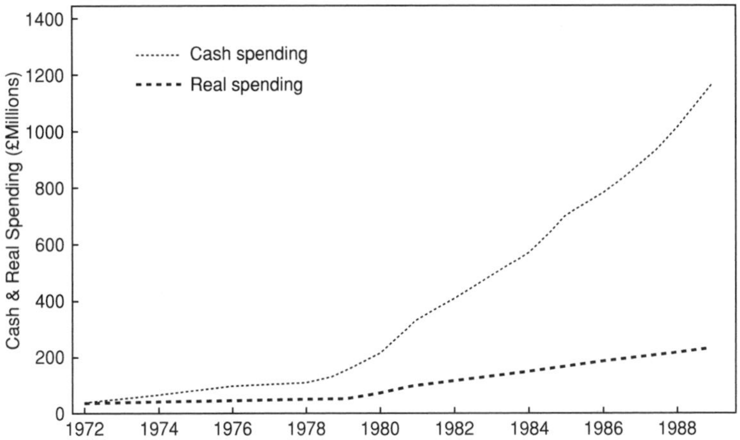

Source: Appleby (1992). Reproduced by kind permission of Open University Press, Buckingham

salary deduction. Previously they had forfeited two-elevenths. Another minor concession was lowering the income limits for tax relief on private health insurance to £8,500.

It seems hardly likely that these changes alone fuelled the growth in health insurance from 5 per cent of the population covered in 1979 to 13 per cent in 1989. More significant were public perceptions of successive 'crises' in the NHS and a desire for more choice over the timing of treatment and the 'hotel' aspects of hospital services.

Figure 4.1 shows the growth in spending on private acute care in cash and real terms (after allowing for general price inflation) between 1972 and 1989. However, the most explosive growth in private health care occurred in long-stay residential and nursing care for the elderly (see Figure 4.2). By the end of the decade the voluntary and private sector had overtaken the statutory sector (local authorities and the NHS) as the main institutional provider, an expansion which had been funded largely out of social security payments. Rather than being the result of deliberate government intention, this reflected the unintended (and embarrassing) consequence of minor regulatory change. The Department of Social Security had always had discretionary power to pay for nursing or residential home care, though this was little known. Klein reports that the total sums spent began a slow rise from the 1970s, reaching £39 million by 1983. In an attempt to prevent this slow creep the department asked each local office to set a maximum upper weekly limit for fees in their area.

Figure 4.2 **Private health care: breakdown by sector (total = £6535 m.)**

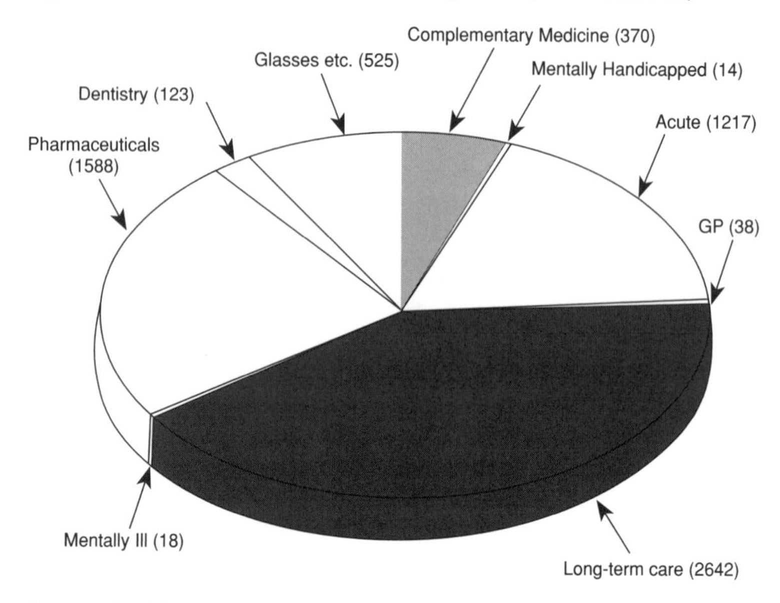

Source: Appleby (1992). Reproduced by kind permission of Open University Press, Buckingham

> The result was precisely the opposite of that intended. The maxima quickly became the minima. More important what had previously been a low-visibility discretionary payment overnight turned into highly visible as-of-right entitlement. Financial need, not medical or social need, was the only criterion.
>
> (Klein 1995: 158)

The result was a sharp rise both in the number of claimants and the fees charged by private homes, subsidised by the Exchequer to the tune of 1 billion pounds by 1988. The government began the attempt to extricate itself after a critical report by the Audit Commission in 1986, which led to comprehensive reviews of community care policies (Audit Commission 1986; Griffiths 1988).

Large increases in prescription charges (from 20p in 1979 to £3.40 in 1991) also led to growth in pharmaceuticals bought over-the-counter privately. In some ways this was a symbolic move, since it raised little revenue: existing exempt groups (children, pensioners, the chronically ill and those on Income Support) retained their right to free prescriptions. In addition higher charges were made for all forms of dental treatment and new charges introduced for sight and dental checks.

The government encouraged the private sector in other ways. In 1983 district health authorities (DHAs) were asked to 'test the effectiveness of their domestic, catering and laundry services by putting them out to tender' (DHSS 1983a). Though the expressed aim of this policy was to improve efficiency, ministers went to considerable lengths to make sure that private firms could compete on favourable terms, initially with little effect since private firms succeeded in gaining only one in four contracts by 1990 (NAHAT 1990).

But for a radical government committed to 'rolling back the state' these changes, though controversial, were not large. Unlike housing and education, health policies were remarkable for their continuity in the 1980s and the NHS finished the decade battered round the edges but largely intact: still the overwhelming supplier of health care in spite of the growth in the independent sector; still tax-funded and for the most part free at the point of use; still growing in real terms even though that did not keep pace with demand in the view of critics. The Prime Minister herself had reaffirmed her commitment to the 'founding principles' of the service in her speech to the Conservative Party conference in 1982 as she sought to allay public suspicion that the health service might not be safe in her hands. By 1990 cash spending on the NHS was two-and-a-half times what it had been in 1979, topping £27 billion and making the Department of Health the second largest spending department. Why had ideology been tempered with pragmatism?

The costs of change

The devotion of the British public to the NHS continued unabated. The NHS consistently achieved high ratings in public opinion polls, irrespective of the party affiliation of respondents, and was consistently thought to merit extra public spending (see, for example, Taylor-Gooby 1985; NAHA 1988). There is evidence, too, that people saw the two sectors of health care as complementary rather than in opposition: they were happy to use private medicine for specific purposes but wanted a strong publicly funded NHS as the backbone of the health care system (Taylor-Gooby 1985). Public opinion buttressed and was shaped by a formidable medical and nursing lobby in the Royal Colleges, British Medical Association and the nursing unions which could consistently command sympathetic media attention. The political costs of abandoning the NHS were simply too high.

So too were the financial costs. Leaked 'think-tank' proposals in 1982 show that the first Thatcher government at least contemplated replacing tax funding by some form of continental health insurance. However, these ideas came to nothing and when interest was revived in 1988, the advantages of the present system appeared to outweigh ideology once again (Timmins 1996).

Nevertheless the government faced the same problem that every other government had faced with the NHS, trying to maintain a balance between a centrally controlled budget and escalating demands, demands shaped by the professional providers of services and the inescapable needs of an ageing population. But this government faced the dilemma from a different ideological perspective. Increasing demands on services estimated at costing 2 per cent more in real terms per year (Benzeval and Robinson 1988) were to be met by increased efficiency rather than by increasing levels of funding to match. There were two strands to the government's strategy, although 'strategy' is probably too strong a word for a policy which evolved opportunistically. The first was to recast management systems, structures, norms and values in line with the perceived virtues of the private sector, in particular its efficiency and dynamism (which Ranade and Haywood (1991) term 'privatising from within'). The most important element of this strand was the introduction of general management in line with the recommendations of the Griffiths Report (DHSS 1983b), which is discussed in detail in Chapter 6.

The second strand of the strategy was to tighten lines of accountability upwards. Under the headings of efficiency and accountability a number of initiatives were introduced which are briefly outlined below. Readers who wish to follow these up in greater detail have a number of good accounts to choose from (see, for example, Harrison *et al.* 1990; Klein 1995; Ham 1992).

The changes: a summary

The efficiency strategy: chronology of events

1979 The White Paper *Patients First* recommends abolishing Area Health Authorities.

1982 District Health Authorities go 'live'.
Rayner efficiency scrutinies begin in the NHS.
Accountability Reviews between Minister and RHA, and RHA and Districts start.

1983 Inquiry into NHS Management (Griffiths Report) (DHSS 1983b) published.
Circular on competitive tendering for the support services sent to health authorities (DHSS 1983a).
First Performance Indicators package.
Introduction of manpower targets.
Review of the NHS Estate.
Korner Committee reviewing the information needs of the service begins its work.

1984 Appointments of general managers begin. Pilots on management budgeting.
DHA reviews of units.
Minimum cost improvement programme introduced.
1985 Second package of Performance Indicators introduced.
1986 Annual performance review of RHAs by NHS Management Board.
1987 Introduction of performance-related pay and individual performance review for general managers.
Resource Management pilots begin in six hospitals and six community sites.
1989 White Papers *Working for Patients* and *Caring for People* published.

The Conservatives inherited the recommendations of the Royal Commission on the National Health Service set up by the preceding Labour government in 1976 (Cmnd. 7615). Its terms of reference were to look at the management of the financial and manpower resources of the NHS. Ignoring most of its recommendations, the new government took a quick decision on one of the major ones, abolishing the area tier of management. The thrust of its White Paper *Patients First* (DHSS 1979) was to give new District Health Authorities (DHAs) more autonomy and devolve decision making down the line to operational units (hospitals, community services). The government's new-found enthusiasm for decentralisation soon ended, however, as the department came under sustained Parliamentary criticism about the lack of accountability in the NHS and the department's failure to develop appropriate mechanisms to ensure it.

As the policy pendulum began to swing back to towards greater centralisation again, two initiatives quickly followed. Annual formal reviews of performance of the 14 Regional Health Authorities (RHAs) by ministers and the DHSS began in 1982, and subsequently extended down the line, with RHA reviews of DHAs and DHA reviews of unit managers. In these reviews the performance of authorities and managers in attaining agreed objectives and targets were discussed, and new objectives agreed for the following year.

The second innovation was the development of performance indicators. In the autumn of 1983 every health authority received from the DHSS a package of 147 indicators in book form to enable them to compare their performance against others on a regional and national basis according to a range of quantitative measures. The indicators covered five broad areas: aspects of clinical activity, finance, the labour force, support services and estate management. The political context determined not only the timing of their introduction but their content as well: 53 indicators were related to finance, 43 to the workforce, 46 to hospital activity. There was nothing on primary care, few related to quality or outcome, and none related to patient satisfaction or ease of public access. The primary concern of the DHSS was the cost and quantity of hospital medicine on which most of the health service budget was spent. Health authorities were asked to respond to the data they received and explain to their RHA any 'outliers', that is, indicators appearing in the top or bottom 15 per cent of the national league table. Performance indicators quickly became used as a diagnostic tool to 'inform' the accountability reviews which in turn developed 'from departmental monitoring of broad strategies to deep monitoring of short-term operational plans and of control systems stretching right down to unit level' (Harrison *et al.* 1990: 129).

The introduction of general management was a vital mechanism for ensuring greater control and demonstrating to the Treasury, Public Accounts and Social Service Committees that the department meant to get a grip on the NHS. The final mechanisms for ensuring managerial accountability up the line were put in place by appointing general managers on short-term contracts, introducing an element of performance-related pay, and installing a system of individual performance review. By 1989 the DOH had installed 'a clear and effective chain of command' upwards from Districts to Regions, the NHS Management Executive and the Secretary of State (DOH 1989a: 13).

Attempts to make clinicians more accountable for the resources they used, another theme of the Griffiths Report, led to pilot projects on management budgeting for clinicians, broadening out to a second phase of pilots in Resource Management in six hospital and six community sites in 1987. Other initiatives which formed part of the efficiency drive were the programme of Rayner efficiency scrutinies, the introduction of workforce targets, and the requirement that health authorities undertake sustained programmes of cash-releasing cost improvements (which included the programme of competitive tendering for laundry, catering and cleaning services).

These initiatives were given extra impetus by reduced rates of revenue growth throughout the 1980s which forced changes in expectations and management behaviour. Increasingly funds for new developments had to be found from redeployment of services and savings. The annual growth in public spending on the hospital and community health services fell from an average of 3 per cent per year in real terms in the late 1970s to less than one-half per cent per year for the hospital and community health services between 1980–81 and 1986–87 (Benzeval and Robinson 1988). The Family Practitioner services did better, averaging 3 per cent per year.

By 1988 the strategy of 'privatising from within' had forced considerable changes in the way the NHS was run. First, a new model of management had been introduced for managers to emulate, based on private-sector practices and precepts. Second, the profile and responsibilities of management had been raised through the introduction of general management throughout the service. Third, the government had introduced new mechanisms to reinforce the accountability of health authorities and managers upwards, and shown considerable political clout in using these mechanisms to enforce its policies.

The government could claim with some truth that it had forced through changes in managerial behaviour so that concepts like efficiency, cost-effectiveness and productivity were accorded more weight in the organisational culture. The cost-improvement programmes had produced annual savings of between 1.1 and 1.5 per cent per year in real terms since they were introduced in 1984–85. The annual growth in the number of patients treated, at 1.9 per cent per year, was more than double the rate of growth in spending (Robinson 1991).

But the changes produced their own set of tensions and contradictions. The limits of introducing into the NHS a model of management based on private-sector practices soon became apparent. Far from possessing similar freedoms, sanctions and incentives as their private-sector colleagues, managers were subject to strong bureaucratic controls and examples of perverse incentives penalising good managerial or clinical performance were legion. In addition, interpreting the activity statistics was impossible in the absence of any information on demand, need, quality of care and outcomes. Critics could argue that higher productivity was being achieved at the cost of pushing patients out of hospital 'quicker and sicker', and increasing the number of patients treated was still consistent with unmet need. This was partly for the reasons discussed in Chapter 3: more elderly people and medical advances which enabled more of them to benefit from treatments like joint replacement at even more advanced ages. The government found it impossible to refute such charges or change the overwhelming climate of opinion which believed the NHS to be seriously underfunded.

The funding debate

Although funding 'crises' are endemic to the NHS, the crisis of 1987 raised more than the usual political storm, and plenty of ammunition for the Opposition in the election campaign of that year. A survey of 106 health authorities undertaken by the National Association of Health Authorities in 1987 showed that most were facing severe financial pressures.

Evaluating charges of 'underfunding' is extremely difficult. Often international comparisons are used, with the charge that Britain spent

Figure 4.3 **Target and Actual Funding 1980–81/1990–91 Hospital and Community Health Service: England (1990–91 prices)**

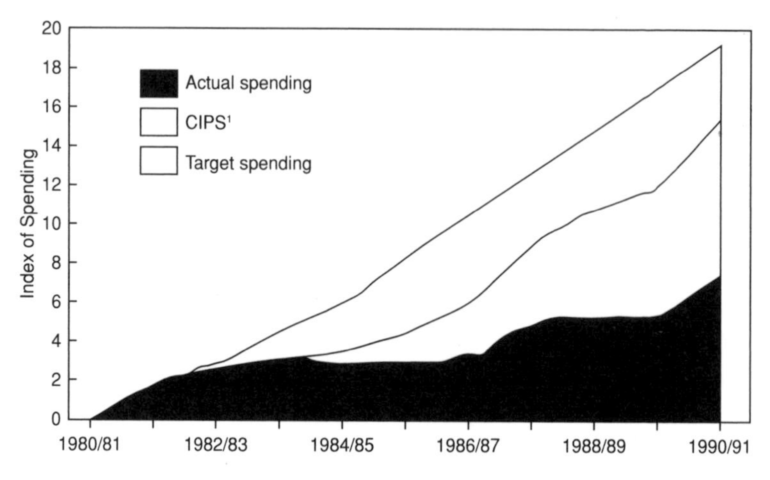

Note:
1 CIPS = Cost-improvement programmes

Source: Appleby (1992). Reproduced by kind permission of Open University Press, Buckingham

less on health care as a proportion of gross domestic product (6 per cent) than any other country in the OECD apart from Turkey, Greece and (marginally) Spain. Appleby (1992), however, has conclusively demonstrated the weaknesses of using international comparisons. Estimates based on demographic pressures, advances in medical technology and the costs of implementing new government policies (such as the introduction of new screening programmes) also have their drawbacks (discussed in Klein 1995: 180) but they represent a pragmatic way of estimating whether funding has been adequate to keep pace with demand pressures over a given number of years. Figure 4.3 shows the difference between actual and target funding for the hospital and community health services throughout the 1980s, taking these three demand pressures into account and allowing for efficiency gains (using cost improvement savings as a proxy for efficiency). Target funding is the estimated budget increase needed to cope with rising demands (on average 2 per cent in real terms each year) against which the actual budget can be compared, with shortfalls accumulated from year to year.

The figures suggest that the crisis of 1987 which precipitated the Prime Minister's Review was the result of cumulative underfunding throughout the 1980s which could not be sufficiently compensated for by internally generated savings and efficiency improvements.

Timmins' recent account (1995) throws fascinating light on the politics of the situation. Before the 1987 election Patrick Jenkin, then Secretary of State for Social Services asked health authorities not to make bed closures to prevent unfavourable pre-election publicity. Without this option for saving money, health authorities turned to another favourite strategem – not paying their creditors. After the June election the incoming Secretary of State, John Moore, inherited the unpaid bills but failed to take action. By July the director of financial management at the NHS Management Executive warned the NHS was 'technically bankrupt' yet still Moore failed to win extra resources for the service. As health authorities realised they were not to be baled out financially, bed closures began in earnest, first in tens, then hundreds, then thousands. The resulting public outcry forced Mrs Thatcher to announce her review of the NHS on television in January 1988, a review which, in Timmins' words 'nobody wanted: NHS professionals for fear of what it would bring. The government because it had no clear idea about what it wanted to do to the NHS, and the public who still did not trust the government with the service' (Timmins 1995: 458).

Strengths and weaknesses of the NHS

In contrast to the secrecy of the official review, the 'alternative reviews' which took place at the same time were valuable forums for informed and open debate, particularly those conducted by the Social Services Committee (1988) and the Institute of Health Services Management (1988). The weight of opinion and evidence bore out the view that 'Britain has one of the fairest, most effective and most socially accountable forms of cost containment of any country' (Barr *et al.* 1988: 11).

There was widespread agreement on the strengths of the NHS. It provides a reasonably equitable and comprehensive service to the whole population at remarkably small cost. Financing the system through general taxation means that financing is linked to the ability to pay which commands considerable public support as fair and equitable. Pooling health care risks on a national basis means that those with fewer health care needs help to subsidise those who need help most.

The system of global cash-limited budgets means that spending is easier to cap and control. Capital spending has always been rigorously controlled, and in general this has permitted a cautious approach to the adoption and dissemination of new expensive technologies. Furthermore, a well-developed system of primary care means that GPs can act as gatekeepers filtering demands made on the more expensive specialist and hospital services. The percentage of all medical practitioners in Britain who are in general practice was 38 per cent in 1995 (DOH

1995: 85) compared to estimates of 12 per cent in the USA (Weiner 1987), but they deal with over 90 per cent of patient episodes.

Because medical practitioners are either salaried or paid on a capitation basis they have no financial incentive to 'overtreat', and the competitive bidding-up of salaries has not been possible when pay and salary structures are nationally negotiated. In addition breaking the link between medical decision-making and the financial self-interest of the doctor enhances professional values and a doctor–patient relationship based on trust.[1]

It is important to realise how the equity aspects of the NHS positively contribute to efficiency rather than detract from it. Universal access means that the costs of checking everyone's eligibility for treatment is avoided. Making services free at the point of use avoids the costs associated with elaborate billing and payment systems. Funding services from income and payroll taxes (which together account for 95 per cent of the total) is cheaper to collect than user charges and avoids the overheads associated with an insurance system or the complexities of means-testing.

These administrative costs can be very high. The American health care system is based on private insurance bought by individuals or by employers as an occupational benefit for their employees, with government-subsidised programmes for the elderly and poor. It succeeds in being the world's most expensive system, consuming 14 per cent of GDP in 1994, yet it leaves 38 million Americans without health insurance and 50 million more with inadequate coverage (Himmelstein and Woolhandler 1992). Administrative overheads consumed 24.7 cents in every health care dollar spent in the US in 1993, $232.3 billion out of a total health expenditure of $939.9 billion, more than enough to provide good basic coverage to every US citizen if private insurance was replaced by a national insurance or tax-funded programme (Hellander *et al.* 1993).

On any objective comparative analysis therefore the NHS has an impressive list of strengths to its credit. In particular it has successfully (perhaps too successfully), contained costs at the macro-level, but the converse of this is that centralised funding decisions are inevitably highly politicised, dependent both on the ideological preferences of the government of the day and the short-term oscillations of the economy. Consumers have little choice over how much to spend on health care or how it is spent, nor, when services are largely free at the point of use, is there any incentive for them to limit their demands or providers to economise in the use of resources. From the politician's viewpoint it also has the unfortunate effect of channelling the blame for funding firmly on central government.

It was a crisis of confidence over NHS funding that triggered the review of 1988 in the first place, and one of its main objectives, according to Mrs Thatcher, was the need for 'a closer, clearer connection between the demand for health care, its cost and the method of paying for it' (Thatcher 1993: 607). However, just as in 1982, most of the alternatives considered by the Review Team seemed to present as many problems as they claimed to solve, and there was no consensus of support around any of them (Timmins 1996: 460–1; Thatcher 1993: 609–10). The method of funding remained unchanged (apart from the ideological concession to Mrs Thatcher of tax reliefs on private health insurance for the over 65s), and attention turned to the organisational dynamics of the system, and the way in which resources were allocated.

The NHS may have been efficient at the macro-level, but this was still consistent with inefficiencies at the micro-level. In common with other health care systems, clinicians and managers lacked good information on the cost, quality and outcomes of treatment to inform their decisions, and a number of perverse incentives in the resource allocation process positively penalised efficiency and clinical excellence. The main examples are outlined below:

Inadequate compensation for cross-boundary flows

Funding allocations to regions, and from them to districts, basically followed a needs-based formula (known as the Resource Allocation Working Party formula or RAWP), adjusted for factors like teaching and research, funding for regional specialities and cross-boundary flows. Cross-boundary flow occurs when a patient resident in one region requires treatment in another. Within regions there were similar flows between districts, often of a substantial kind. The RAWP compensation mechanisms for these cross-boundary flows suffered from a number of flaws which did not properly compensate patient-receiving districts, nor reward cost-effective patterns of treatment (for example, ambulatory as opposed to inpatient care.)

Inappropriate incentives for managers and clinicians

Examples of inappropriate incentives for managers and clinicians were legion. For example:

- With cash-limited budgets, efficient authorities who treated more patients simply increased their costs, not their revenue (the efficiency trap). This often led to unused spare capacity, as beds were closed and surgeons idle towards the end of the financial year.
- A reputation for shorter waiting times or clinical excellence attracted more referrals from GPs but no extra money.
- A poor service meant that GPs referred patients to another district, and the district providing the poor service was rewarded by less work but no deduction from its budget.

- Clinicians who built up their NHS waiting lists created demand for their services in private practice. Their colleagues who worked hard to reduce their waiting lists only attracted more work.

Disincentives applied at the level of general practice as well. Cost-effective behaviour (prevention work, carrying out more minor surgery) was not rewarded and GPs lacked information signalling the relative cost-effectiveness of different therapies and packages of care (Bevan *et al.* 1988). This resulted in wide variations in the range and quality of services provided (RCGP 1985), in the rate of referrals for outpatient, diagnostic and inpatient treatment and in prescribing costs per head. The effect of these variations on health outcomes was simply unknown.

Lack of responsiveness to consumers

It was a familiar complaint from right-wing analysts that the monopoly power of the NHS made it unresponsive to consumers, but as discussed in Chapter 2 they were not alone in this criticism. From rather different standpoints feminists, radicals and Marxists have criticised the paternalist and even oppressive nature of relations between providers and consumers of health care, and from the perspective of a businessman, Griffiths challenged the NHS to become more aware of the needs of its users.

While there was substantial agreement on the nature of the problems (see for instance IHSM 1988; Culyer 1988; Klein and Day 1988) there was less agreement on how to put them right, but the analysis and prescription of the American market economist, Alain Enthoven, written after a visit to Britain in 1985, chimed well with the Review Group's thinking. Enthoven argued that the NHS was caught in a gridlock of forces that made change exceedingly difficult to accomplish, and gave managers neither the incentive nor the power to address the service's failings. Yet the need for change was indisputable to cope with changing technologies and patterns of health needs. 'There is a need to work at loosening up the system so that new things can be tried and so that successful innovations can spread' (Enthoven 1985: 12).

What were the solutions? The government's answer had been to increase the responsibilities and accountability of management and to put a good deal of political energy into the efficiency strategy. But this left unresolved the basic problem that 'those who take the decisions about what to spend money on are not the same people who have to account for it' (Gretton and Harrison 1988). As Enthoven pointed out, clinical domination of the service was still relatively intact and managers possessed relatively few formal controls over consultants, not even holding their contracts outside teaching districts. The pilot studies on management budgeting which had tried to make clinicians accountable for a budget related to agreed workload targets demonstrated the difficulties of getting clinical cooperation on a voluntary basis and the massive efforts of persuasion and education needed for success (Harrison *et al.* 1989).

The improvements that had taken place relied on the voluntary efforts of enthusiasts or political clout expended on particular initiatives. Inevitably this meant wide variations in performance, for example, in achieving cost improvement targets (National Audit Office 1986; Haywood *et al.* 1989); in clinical productivity, and other measures of efficiency such as theatre and bed usage or rates of day surgery (Yates 1985, 1987; Audit Commission 1991). This in turn led to massive variations in waiting times and waiting lists, an issue of high public and political salience.

Enthoven argued that a possible solution lay in mimicking market incentives by separating responsibility for the purchase of health care from its provision and management, and subjecting providers to an element of competition for contracts.

Once 'money followed the patient', providers would have systematic financial incentives to cut costs, improve quality and be more responsive to what consumers wanted. Purchasers in turn, since they would still be cash-limited, would have an incentive to bargain for improved value-for-money on behalf of patients. The cross-boundary flow problem would disappear, since districts would now directly pay for the services they purchased on behalf of their residents. It was this idea of the internal market which became the centre piece of the Review Team's proposals, in *Working for Patients* (hereafter *WFP*) (DOH 1989a) which was also recommended for community care by Roy Griffiths in his second report for the government (Griffiths 1988, see below).

Working for patients: summary of main proposals

The three main aims are to:

- Extend patient choice;
- Devolve responsibility;
- Secure better value for money.

The seven key features are

1 Devolution.
All services currently provided by regions and districts not essential to their new roles devolved to lower levels of management or hived off into trading agencies unless retention is still the most cost-effective option.

continued

2 Management changes.

- At central level: A new policy board chaired by Secretary of State to oversee strategic direction of the service and a NHS Management Executive chaired by the Chief Executive to carry it out.
- Regions and Districts: Health authorities reduced from previous 16–19 members to five executive members (which includes the general manager and finance director), and five non-executive members appointed for their individual skills and experience by the Secretary of State/RHA. Non-executive members paid for the first time.
- Family Health Service Authorities: Membership reduced from previous maximum of 15 professional and 15 lay members to a maximum of 11 (five professional, five lay members and a chair appointed by the Secretary of State). Chief Executives to be appointed and management teams strengthened.
- Resource management: Implementation speeded up – all major acute hospitals could join the programme by March 1992.

3 Money follows the patient.
A weighted capitation system of funding replaces RAWP, phased in over five years. DHAs receive allocations for their resident populations and pay each other directly for services provided across their boundaries.

4 Self-governing trusts.
Hospitals and community units who can satisfy specified management criteria allowed to apply for self-governing status independent of health authority control. Trusts are run by boards of directors and raise their income from contracts won from health authorities, GP fundholders and private patients.

5 GP fundholding.
General practices who satisfy certain criteria may opt to hold their practice budget and buy a defined range of hospital services for their patients. Non-fundholding practices receive indicative prescribing budgets monitored by the FHSA.

6 Purchaser–provider split.
The main role of DHAs will be assessing the health needs of the population and purchasing services to meet those needs, not the provision and management of services. The DHA is free to purchase services from its own directly managed units, self-governing trusts, hospitals in other districts and the private and voluntary sector.

continued

7 Medical audit.
- In hospitals: Local medical audit advisory committees chaired by a senior clinician set up in every hospital. Royal Colleges are encouraged to make participation in audit a condition for a hospital receiving training approval, and audit participation will be a condition for gaining self-governing status.
- In primary care: Comprehensive system of medical audit for general practice to be in place within three years, supervised by medical audit advisory group accountable to the FHSA.

Many of the proposals in *WFP* consolidated and reinforced the managerialist trends of the previous decade, and gave managers further tools to discipline doctors and make medical practice more transparent and accountable. For example, the proposals on medical audit, the involvement of managers in the renegotiation of consultant contracts and in the merit awards process, the formation of smaller, more managerially oriented health authority boards and further devolution of management responsibilities to units. More significant still was the creation of self-governing trust status for those units thought to have the managerial capability to run themselves. This proposal was modelled on similar developments being proposed for schools under the 1988 Education Act, but also reflected the interest of some of the teaching hospitals in returning to the independence they had enjoyed up to 1974 (Timmins 1996: 462).

The radical core of the reforms was, of course, the internal market and the structural changes which this necessitated – the separation of purchasing and providing functions, the designation of the purchasers and the requisite changes in the resource allocation process. The concept of the internal market, and the process by which the Review Team arrived at this particular model will be discussed more fully in Chapter 5. Here we give only the outline of its main features.

On the demand side, there were three categories of budget holder acting as purchasers of services for patients. As the main purchasing authority, DHAs were given the responsibility for ensuring that the health care needs of their resident population were met. After a transition period they would receive cash-limited allocations from the RHA based on the number and characteristics of their resident population and would be free to purchase services from within or without the district (subject to certain safeguards), from NHS, private and voluntary suppliers. The second category of budget-holder were general practitioners. Eligible practices could opt to receive their practice budgets directly from the RHA. This included a drug budget, 70 per cent of practice team staffing costs, improvements to premises and monies to buy a defined range of hospital treatments for patients.

The cost of these services was deducted from the allocation made to the relevant DHA. The third category of purchaser was private patients and insurers such as BUPA.

On the supply side, services would be provided by hospitals still directly managed by health authorities, hospitals and community units who opted out of health authority control and became self-governing NHS trusts, and private and voluntary suppliers of services. Trusts were promised further freedoms such as the right to employ their own staff (including consultants), to vary pay rates and conditions of service, and to raise investment capital subject to certain controls. In the interests of maintaining 'fair competition' between public and private providers and the efficient use of capital, a system of capital charges was introduced into the NHS for the first time, and all hospitals were made responsible for meeting the interest and depreciation costs of their existing assets and new investment.

Contracts or service agreements were the method by which purchasers and providers did business. These set out prices, treatment levels and quality standards and enabled purchasers to hold providers accountable for their performance. Cross-boundary flow adjustments to allocations would be replaced by direct billing for services rendered.

The quasi-market was therefore an attempt to expose providers to competitive tests of cost-effectiveness and quality while retaining safeguards for the consumer. It was a highly artificial construct with no precise parallel in any other health care system, and predictions about its performance were hard to make. The NHS was sailing into uncharted territory.

Developments in primary care

Primary care did not escape the attention of the Thatcher government either. Here the aims were three-fold: curbing expenditure, raising standards and giving greater emphasis to health promotion and illness prevention. As the most individualistic and autonomous arm of medicine, general practice had maintained its position virtually unscathed since the National Insurance Act of 1911 established its main institutional features. The Act introduced the self-employed contractor status of the GP, care for a defined list of patients, the capitation fee and referral system and a medical record system still in use today.

The establishment of the NHS in 1948 represented the formalisation and development of the principles adopted in 1911, with general practitioners playing a pivotal role as 'gatekeepers' to the health care system. Apart from the agitation over conditions and pay in the mid-1960s, which led to a new contract and the 'renaissance of general practice', the profession was virtually untouched by governments of either party, although the escalating demands on the hospital service which successive governments tried to grapple with were largely GP-induced. As Klein points out, GP referral rates increased over the history of the NHS, whereas the annual rate of GP consultations made by the public fell (Klein 1989). Demand was therefore shaped by the professionals rather than consumers.

Although no government willingly tangled with the BMA, it became increasingly clear to the Thatcher government that the financial costs of avoiding a confrontation with the profession might outweigh any political costs. Primary care was an obvious source of concern to a government anxious to control government spending. It represented an open-ended public expenditure commitment with no way of imposing cash limits on the amount spent on prescribing and seemingly no way to check the number of people GPs referred to hospital. In addition there was little evidence that increased investment in general practice was yielding any return, although in theory primary care should be able to treat many conditions less expensively than the hospital sector. The government also realised that an increased emphasis on health promotion in the GP's surgery might pay dividends, given the preventable nature of much modern morbidity.

The government's more active stance towards primary care began with attempts to control the prescribing budget through the 'limited list' in 1984. Vociferously opposed by both the profession and the pharmaceutical industry, compromises were made which both reduced the scope for potential savings and did little to impinge on clinical autonomy. Nevertheless, an important principle had been established, that clinical autonomy did not mean an automatic right to use public monies without scrutiny or limits.

Further moves quickly followed. A consultative document in 1986 was followed up by the White Paper *Promoting Better Health* (DHSS 1987). The same themes of consumerism and better 'value for money' through stronger management which characterised policy in the hospital and community health sector are also reflected in government aims for primary care, with the additional aim of giving higher priority to health promotion and illness prevention.

Many of the proposals in the White Paper were introduced through the new contracts for general practitioners which took effect in April 1990, in spite of strong resistance. There were three main ways in which the government hoped to achieve its aims. First there were proposals to give patients a 'better deal'. GPs were required to provide fuller information on the services they provided through practice leaflets. Family Health Service Authorities (FHSAs), the successor bodies to Family Practitioner Committees established under the 1990 legislation, had to publish directories giving information on the sex, qualifications, services and deputising arrangements of GPs in their area. GPs were allowed to advertise their practices subject to certain safeguards, and arrangements for changing GPs and making complaints were simplified.

Second, the services that GPs had to provide under the contract were made more specific to reflect the government's view of 'good general practice', and included a range of health promotion services. The management role of FHSAs in monitoring the contracts, encouraging high standards and developing primary care generally was strengthened.

Third, the remuneration system became performance-related. By increasing the proportion of the GP's income derived from capitation fees from the average of 45 per cent to 60 per cent, GPs were encouraged to 'compete' for more patients by offering higher standards of care. There were also extra payments for doctors practising in deprived or isolated areas, target payments encouraging GPs to achieve higher levels of cover for childhood immunisation and cervical screening, and incentives for the provision of minor surgery and health promotion clinics.

In conclusion 'Promoting Better Health' and its implementation through the new contract can be seen as the starting point for the subsequent reforms in *Working for Patients* (*WFP*). The Conservative government not only showed its willingness to challenge general practice and scrutinise its procedures and use of resources but also a strengthened commitment to health promotion. But the contract was imposed on an unwilling and angry profession, already alarmed by the publication of *WFP* in January 1989 and threatened by what seemed potentially strong curbs on their independence.

Developments in community care

'Community care' has always been difficult to define, since it covers such a diverse set of needs met by a variety of providers. It is generally taken to mean services provided in a variety of non-hospital settings to meet the long-term health and social care needs of groups with chronic disabilities and illnesses of either a physical or mental kind. However, this is not a complete definition. Some services for these groups such as respite care or rehabilitation may still be provided by hospitals.

In terms of provision services are diverse and fragmented.

- The health service provides general home nursing as well as a variety of specialist nursing services (pain relief, psychiatry, care of the elderly, incontinence advisers), physiotherapy; chiropody; respite care, etc. The staff may work for community or mental health units (now trusts) or be attached to GP surgeries and be part of the primary health care team;

- Local authority social service departments provide a wide range of social care services such as social workers, home helps and care assistants, meals, aids and adaptations, various kinds of residential accommodation, day centres, etc;
- The voluntary sector, which includes self-help and pressure groups for the various 'client groups' and housing associations, provides a wide range of residential, community and domiciliary services, often in partnership with statutory agencies. The voluntary sector often tries to 'plug the gaps' by providing services the statutory sector ignores or is ill-equipped to do well e.g. sitting services for carers, drop-in centres for the homeless, sheltered employment schemes;
- The private sector is the main provider of residential and nursing homes for the elderly. To a smaller extent it provides residential care for those with learning disabilities and mental illnesses;
- Finally the 'informal sector' refers to the care given to dependents by family members, friends and neighbours, which still covers the main bulk of caring services. Government estimates in 1988 were that six million people in Britain were carers, with 1.4 million spending more than 10 hours a week on caring tasks (Green 1988).

In most people's minds 'community care' is closely associated with the closure of long-stay hospitals for people with mental illnesses, learning disabilities and the elderly and the development of community facilities to replace them. This has been the declared policy of successive governments since at least the early seventies (DHSS 1971, 1975) and its origins can be traced back as far as the Mental Health Act of 1959. Conservative policies in the 1980s reiterated the commitment to community care for these groups and intensified the speed of hospital rundowns but critics argued that in terms of alternative services provided for patients, care *in* the community was less evident than care *by* the community, and specifically the family. Indeed policy documents such as the 1981 White Paper, *Growing Older*, openly argued that the care of dependents should be everyone's business.

> Providing adequate support and care for elderly people in all their varying personal circumstances is a matter which concerns – and should involve – the whole community, not just politicians and officials, or charitable bodies. It is a responsibility which must be shared by everyone.

It went on to state:

> Whatever level of public expenditure proves practicable and however it is distributed the primary sources of support and care are informal and voluntary. These spring from the personal ties of kinship, friendship and neighbourhood. They are irreplaceable. It is the role of public authorities to sustain and where necessary develop but never to displace such support and care.
>
> (DHSS 1981: 3)

Feminist writers and bodies like the Equal Opportunities Commission showed that the 'family' was simply a euphemism for women, who shouldered a large and growing burden of care for disabled and elderly dependents, with little acknowledgment of their own needs or support from statutory agencies (Equal Opportunity Commission 1982; Pascal 1986; Finch and Groves 1983). The idea that neighbours and friends could be induced to do more caring tasks flew in the face of trends like growing female employment, and the evidence suggested that in any case they were likely to provide help in the least arduous aspects of caring – shopping, gardening or occasional 'minding'. The worst aspects were the heavy physical tasks of 'tending' – lifting, washing, dressing, feeding – plus the mental and emotional effort needed to manage the complex process of care day after day.

> This is the unromantic uncomfortable reality of a great deal of caring work: hard manual labour, dirty jobs, sleepless nights and mental stress.
>
> (Walker 1987: 377)

The financial pressures experienced by both local authorities and health authorities throughout the 1980s as the government sought to control public expenditure were a major reason for the slow build-up of community provision. However, no such restraints impeded the growth of private residential and nursing homes, which was fuelled by entitlements to social security payments, as discussed earlier in this chapter. The health service also benefited, with many health authorities contracting out the care of long-stay elderly patients to the voluntary or private sector where the revenue costs would be covered by the DHSS.

A highly critical report by the Audit Commission in 1986 argued that community care policy was in a mess, fragmented organisationally and financially, marked by perverse incentives which encouraged the growth of the most expensive forms of provision – residential and nursing home care – with no assessment of need, and penalised more cost-effective alternatives provided by local authorities. Local authorities were hardly likely to take the policy seriously and try to provide decent domiciliary and community services when they ran the risk of being rate-capped by the government if they exceeded their stringent budgetary limits. A further handicap was the lack of any bridging finance needed to develop community facilities in advance of any savings that might be made from the closure of large institutions once their residents had been discharged (Audit Commission 1986).

The deficiencies of community care policies for the mentally ill and handicapped were further highlighted in a report by the Parliamentary Social Services Committee in 1985. It was on the basis of these critical reports that the now knighted Sir Roy Griffiths was once again asked to make his own enquiries in December 1986 and make recommendations to the Secretary of State on the 'way in which public funds are used to support community care policy and . . . on the options for action that would improve the use of those funds as a contribution to more effective community care' (Griffiths 1988: iii). The brief did not extend to looking at the policy itself nor to the adequacy of funding, although Griffiths could not resist making the remark that in trying to grapple with the problems at local level many local authorities and voluntary organisations 'certainly felt that the Israelites faced with the requirement to make bricks without straw had a comparatively routine and possible task' (Griffiths 1988: iii).

The report was presented in February 1988, and the analysis was clear and cogent. Griffiths argued that policy and resources must be brought into a 'reasonable relationship' otherwise community care would exist only in rhetoric. Fragmentation of responsibility at central government level (between the two arms of the Department of Health and Social Security and the Department of Environment) was paralleled by the organisational fragmentation at local level, and meant there was no clear leadership or direction. Community care was 'a poor relation, everybody's distant relative but nobody's baby' (Griffiths 1988: iv). There was a need to specify clear responsibilities at all levels, insist on accountable performance and tailor appropriate incentives and sanctions to encourage collaborative working.

His main recommendations were for a Minister of Community Care within the DHSS, with local authorities taking responsibility for assessing needs and planning services at a local level in collaboration with health authorities. Care managers would be responsible for seeing that individual needs (including those of carers) were met by constructing a care package, building on the contribution that informal carers could offer. The role of local authorities would change. Griffiths was clear that they should be the 'designers, organisers and purchasers of non-health care services' (p. 1), not primarily providers. The onus should be on local authorities to show that they stimulated a competitive market, and made maximum use of the private and voluntary sector to widen choice and encourage efficiency.

To eliminate the perverse incentives in the social security system favouring residential care and to further encourage collaboration he wanted to see a unified community care budget allocated to local authorities through a specific grant, with 45–50 per cent being provided by central government. The grant would have been conditional on the submission of local plans which provided evidence of local consultation on needs, collaborative planning and the mixed economy of care, thus providing an important tool of political accountability to central government.

The report was therefore a clear statement of the 'enabling' role of local authorities, which was likely to appeal to the government and echoed what was happening in education with the local management of schools. The transfer of new responsibilities and large additional budgets to local authorities was far more contentious and almost certainly the reason why the government's response to the report was delayed for over a year, finally appearing in the White Paper, *Caring for People*, in July 1989 (DOH 1989, see below). When it did respond local authorities were given the lead role after all, but the Griffiths' proposal for a specific grant was rejected in favour of the general rate support grant, with no ring fencing which would have safeguarded the community care element. The link between plans and resource allocation which Griffiths insisted was essential was broken.

Caring for People

Six main objectives

1 Services which allow people to remain in their own home wherever possible.
2 High priority to supporting carers.
3 Quality care to be based on needs assessment and good case management.
4 To promote a mixed economy of care.
5 To clarify responsibilities.
6 Better value for money.

Main features:

1 Local authority as the lead agency: Local authority social service departments are given lead responsibility for community care. Their role will include:
   - assessing individual care need (in collaboration with health authority staff);
   - appointing care managers to design individually tailored packages of care;
   - providing services and purchasing them from other providers;
   - monitoring quality and cost-effectiveness;
   - assessing clients' ability to help pay for the care they receive.
2 Developing a mixed economy of care: Local authorities will be expected to use a variety of voluntary and private providers as well as their own services, making more use of competitive tendering for care contracts to secure value for money.

continued

3 Planning and collaboration: Local authorities to publish community care plans for approval by April 1991 in consultation with health, housing and family health service authorities. Joint planning with health authorities to be based on 'planning agreements' which set out common goals for community care, funding arrangements, agreed operational policies in key areas, etc.

4 Quality control: Local authorities to set up 'arms-length' inspection units to monitor the quality of all public and private residential homes according to uniform standards.

5 Resources: Interim specific grant paid by RHAs to local authorities from 1991–1992 to set up priority community care projects for people with mental illness. New unified budget to cover the cost of social care whether this is in the person's own home or in a residential care or nursing home. The new budget to be paid to local authorities will include the care element of social security payments to people in private and voluntary homes. The rights of those already in homes to be protected but in future local authorities will determine whether residential care is appropriate to the person's needs and what proportion of the costs should be met from public funds.

In addition only £2 million was allocated for implementation in contrast to the £85 million given to the NHS for implementing *WFP* in 1989–90 (which rose to £300 million in 1990–91). Full implementation of the policy was delayed until April 1993, partly to avoid extra costs to the charge payer before an election (after the Community Charge had replaced local rates), partly because of difficulties in finding a formula for transferring funds for residential care for publicly funded residents from the social security budget to local authorities. In the event when the financial allocation to local authorities was announced in November 1992 ring-fencing was restored for a transitional period, but in the first year of operation 85 per cent of the monies transferred had to be spent in the private sector. The rebirth of community care was therefore both protracted and difficult, in spite of its immaculate conception in the Griffiths report which some commentators argued was 'visionary by international standards' (Bleddyn Davies 1994).

Conclusions

Although many aspects of *Working for Patients* and *Caring for People* can be seen as evolutionary extensions of Conservative policies for the

NHS and social services throughout the 1980s, there is also a sense in which their publication marked a defining moment. Both services embarked on a new trajectory of change which would start to break the mould of established power structures, systems and values. Bureaucracy, hierarchy, professionalism and paternalism were yesterday's words: markets, networks, consumerism and user rights were those of today.

But whereas the reforms in community care were based on a coherent model of the ends and means of community care (whether one agreed with it or not) and the policies necessary to bring them about in the Griffiths Report, the NHS reforms were characterised by a mode of policy-making that destabilised the status quo but had no clear end in sight. Timmins' account of the NHS Review shows that even at the last moment the most senior managers in the NHS could not reassure Mrs. Thatcher that 'her' reforms would work, and she seriously contemplated stopping them until a great deal more preparatory work had been done (Timmins 1996: 472). Even Secretary of State Kenneth Clarke's Minister of Health, David Mellor, conceded he had 'no idea what the NHS would look like' in five or six years time (Butler 1992: 48). In Klein's words 'The Government had created – whether by intention or by inadvertence – an institution which would invent its own future in a process of trial and error' (Klein 1995: 199).

Note

1 This is not entirely true for those doctors who practice both in the NHS and in private practice, where there is a financial incentive for the doctor to persuade patients they could be treated more quickly or more efficiently in the private sector.

References

Appleby, J. (1992) *Financing Health Care in the 1990s*, Buckingham: Open University Press.

Audit Commission (1986) *Making a Reality of Community Care*, London: HMSO.

—— (1991) *A Short Cut to Better Services: Day Surgery in England and Wales*, London: HMSO.

Barr, N., Glennerster, H. and Le Grand, J. (1988) *Memorandum of Evidence to Social Service Committee H.C. 613 p. 11*, London: HMSO.

Benzeval, M. and Robinson, R. (1988) *Healthcare Finance: Assessing the Options*, Briefing Paper 4, London: King's Fund Institute.

Bevan, G., Maynard, A., Holland, W. and Mays, N. (1988) *Reforming UK Healthcare to Improve Health: the Case for Research and Experiment*, York: Centre for Health Economics, University of York.

Bleddyn Davies (1994) 'Maintaining the pressure in community care', *Social Policy and Administration*, 28 (3): 197–205.

Brazier, J., Hutton, J. and Jeavons, R. (1988) *Reforming the UK Healthcare System*, Discussion Paper 47, York: Centre for Health Economics, University of York.

Butler, J. (1992) *Patients, Policies and Politics: Before and After Working for Patients*, Buckingham: Open University Press.

Culyer, A. (1988) *The Radical Reforms the NHS Needs – and Doesn't*, York: Centre for Health Economics, University of York.

Dept. of Health (DOH) (1989a) *Working for Patients*, Cmnd. 555, London: HMSO.

—— (1989b) *Caring for People*, Cmnd. 7615, London: HMSO.

—— (1996) *Health and Social Service Statistics for England 1995*, London: HMSO.

Dept. of Health and Social Security (DHSS) (1971) *Better Services for the Mentally Handicapped*, London: HMSO.

—— (1975) *Better Services for the Mentally Ill*, London: HMSO.

—— (1981) *Growing Older*, Cmnd. 8173, London: HMSO.

—— (1983a) Health Circular HC(83)18 *Health Services Management: Competitive Tendering in the Provision of Domestic, Catering and Laundry Services*, London: DHSS.

—— (1983b) *Inquiry into NHS Management* (The Griffiths Report), London: HMSO.

—— (1987) *Promoting Better Health*, Cmnd. 249, London: HMSO.

Dept. of Health and Social Security and Welsh Office (1979) *Patients First: Consultative Paper on the Structure and Management of the National Health Service in England and Wales*, London: HMSO.

Equal Opportunity Commission (1982) *Caring for the Elderly and Handicapped: Community Care Policies and Women's Lives*, Manchester: EOC.

Enthoven, A. (1985) *Reflections on the Management of the National Health Service*, London: Nuffield Provincial Hospitals Trust.

Enthoven, A. (1989) 'What can Europeans learn from Americans about financing and organisation of healthcare?' *Healthcare Financing Review*, Annual Supplement.

Finch, J. and Groves, D. (1983) *A Labour of Love: Women, Work and Caring*, London: Routledge and Kegan Paul.

Gretton, J. and Harrison, A. (1988) 'Stand up and deliver', *Health Service Journal*, 98, 5100.

Griffiths, Sir R. (1988) *Community Care: An Agenda for Action*, London, HMSO.

Ham, C. (1992) *Health Policy in Britain*, 3rd edn., London: Macmillan.

Harrison, S., Hunter, D., Marnoch, G. and Pollitt, C. (1989) *The Impact of General Management in the NHS*, Nuffield Institute, University of Leeds and the Open University.

Harrison, S., Hunter, D. and Pollitt, C. (1990) *The Dynamics of British Health Policy*, London: Unwin Hyman.

Haywood, S., Monks, A. and Webster, D. (1989) *Efficiency in the National Health Service*, Discussion Paper 24, Birmingham: Health Services Management Centre, University of Birmingham.

Hellander, I., Himmelstein, D., Woolhandler, S. and Wolfe S. (1993) 'Health care paper chase 1993: the cost to the nation, the states, and the District of Columbia', *International Journal of Health Services*, 24(1): 1–9.

Himmelstein, D. and Woolhandler, S. (1992) *The National Health Program Chartbook*, Cambridge, Mass.: Harvard Medical School.

Institute of Health Services Management (1988) *Final Report of the Working Party on Alternative Delivery and Funding of Health Services*, London: IHSM.

Klein, R. and Day, P. (1988) 'Future Options for Healthcare' in Social Services Committee Session 1987–88 *Resourcing the National Health Service: Memoranda Laid before the Committee,* HC Papers 284 IV pps. 48–51, London: HMSO.

Klein, R. (1995) *The New Politics of the NHS*, 3rd edn, London: Longman.

Millar, B. (1989) 'Cloud of doubts may spell an uncertain takeoff', *Health Service Journal*, 99(5161): 905.

National Association of Health Authorities (NAHA) (1988) 'Extra money for the NHS should come from taxation', *NAHA News*, June.

National Association of Health Authorities and Trusts (NAHAT) (1990) *Healthcare Economic Review 1990*, Birmingham: NAHAT.

National Audit Office (1986) *Report by the Controller and Auditor General: Value for Money Developments in the NHS*, HC Papers 85–6 212, London: HMSO.

Packwood, T., Buxton M. and Keen, J. (1990) 'Resource Management in the National Health Service: a first case history' *Policy and Politics*, 18(4): 245–55.

Pascal, G. (1986) *Social Policy: a Feminist Analysis*, London: Tavistock.

Ranade, W. and Appleby, J. (1989) *To Market, To Market. . . .*, Research Paper 1, Birmingham: NAHA.

Ranade, W. and Haywood, S. (1991) 'Privatising from within: the National Health Service under Thatcher', in C. Altenstetter and S. Haywood (eds) *From Rhetoric to Reality: Healthcare and the New Right*, London: Macmillan.

Robinson, R. (1991) 'Health expenditures: recent trends and prospects for the 1990s', *Public Money and Management*, Winter, 11(4): 19–24.

Royal College of General Practitioners (RCGP) (1985) *Quality in General Practice*, London: RCGP.

Royal Commission on the National Health Service (1979) Cmnd. 7615 *(The Merrison Report*), London: HMSO.

Social Services Committee (1988) *The Future of the National Health Service, Fifth Report, Session 1987–88*, H.C. 613, London: HMSO.

Stocking, B. (1988) 'Medical technology in the United Kingdom', *Journal of Technology Assessment in Health Care*, 4(2): 171–83.

Taylor-Gooby, P. (1985) 'The politics of welfare: public attitudes and behaviour', in R. Klein and M O'Higgins (eds) *The Future of Welfare*, London: Blackwell.

—— (1987) 'Citizenship and welfare' in R. Jowell, S. Witherspoon and L. Brooks (eds) *British Social Attitudes 1987*, Aldershot: Gower.

Thatcher, M. (1993) *The Downing Street Years*, London: HarperCollins.

Timmins, N. (1996) *The Five Giants: A Biography of the Welfare State*, London: Fontana.

Walker, A. (1987) 'Enlarging the caring capacity of the community: Informal support networks and the Welfare State' *International Journal of Health Services*, 17(2): 369–85.

Weiner, J. (1987) 'Primary care delivery in the United States and four North-west European countries: comparing the "corporatized" with the "socialised"', *Milbank Quarterly*, 65(3): 426–61.

Yates, J. (1985) 'In search of efficiency', *Health Service Journal*, Centre Eight Supplement XCIV (4957): 5.

—— (1987) *Why are We Waiting?* Oxford: Oxford University Press.

CHAPTER 5

Setting out to market

Introducing market-like mechanisms into a planned system of health care was never going to be easy. Against the timescales set by the government, that contracts for all services be in place by April 1991, it proved a stern test of general management. The first important step was to separate the purchasing and providing functions and devolve services such as personnel and finance to units. This was complicated by the desire of some hospitals and community services to apply for self-governing status and achieve total independence from health authority control, which often led to local conflicts. Public suspicion that the real motives and intentions of the government lay in 'creeping privatisation' were particularly focused on trusts. The conflict was exacerbated by the way in which the issue was handled by the National Health Service Management Executive (NHSME), with the chief executive writing directly to Unit General Managers (UGMs), 'inviting' them to express an interest in self-governing status, over the heads of their health authorities and often against the latter's express wishes. Such an approach cut a wedge between health authorities and their units, and was guaranteed to create even greater local furore.

Preparing for contracts also imposed a massive management agenda on both purchasers and providers, requiring them to address the information deficiencies of many years in 18 months. Simply describing, assessing and costing the present pattern of services was a massive task, but in addition, new information and accounting systems for contract monitoring, invoicing and capital charging had to be installed and capital asset registers compiled for every asset worth more than £2,000.

For their part, provider units had to think more like commercial organisations and acquire new skills in business planning, marketing, contract construction and negotiation.

The headlong rush to implement the reforms without pilots or experiments, when the information base was so poor, provoked much critical comment from observers (see, for example, Social Services Committee 1990) as well as managers and professionals in the service (Appleby *et al.* 1991a). Enthoven himself had urged the case for demonstration projects to 'work at it till you work it out well in a few places – till you debug it' (Health Service Journal 1989). The price for not doing so was costly mistakes and severe stress.

There was an alternative view, however, that forcing the pace was necessary if real change was to be effected. As one manager expressed it: 'If you want to move an elephant you have to be pretty rude about it.' The Griffiths Report had summed up the service's capacity for inertia and resistance to change just as graphically:

> To the outsider it appears that when change of any kind is required, the NHS is so structured as to resemble a 'mobile': designed to move with any breath of air, but which in fact never changes its position and gives no clear indication of direction.
>
> (DHSS 1983: 12)

Theorists of cultural change in organisations support the view that breaking down the 'disbelief system' which prevents acceptance of new ways of functioning calls for 'toughness, single-mindedness and even ruthlessness' (Richards 1989) before a 'new paradigm which will frame the organisational culture in future can be built'. However, it was precisely this paradigm, symbolised by the Thatcherite language of markets and business, products and customers, that so many within the service found offensive. This was particularly true of doctors, the high priests of the old cultural order.

But what kind of 'market' was being introduced and how did it develop? The next section traces the traditional arguments for and against health care markets to set against the peculiar hybrid that was introduced into the NHS.

Markets and health care

In free-market economics perfectly competitive markets achieve an efficient allocation of resources by balancing demand and supply through the price mechanism. The assumptions underpinning the theory are that new suppliers can easily enter the market and there are no restraints on trade; that consumers are well-informed about their wants and the choices open to them and can exert leverage over sellers by threatening to take their business elsewhere. This creates the appropriate incentives for sellers to increase their efficiency (and reduce cost) and improve the quality or attractiveness of their products to buyers. Some New Right economists such as Lees (1961), Friedman (1980) and their proponents in right-wing think tanks such as Seldon (1981) have argued that the model, with appropriate modifications, is applicable to health care, which they deem to be a consumption rather than an investment good (the opposite view to that of Beveridge and the Fabian Socialists). The demand for health care, it is argued, is similar to the demand for any other commodity. Once consumers have to pay a price which reflects the real costs of providing health care, frivolous demand will be curbed and demand will be more likely to reflect perceived need (although there is considerable suspicion about the concept of 'need' in health care as distinct from demand). The absence of a price mechanism in state-provided health care distorts the relationship between demand and supply and forces a form of political or professional rationing which is more arbitrary and unfair than rationing by price. Consumers are not free to express their real preferences and suppliers are not subject to competitive tests of efficiency and quality.

The counter-arguments, however, are that in practice health care markets are highly imperfect both on the demand and supply sides. On the demand side, consumer sovereignty is not possible since the consumers are not as well-informed about their conditions and treatments as the supplier. Demand is shaped by the suppliers themselves and ignorance makes consumers relatively powerless. Second, health care cannot be treated like any other commodity since health is a prerequisite for every other activity of living, and denying appropriate care to those unable to pay is morally unacceptable. (In practice, of course, a good deal of health care is either inappropriate, useless or positively harmful.) The uncertainty of catastrophic or chronic illness and the costs incurred means that no developed country leaves health care entirely to the market, even the United States which most nearly fits the New Right model. As consumers pay either through insurance or income tax for health services, there is no true test of the New Right model of suppliers reacting directly to consumer preferences in the market-place. The choice is between a national system of health care and some form of insurance with extensive government subsidies to those 'bad risks' – the poor, elderly and chronically ill – who cannot get cover. As Bosanquet (1983) points out, this in itself suggests that the relationship between demand and need is not as close as some New Right economists believe, and in any case introduces a very different set of arguments about the relative advantages and disadvantages of both systems.

On the supply side, there are two main sources of market failure. First, the relative powerlessness of the patient in the face of the doctor's superior knowledge can be exploited, particularly if the doctor has a direct financial interest in the outcome (the 'overtreatment' problem, for example). This is tackled through the ethical system of values socialised into doctors through the long process of training and, in many countries, by trying to break the link between clinical decision making and the financial self-interest of the doctor through third-party payment or salaried service.

Second, competition is difficult to ensure, giving scope for monopolistic abuse. Health care markets are not easily 'contestable' (Baumol

1982) since there are many barriers to entry against potential new suppliers, for example, the heavy costs of new hospital development and technologies, and the legal monopoly given to doctors controlling entry to the profession.

To these traditional criticisms can be added more recent ones. There is no guarantee that competitive markets and more direct consumer choice lead to a more efficient and effective deployment of health care resources. The evidence from America suggests the reverse, with the inappropriate overuse and duplication of expensive treatments and technologies and a lopsided emphasis on individualistic curative medicine at the expense of population-based prevention and public health.

The NHS reforms attempt to gain some of the advantages of markets within a public health system, without their inequities and inefficiencies, by a managed form of competition. Enthoven's original term to describe this was the 'internal market', but after some semantic uncertainty this has changed to 'quasi-market' to describe a general concept, and this will be the term used here. In the UK quasi-markets have been introduced into education, housing and community care as well as the health service, and they underpin health care reforms in several other countries. They are 'markets' inasmuch as they replace monopolistic state providers with competitive independent ones, but they are 'quasi' because they differ from conventional markets in significant ways. Le Grand and Bartlett (1993) outline three principal differences:

- Although a number of service providers compete for contracts they may not be privately owned nor are they necessarily seeking to maximise their profits. For example, in the NHS, publicly owned trust hospitals, not-for-profit voluntary organisations, and private hospitals compete for public contracts;
- Buyers may not be the ultimate consumers of the service but agents acting on their behalf such as DHAs and GP fundholders;
- Purchasing power is centralised into a budget given to one or more agencies (DHAs, local authorities) or takes the form of an earmarked budget or 'voucher' which individuals can use for a specific service (choice of school or residential home).

Designing the quasi-market

In principle, quasi-markets can be 'designed' to achieve different objectives, although in practice choice may be constrained by the institutional arrangements for health care which already exist. Various models have been suggested in the UK. Enthoven's was clearly the most influential, and his was designed to improve incentives for micro-efficiency, patient responsiveness and innovation in the health service while retaining its present strengths of cost containment and equity. The District Health Authority (DHA) was the sole budget holder, receiving a revenue and capital allocation with which to provide and pay for comprehensive health care for its resident population. It received considerable freedoms in doing this: to raise capital, dispose of assets, negotiate directly with GPs and consultants and experiment with different forms of employment and service contract.

Enthoven's model for the new DHA was the health maintenance organisation (HMO) in the United States, which had provoked great interest in the UK. HMOs take the responsibility for providing comprehensive health services to an enrolled population in return for annual premiums. Enrolment is on an annual basis, and HMOs compete for subscribers. The HMO provides a family doctor service but also provides or purchases secondary care for enrollees. Since the costs have to be met from a fixed budget, the HMO has an incentive not to refer patients to expensive hospital services unnecessarily, and to promote the good health of enrollees. The performance and equity consequences of HMOs have been subject to growing critical scrutiny (Light 1994; Miller and Luft 1994) but Enthoven is still one of the main advocates of HMOs in the United States, and they are a principal feature of his plans to reform the American health care system along 'managed competition' lines (Enthoven and Kronick 1989; Enthoven 1993).

Some of Mrs Thatcher's advisers, for example, Goldsmith and Willetts (1988) argued for a similar system of competing HMO-style intermediaries here to enhance direct consumer choice and market incentives. Enthoven also believed this to be desirable but unacceptably radical in the British context. His proposals for the NHS were relatively modest and evolutionary, building on the managerial reforms of the 1980s. Competition was relatively constrained and DHAs used the *threat* of buying elsewhere to force changes in behaviour from their own, still directly managed providers. In practice, the government went further than Enthoven suggested in giving greater independence to NHS providers, but drew back from implementing another of his recommendations, curtailing GP freedom of referral to any consultant of their choice.

A second group of proposals was also influenced by the American literature on HMOs but made the GP the main budget-holder (Maynard 1986, see also Bosanquet 1985, Culyer 1988). An early paper by Alan Maynard, Professor of Health Economics at York University, argued that the 'assymetry of information' which characterised health care markets could be partially redressed by making GPs – who were well placed to know the needs and preferences of their patients – act as expert proxy consumers on their behalf, so improving choice and responsiveness within the British context. In a later joint paper with

Bevan, Holland and Mays (1988) Maynard argued there was also greater potential for achieving substantial cost savings in health care by giving a greater role to primary and community care, than in promoting competition between hospitals (largely the premise of the Enthoven model).

Glennerster and his colleagues (1992) note how these ideas had been picked up both by the Treasury and the DOH in the late 1980s, but only found their way into policy when Kenneth Clarke added GP fundholding to the NHS package of reforms as an experimental appendage at a late stage, with GP fundholders restricted to buying a narrow range of services. However, fundholding spread more rapidly than expected, The first phase only accounted for 3 to 4 per cent of practices, but by 1994 accounted for 8,000 GPs in 2,000 practices serving 36 per cent of the population. The services they were allowed to purchase also increased. At first these were restricted to diagnostic, outpatient and inpatient treatments of a relatively standard kind (mostly elective surgery). Community health services were added later. High-technology procedures and emergency care were still the responsibility of the DHA, but every fundholding budget meant a corresponding reduction in the DHA's budget. This decreased their ability to balance demands for emergency and elective care (which still had to be purchased for non-fundholders) and led to claims that the patients of non-fundholders were disadvantaged in access to such treatments. In the early years of the reforms, therefore, the issue of how these two forms of purchasing were meant to relate, and who would emerge as the 'primary purchaser' of health care was a contentious and much-debated issue.

What did the government hope its own quasi-market model would achieve? There is little discussion of aims and objectives in *Working for Patients* (WFP), but Le Grand and Bartlett (1993) argue that explicitly or implicitly four aims can be discerned: improvements in productive efficiency, responsiveness, patient choice and equity. Productive efficiency is equated with the rather vague concept of 'value for money', which Mrs Thatcher promulgates in her foreword to *WFP*. Le Grand and Bartlett (p. 15) define this as providing a given quantity and quality of service at minimum cost, to differentiate it from cruder definitions of efficiency which relate solely to unit costs and do not take issues of quality into account. These aims may, however, be incompatible. Choice may have to be compromised in the interests of efficiency; the freedoms necessary for ensuring efficiency curbed in the interests of equity. The next section throws more light on these dilemmas.

Theorising the quasi-market

Theoretical analyses and predictions about the quasi-market have, not surprisingly, been dominated by economists. Underlying most of their critiques is the fundamental point that politicians simply misunderstood how markets work and the conditions which are necessary if the government's objectives were to be achieved.

Some of the causes of market failure in health care have already been discussed earlier this chapter, but these are worth elaborating in the context of the NHS quasi-market.

Limits to contestability

Theoretically, conventional markets achieve an efficient allocation of resources by competition between sellers and buyers where no one individual or firm is able to influence the price by their decisions. In practice, many markets display significant elements of monopoly or oligopoly (domination by a few suppliers), but this may not matter if the market is contestable, that is, if new suppliers can enter the market relatively easily and inefficient suppliers can be driven out of business. The threat of competition is sufficient to prevent suppliers abusing their monopoly position. Monopsony (domination of the market by one buyer) can also lead to distortions, if market power is used to exploit suppliers.

Analyses of market structure in health care are complicated by the fact that there are numerous health care 'products' and a variety of different submarkets from liver transplants to chiropody (Boyle and Darkin 1994). Some, such as Accident and Emergency services are natural monopolies designed to serve populations of at least two million people because of the cost and complexity of the services they provide, and they are not easily contestable. Others, such as general surgery, may be both more competitive (Appleby *et al.* 1991b), particularly in metropolitan areas, and contestable. In practice, even where choices are theoretically available for purchasers, the local service may enjoy a de facto monopoly if patients are not willing or able to travel to other hospitals (Ranade and Appleby 1989; Mahon *et al.* 1994) or where the political costs of allowing a facility to close appear too great.

Restricted capital and labour markets

In conventional markets providers improve productivity by substituting more expensive inputs (either capital or labour) by less expensive ones, but once again there are restrictions on the ability of NHS providers to do the same. For example, trusts were promised much greater personnel freedoms but progress has been slow and incremental (Buchan and Seccombe 1994) and the transition to local pay bargaining fraught with political and practical problems.

Similar controls operate in the capital market. Although freedom to borrow on the private capital market was a major initial incentive persuading units to apply for trust status, in practice this freedom was severely constrained by Treasury fears of expanding the public sector borrowing requirement. On existing capital, trusts are required to show a rate of return of 6 per cent, but cannot hold or carry surpluses from one year to another and their working cash balances are small.

Competition among purchasers

Turning to the purchasing side of the market, Le Grand and Bartlett (1993) argue that the requirement for competitive purchasers is only met in the case of GP fundholders and the services they purchase. Patients have a choice of GP but no choice of DHA, who are local monopolies.

Information

Both sides of the market need cheap and accurate information on costs and quality if prices are to serve as reliable indicators of comparative efficiency. However, cost and quality information in the NHS was rudimentary, and though many advances have been made, problems still exist. For example, in drawing up their contracts, trusts are expected to price their services equal to their own average costs with no cross-subsidisation between services. In practice, purchasers cannot use these prices as reliable value-for-money comparisons. Average speciality costs disguise differences in case mix within a speciality, there is still no agreed uniform definition about what procedures should be included under a particular speciality heading and providers vary considerably in the sophistication of the costing procedures.

Another serious difficulty revolves around the issue of contract monitoring. This is essential in the quasi-market, otherwise providers could indulge in opportunistic behaviour (Robinson and Le Grand 1995: 35); for example, skimping on the standards they have agreed to in the contract, distorting or selectively disclosing information. In theory this should be controlled through the contracting process and the way contracts are enforced but this is not easy with NHS contracts (which in any case are not legally enforceable). There are three types of NHS contracts:

1 Block contracts which specify access to a defined range of services in return for an annual fee or block with 'floors and ceilings' which specify minimum and maximum levels of activity
2 Cost and volume which specify that a provider will supply a given number of treatments at a given price
3 Costs per case which specify in detail both the service to be provided at an individual patient level and the price.

Given poor information on cost and quality, DHAs had to rely mainly on block contracts in the first two years (although GP fundholders were often insisting on costs-per-case contracts), but these allow ample opportunity for providers to 'game' the system (for example, maximise the throughput of minor cases at the expense of more complex, costly ones), which purchasers find difficult and costly to monitor (Light 1990; Ranade 1995). As more refined cost information becomes available, purchasers are using more sophisticated cost and volume and cost-per-case contracts, which makes opportunistic practices more difficult, but this is at the expense of high transaction costs, as discussed below.

Accurate information on quality of care is also difficult for purchasers to collect, particularly on the outcomes of care. Advocates of fundholding argue that GPs are better placed than DHAs to assess outcomes, since they are both medically trained and closer to patients (Glennerster *et al.* 1994; Le Grand and Bartlet 1993).

The costs of contracting

The transaction costs associated with market exchange (drafting, negotiating, placing and monitoring contracts; installing and running billing and payments systems), are likely to be high in health care markets. An important stream of criticism about the quasi-market has focussed on the theoretical work of Williamson (1975, 1985) which suggests that markets are a more efficient form of allocating resources than bureaucratic hierarchies only when products are relatively standard, information on outcomes, risks and associated costs are relatively predictable and known, and the technology used to produce the product is not highly specific to the transaction in question. Where these conditions do not prevail – as in health care – writing, setting and enforcing comprehensive contracts which try to predict all contingencies and deal with all possible risks becomes very difficult and costly (Burke and Goddard 1991; Bartlett 1991). In practice such comprehensiveness becomes impossible, and this provides fertile ground for opportunism or for sellers to try and over-protect themselves against risk, which drives up prices. At the same time, if buyers and sellers are locked into each other because of reliance on specific and costly technology, competition cannot act as a check on bad faith or malfeasance. and this explains why other institutional responses (such as bureaucratic hierarchies) have evolved.

However, the analysis is still underpinned by economic assumptions about behaviour and motivation which reduces everything to an economic calculus of short-term market advantage. Hence the starting presumption of low trust, and the need to control opportunism and deceit. In the real world, cooperation and trust are a common response to the problems identified by Williamson because they are perceived to bring benefits to each side. Chambers argues that many markets which share some of the characteristics of the health care market – uncertainty, risk, imperfect information – are characterised by long-term relationships between buyer and seller based on trust, track record and a reputation for quality and reliability. At the same time, they have developed an agreed body of industry-wide procedures to regulate the risks both share (Chambers 1990). Ford (1990) argues that a 'relational market' with similar characteristics will develop where there are a small number of suppliers and corporate consumers, which is largely the case in the NHS (see also Propper 1993). Such markets are increasingly common in the commercial world, often based on integrated information or production processes, and close co-operation on product or technology development.

Motivation

Providers must be motivated at least in part by financial self-interest, otherwise they will not respond appropriately to price signals. The requirement appears to be met if providers believe their survival depends on their ability to attract profitable business, and lessens to the extent that they would be protected and 'baled out' if they made losses. It may be difficult to let some providers 'exit' the market, however, particularly where there are no alternative sources of supply, thus reducing the incentives for efficiency. For their part, purchasers must be motivated by the needs and wishes of users when placing their contracts, given there is an agency relationship between purchasers and the ultimate consumers of services. Advocates of GP fundholding have argued that GPs are better placed to know user needs and preferences than 'remote' DHAs but factors such as the medical bias of GPs, communication problems with lower socio-economic groups and gender stereotyping suggest that GPs perceptions are often distorted (see for example, Cartwright and O'Brien 1976; Cartwright and Anderson 1981; Oakley 1980).

Cream-skimming

In theory, users will still receive services on the basis of clinical need, not the ability to pay, so in principle there should be no loss of equity unless 'cream-skimming' occurs. This refers to the opportunities for both purchasers and providers to practice 'adverse selection' – choosing not to buy or provide services for high-cost patients. Equity will only be achieved if there is no incentive for either side to discriminate against such patients. Adverse selection could be practised by DHAs, who still have to ration services, and GP fundholders discriminating against high-cost patients (although partial protection is provided by the fact that over £6,000 the DHA picks up the bill). Opportunities for cream-skimming on the provider side are particularly likely with block contracts, which allow providers considerable freedom in the delivery of services.

In conclusion, economic analysis seems to provide a useful theoretical framework for clarifying the conceptual weaknesses and practical difficulties of operating the NHS quasi-market. Indeed its development over the last five years largely reflects attempts to reconcile the contradictions and dilemmas exposed by this analysis, and health economists have been prominently involved in suggesting remedies (see for example, Boyle and Darkin 1994; Smee 1995; Robinson and Le Grand 1995; Saltman and Von Otter 1992, Culyer *et al.* 1990 as well as a stream of papers by several authors from the Centre for Health Economics, University of York). But the analysis is still narrowly based on the core assumptions of neoclassical economics about human behaviour and motivation. The 'embeddedness' (Granovetter 1985) of economic behaviour in wider patterns of social relationships, the influence of social norms, cultural or professional values (including public service values), the exercise of political power – all receive scant recognition; yet these powerfully shape policy outcomes. Non-economic motives – care, compassion, altruism, professional integrity – figure prominently in health care systems, but find little place in economic theory.

In the rest of this chapter we examine how in practice the NHS quasi-market has developed over the last five years, and with what results. In doing so we draw on a number of research studies, including survey and case study evidence from a major monitoring study of the quasi-market in the West Midlands[1].

The evolution of the quasi-market

Perceptions and expectations

Given the lead role that the new cadre of general managers were expected to take in implementing the reforms, their perceptions and attitudes assumed considerable importance. A national survey of District General Managers (DGMs) and one among Unit General Managers (UGMs) in the West Midlands in November/December 1990 showed that, in general, they supported many of the main principles of the reforms (Appleby *et al.* 1991a, 1991c) and 85 per cent approved of the NHS and Community Care Act 1990 'with some reservations'. The most popular aspect was the purchaser-provider split, approved of by 90 per cent of both sets of managers, but this was differentiated from the introduction of market concepts into the NHS. Only 50 per cent of DGMs thought a market could work successfully to the benefit of patients (60 per cent of UGMs), 25 per cent disagreed and 17 per cent were unsure.

In fact, the most important potential advantages of the reforms as perceived by managers had nothing to do with the market at all but revolved around greater clarity of roles. As DHAs relinquished their responsibility for managing services, they could concentrate on a more strategic public health role, assessing the health needs of the population, and purchasing services to meet them. This gave them the opportunity of restructuring services in ways which produced greater health benefit. In addition, many managers showed enthusiasm in acting as 'the champions of the people' as they were exhorted to do by the DOH (1990). There was a clear presumption that they would be changing their health care priorities to switch resources out of hospitals and into community and primary health care services in line with their needs assessment process and consumer research. How to reconcile this strategic role with the concept of GP fundholding was seen as problematic, however.

An awareness that quality issues would now assume a much higher profile, and that they must begin to get to grips with the issues of defining, measuring and monitoring quality of care and outcomes, was also thought to be a major but worthwhile challenge. UGMs also welcomed the greater freedoms and wider responsibilities devolved down to them from DHAs. Finally, the role of contracts in clarifying choices and forcing greater accountability on providers was seen as an advantage of the new arrangements. Previously many managers at DHA level had been frustrated at the provider-led nature of the service, which they now believed they had the opportunity to change.

> For some time now we felt as directors that the organisation was being run by the units, but it is not like that now . . . Units are not too keen on that view and say, oh, its all the same, not really changed but it bloody well is going to be!
>
> (Director of Quality Assurance, DHA)

For some the quasi-market was an important mechanism for starting to exert greater control over professionals and would provide:

> . . . a lot of levers to shift some of the vested interests around . . . be able to get at some of the clinical practices because of the dynamics of someone else having the money and having to specify what sort of services would be provided.
>
> (DGM, DHA)

From stable state to take-off

In the first year of contracting the DOH and NHSME were concerned to prevent destabilisation in a pre-election period and purchasers were instructed to place contracts with their providers according to the previous year's referral patterns and volumes of work. To ensure a 'smooth take-off' for the reforms effectively meant refusing to allow the market to operate at all. The main concern of the centre and Regional Health Authorities (RHAs) was to ensure the viability of providers and their readiness for trust status. DHAs were also concerned to protect their own local units and there seemed little appetite for making changes, even if this had been allowed (Appleby *et al.* 1991a; Baeza *et al.* 1993).

The first wave of GP fundholders were not bound by these restrictions, however, and quickly began to make their presence felt as purchasers. The motivation for many of the first-wave practices to become fundholders was often irritation, over many years, with unresponsive hospitals or rude consultants (Glennerster *et al.* 1994). Now they had the freedom to make changes, and in a remarkably short time it was clear that the balance of power between consultants and GPs had started to tip in the latter's direction.

Fundholders began to insist that they talk to consultants about how service improvements could be brought about and agreed in the contract: Glennerster and his colleagues record the reaction of one of them when this first happened:

> As I sat down and I realised what we were about to do, I thought, this is a revolution happening here. No consultant has ever talked to me about what I might think of his service or any general problems we have had in 20 years of professional life.
>
> (Quoted in Glennerster *et al.* 1994: 193)

In the four West Midlands case study districts many managers still had misgivings about the 'wild card' of fundholding, and where it would eventually lead but while their numbers were limited, they could appreciate the benefits the fundholders were winning from providers, which often made it easier for the DHA to argue for similar improvements. As one Chief Executive with two first-wave fundholders remarked: '*. . . they are biting the ankles of our provider unit at present and that suits me very well*' (CEO, DHA).

In year two, some of the restrictions on DHAs were cautiously lifted, and districts responded by making changes to their 1992–93 contracts to reflect their needs assessment activity, or get better value for money (Appleby *et al.* 1992). Sometimes changes were made with little regard for their effects on providers. Unilateral action could impose damaging cuts in workload or activity, which could raise unit costs, and make certain services uneconomic. Attitudes towards service change (a more rapid build-up of community services, for example,) could become entrenched as hospitals fought for survival, and regions were called in to arbitrate as relations between purchasers and providers worsened. The effects were most clearly seen in London, as referrals to hospitals from out-of-London districts dropped, triggering the Tomlinson Inquiry into the future of London's health services and the subsequent recommendation that some of the most prestigious teaching hospitals should merge or close altogether (Tomlinson 1992). Similar problems developed on a smaller scale in other cities like Birmingham and Newcastle, prompting a wave of acute service reviews and proposals to rationalise hospital provision, often against considerable public opposition. Market pressures had pushed long-standing problems back onto the agenda and made them impossible to ignore, but illustrated the fact that restructuring services and closing hospitals will always require political courage and a planned and coordinated approach over a number of years to succeed. In this and other ways, the new market was already showing its muscle but the political consequences were not always welcome, and ministers or the NHSME often intervened to limit or reverse its effects.

Role and relationships

Three clear roles have emerged in the quasi-market, purchaser, provider and regulator, but how these are fulfilled, by whom, and through what kind of structures continually changed and developed.

The *provider role* was relatively clear-cut and developed most quickly, as wave after wave of district managed units assumed independent trust status. The first wave of 57 trusts started operating in April 1991, accounting for 13.5 per cent of NHS revenue expenditure. By the time the fourth wave became operational in April 1994, this had increased to 95 per cent of expenditure (Smee 1995: 181).

As discussed earlier, the financial freedoms trusts had been promised did not materialise and trusts were relatively slow in exploiting their personnel freedoms, which was partly due to lack of appropriate skills, and partly due to other more pressing priorities (Buchan and Seccombe 1994), although a decisive shift which firmly established the principle of local pay bargaining took place after the outcome of the 1995 pay round. Access to capital was still largely through public funds, but this is starting to change through the development of the Private Finance Initiative (PFI), which started in 1992. Trusts are required to put capital projects out to tender to try and attract private finance, before any case for public investment will be considered. The process is both bureaucratic and complex and few projects have successfully been completed under the initiative to date, but this may change in future, with far-reaching implications. The consequences of a larger reliance on private capital by the NHS, and the development of the PFI itself, are discussed in greater detail in the final chapter.

Managerially, providers did begin to exploit their growing autonomy which seemed to release a lot of creative energy and innovation. Strongly managed trusts took the lead in suggesting new patterns of provision and improving existing services. These ranged from the establishment of patient hotels to the better utilisation of theatres, improving the physical environment of waiting areas to new forms of care for people with mental health problems. A wave of trust mergers also took place, demonstrating an early prediction made by Ranade and Appleby (1989: 14) that although the introduction of the quasi-market was intended to replace planning (certainty) by market forces (uncertainty), uncertainty was the one characteristic of markets which they themselves try to overcome by the creation of cartels or monopolies to eliminate competition and control prices and output.

The *purchasing function* by contrast developed more slowly and weakly across the board. Although this has increasingly been seen as the heart of the NHS reforms, there was no clear understanding of this at first at government level and therefore clear leadership was lacking. A number of factors impeded its development. First, DHAs had continuing responsibilities for directly managed units and their transition to trust status. Secondly, many underwent further reorganisations and mergers, either with other DHAs or with FHSAs or both. Some authorities were involved in up to three rounds of reorganisation, often imposed from above by RHAs. DHA mergers were defended on the grounds that the quasi-market needed larger authorities to make more economic use of scarce skills (public health medicine, IT specialists); to give greater scope for both competition and complementarity of services; and to provide greater bargaining leverage with providers and easier collaboration across agency boundaries. At the same time DHAs found it necessary to work closely with FHSAs to prevent duplication and coordinate primary and secondary care. A second national survey of purchasers in December 1991 found that 80 per cent were working jointly on needs assessment, information systems and service planning; 65 per cent on joint commissioning of services, and 50 per cent on consumer research. Not surprisingly 83 per cent of DGMs agreed with the statement that 'it would be better all round if this DHA and FHSA merged' (Appleby *et al.* 1992). Many did merge their management arrangements but the creation of a unified authority required primary legislation. This was announced in April 1993, and involved the dissolution of all the existing authorities and the creation of new unified Health Authorities which started work in April 1996.

Only in 1993 did ministers give due importance to the purchasing function with a series of speeches by the new Minister for Health, Brian Mawhinney. Mawhinney argued that the main goal of purchasing was to secure 'tangible improvements in people's health' (Mawhinney 1993: 24) achieved through seven steps:

- strategic planning;
- effective contracting to achieve incremental improvements in quality and efficiency;
- knowledge-based health care;
- responsiveness to local people;
- cooperative relations with providers;
- local alliances;
- appropriate organisational capacity.

The speeches were important for setting out a much-needed framework for purchasing, but glossed over many of the difficulties facing authorities in trying to attain it, and the timescales involved. Health authorities had been saddled with a huge agenda which they had neither the expertise nor the appropriate support to fulfil, and were continually asked to absorb new responsibilities and tasks, notably after the *Health of the Nation* White Paper and the Patient's Charter were published in 1992 (DOH 1992a, 1992b). The former set out 27 national health targets in five key areas such as coronary heart disease and cancers (discussed in more detail in Chapter 8), while the latter set out standards which patients had a right to expect on service aspects like waiting times (see Chapter 7), which were to be continuously reviewed and improved. The implementation of the community care reforms also presented another raft of challenges and demands, requiring health and local authorities to work together in new ways.

At the micro-purchasing level, the number of GP fundholders increased steadily to cover half the population by 1996 (Audit Commission 1996a), though there were regional disparities with the scheme attracting more applicants in southern parts of the country than the north or Scotland, and in rural and suburban areas more than inner cities. Applicants were at first restricted to larger practices with list sizes in excess of 9,000 patients (subsequently reduced to 7,000). Since then further work has been done to facilitate the entry of even smaller practices, by grouping them into consortia or multifunds, for example, and one-third of practices entering the scheme in 1995–96 were grouped in this way compared to only 2 per cent of first-wave practices in 1991–92 (Audit Commission 1996b: 17). The average standard fundholding practice received a budget of £1.7 million in 1995–96, though there is a three-fold variation between the extremes. Of this budgeted amount about 55 per cent is used for hospital and community care, 38 per cent to pay for drugs prescribed by the practice's GPs, and about 7 per cent on practice staff. Fundholders pay for 20 per cent of the hospital care their patients receive by value, of which one-third is spent on planned operations, and about 40 per cent on medical and surgical outpatient treatment (Audit Commission 1996b: 6).

Early research on fundholding largely applied to the first-wave practices which appeared to be differentiated by a 'lower aversion to the financial risk involved, managerial competence, the existence of well-established computerised data systems and perhaps particular ideological and political loyalties' (Smee 1995: 195). In terms of effects, they were shown to be more successful than non-fundholders in introducing generic prescribing, reducing the volume of prescriptions and limiting total prescribing costs (Penhale *et al.* 1993; Coulter and Bradlow 1993). They also appeared to be highly successful in expanding the services they provided for their patients or improving quality and choice; for example, reduced waiting times, direct access to physiotherapy services, consultant outreach clinics (Glennerster *et al.* 1994). Whether these advantages would apply to the majority of practices was a matter of argument (this is discussed further at the end of the chapter) but the growing numbers and financial importance of GP fundholders had major implications for DHAs, as well as trusts. Mawhinney (1993) had argued that health authorities must work with GP fundholders to develop 'shared purchasing' arrangements which agreed on priorities, avoided duplication and pooled skills, but dodged the problem of what DHAs could do if GPs decided not to cooperate.

In reality, most authorities had found it necessary to work more collaboratively with all their GPs and many were experimenting with innovatory forms of primary-care led models of purchasing or commissioning, apart from orthodox fundholding. Purchasing simply means buying existing services; commissioning goes a stage further and is defined by Higgins and Girling (1994) as 'the process of seeing the right services are in place either by direct purchasing or by influencing the purchasing decisions of others'. Commissioning may also involve a degree of 'market development', persuading other agencies or providers to enter the market, develop new services or address unmet needs. As Balogh (1996) points out, the earliest experiments with devolved forms of purchasing or commissioning sought to involve a wide range of stakeholders, whereas those initiated since 1992 have focussed their attention primarily on GPs, in acknowledgement both of the direction of policy and the shifting balance of power.

A decisive move to make primary care take the lead in purchasing was made in April 1994, when the Secretary of State announced further extensions to the fund-holding scheme (NHS Executive 1994a). There are now three categories of fund-holding:

1 *Community fundholding*: for practices of 3,000 or more patients or for those who do not wish to take on standard fundholding.
2 *Standard fundholding*: available for practices of above 5,000 patients.

Includes virtually all elective surgery, outpatients and community health services.

3 *Total purchasing*: about 50 pilot schemes where GPs in a locality normally form a consortium to purchase the full range of services for their patients, apart from expensive treatments for rare conditions.

What had started as an experimental appendage, tacked onto the reforms at a late stage, now came centre stage: 'a primary-care-led service' had become the new mantra of the NHS. Once again there were implications for the new health authorities whose role has changed again. Increasingly their direct role in purchasing will lessen as GPs take greater responsibility for this in a variety of ways, through the fund-holding scheme and through other forms of primary-care-led commissioning and purchasing of services. In a review of different models, Shapiro *et al.* (1996) argue that there are now so many variants that it is impossible to categorise them by structure: they include total purchasing multifunds, standard multifunds, GPs sitting on the health authority's executive board; multi-agency commissioning (sometimes including the local authority as well); various forms of GP commissioning groups and other forms of health authority/GP alliance.

The new roles of the health authority as defined by the NHS Executive are:

- assessing the health needs of the local population;
- developing a local strategy to meet these, in conjunction with GPs, local people and other agencies;
- monitoring and management oversight of GP budgets and performance;
- providing support, development and training for GPs to support them in both their providing and purchasing roles;
- continuing to purchase those services which require a broad population base to purchase efficiently (low-volume, high-value services such as bone marrow transplants, for example).

The notable feature of present developments is the way in which much of the implementation is left to individual authorities and their GPs, giving rise to great diversity in arrangements, an enormous change from the detailed centralist prescriptions of NHS history, notably the 1974 reorganisation which was accompanied by job descriptions for every management role.

Managing the market – the regulatory role

Achieving the right balance between market freedoms and the need for regulation has proved difficult to manage, as predicted by Ranade and Appleby in 1989:

The imperatives of the market may still clash with the imperatives of a public service – centrally funded, cash-limited and politically highly sensitive. The 'market' must either be regulated to prevent politically unacceptable variation in access and standards, and will therefore be unable to achieve what a natural market does, or it must be freed from restraint still further. Ultimately at what point does regulation essentially become planning?

(Ranade and Appleby 1989: 22)

The history of the quasi-market to date validates that view. Initially, Regional Health Authorities performed the regulatory role together with the NHSME and DOH, as well as overseeing management performance in purchasing authorities. Management oversight of trusts was carried out by regional outposts of the NHSME, who were responsible for approving annual business plans and monitoring financial performance against target.

Prompted by the need to streamline central management as more responsibilities were devolved to trusts and purchasing authorities, the Secretary of State commissioned a review of Functions and Manpower in 1992 which was undertaken by Kate Jenkins from the NHS Policy Board, and Alan Langlands, then Deputy Chief Executive of the NHS Management Executive, and who is now Chief Executive. Their review reported in 1993 and recommended three main changes, the first two of which required primary legislation:

1 the unification of DHA and FHSAs into single authorities, to which we have already referred;
2 the abolition of Regional Health Authorities;
3 a more streamlined NHSME (to be known in future as the NHS Executive) with eight regional offices. These would replace both RHAs and the existing management outposts, and would be headed by a regional director and non-executive appointed chair

The government confirmed its commitment to these changes in July 1994 in *Functions and Responsibilities in the new NHS* (DOH 1994a), and produced two further reports to complete these administrative reviews – the so-called Banks Review, which proposed a series of changes in the Department of Health and NHS Executive (DOH 1994b), and one which dealt with arrangements for the public health function (DOH 1994c). The changes were largely seen by the Executive as 'unfinished business', a tidying-up operation which was promoted as supporting 'the continued drive towards decentralisation in the NHS, with responsibility and decision making devolved as far as possible to local level' (DOH 1993: 4). Yet, as Klein (1995) points out, in practice the line of central control over health authorities had tightened with the abolition of the RHAs as a buffer.

Figure 5.1 **Structure of the NHS – March 1993**

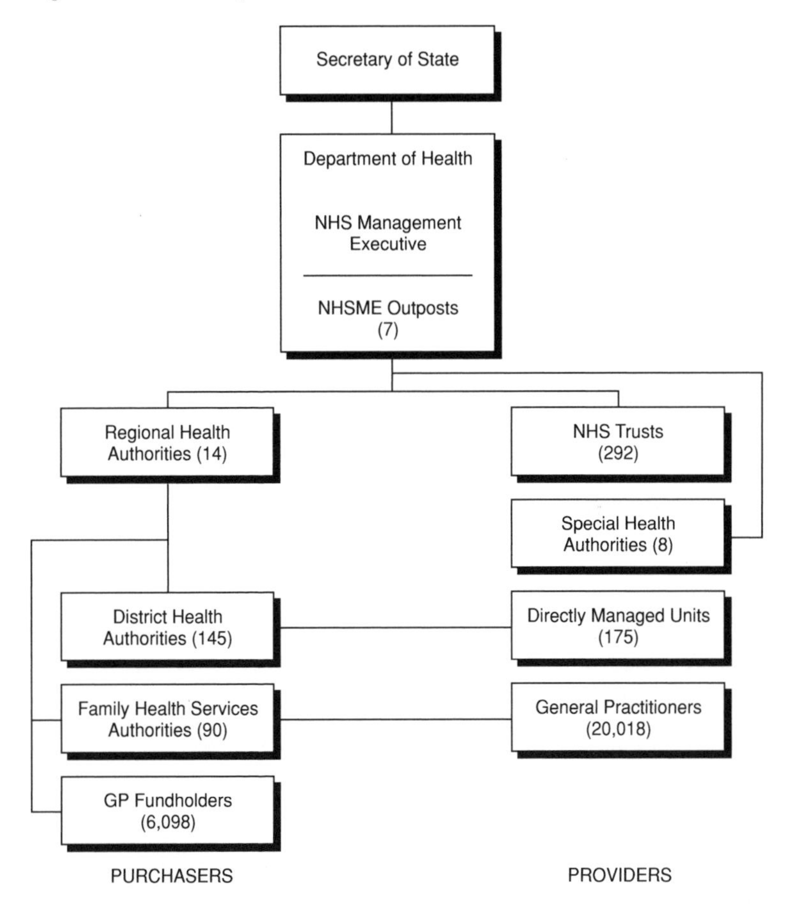

Source: Department of Health: *Managing the New NHS* (1993)
Crown copyright is reproduced with the permission of the Controller of Her Majesty's Stationery Office.

The Functions Review also confirmed the government's commitment to a competitive market and argued that regulation should promote competition whenever possible, with clear and consistent rules guiding intervention. However, as Harrison (1995) points out, there was little analysis of the factors which would determine on what basis a local market would be deemed competitive or not (for more detailed discussion see Appleby *et al.* 1991c; Propper 1995) or the specific measures necessary to promote a competitive market. More detailed guidance appeared in December 1994 which aimed to provide 'a simple set of ground rules' for the quasi-market, detailing the circumstances when central intervention in local decisions would be made in the

Figure 5.2 **New structure of the NHS – from 1993**

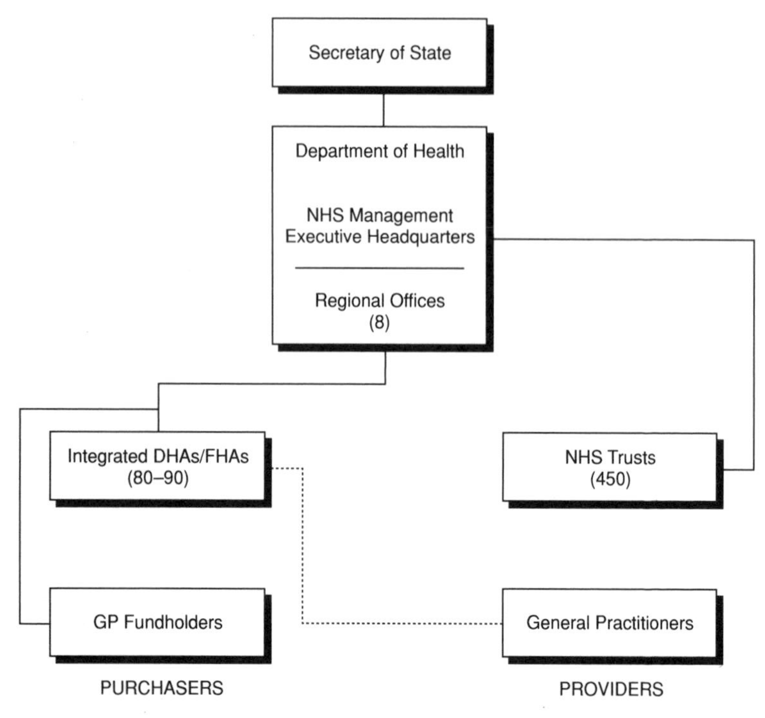

Source: Department of Health: *Managing the New NHS* (1993)

interests of 'market management'. But the guidance simply reinforced current uncertainties, as the NHS Executive wrestled with the contradictions of simultaneously encouraging a competitive market while recognising that, in large part, the effective delivery of health care involves a high degree of cooperation. How to distinguish 'constructive cooperation' (good) from 'market collusion' (bad) left everyone more baffled than before (NHS Executive 1994b).

In practice, competition for most services has been replaced by contestability, and even that may not be possible in some areas and for some services. The extension of competitive tendering to clinical services has proceeded only at the margins of activity (Appleby 1995).

Evaluating the results

Has the quasi-market achieved its original objectives – improvements in productive efficiency, choice, responsiveness and no loss of equity?

Evaluating the results is a very difficult task for several reasons. To begin with, the reforms were implemented as a package, and it is not possible to isolate the independent effect of only one aspect of them, the quasi-market. Secondly, as we have seen, the quasi-market itself has been subject to five years of almost continuous policy development and evolution. Finally, there are a number of other confounding factors, for example, the impact of the Patient's Charter, changes in the technology of care or the unusually generous budget allocations the NHS received in 1991–92 (6.1 per cent in real terms) and 1992–93 (5.5 per cent in real terms) which add to the ambiguity of the evidence.

The indicators used to measure 'success' are also problematic. The government uses increases in activity as an important measure, citing an increase of 18 per cent in 'finished consultant episodes' between 1990–1991 and 1993–1994 (with a further 6.5 per cent increase the following year (BMJ 1996)), and an increase in day cases by 66 per cent in the same period. For a service trying to *promote* health and *prevent* illness, this seems a rather ambiguous indicator of success, but in addition, as Klein (1995) points out, it is difficult to tell whether the *rate* of increase has speeded up after 1991 or not, since the figures show a drop in the annual increase in the number of inpatients by nearly one-half in those years (compared to the whole period since 1979) but a doubling in the number of day patients, reflecting the rapid pace of technological development which allowed this substitution to occur (DOH 1994d).

Waiting times are also an ambiguous indicator. In March 1994, just over one million people were waiting for treatment, but there were big reductions in the numbers waiting more than one year and 70 per cent of the total were waiting for less than six months. Once again these results have to be seen in context. Waiting times have certainly reduced, but this is due to the estimated £250 million on targeted funding and the enormous political energy put behind the achievement of Patient's Charter targets. The sustainability of current improvements is also in doubt. Recently hospitals have faced an unprecedented increase in emergency admissions which is impacting on waiting times for elective treatments and causing them to rise once again.

Direct research evidence of the reforms' impact on patients is summarised by Robinson and Le Grand (1994), but this only covers the early years (up to 1993). On consumer choice, there was little evidence that patients had any greater choice of hospital or consultant (Mahon *et al.* 1994: Jones *et al.* 1994) and are reluctant to exercise their choice to change GPs. The freedom of non-fundholding GPs to refer to any consultant is also restricted in practice since they can only refer to the providers with whom the DHA has contracts, unless they get prior permission to make an extra contractual referral. On quality and

Figure 5.3 ***Benefits achieved by majority of fundholders according to the Audit Commission, 1996***

Objective	*Benefits (examples)*	*Indicators*
Closer focus on individual needs	Better information from consultants improving care of the patient when discharged from hospital	Quicker and more informative clinical letters
Better quality services	Solutions to longstanding problems such as access, lack of courtesy to patients, inconvenient pathology collection times, etc.	Local difficulties solved; faster rate of change
Increased efficiency	More cost-effective prescribing; Benefit to patients via fundholder savings	Less inappropriate prescribing, more generics Planned savings spent in line with regulations
Wider choice for patients	Freedom to refer where GP wishes	Referral range protected/ increased

Source: Audit Commission 1996a: 38–9

responsiveness the evidence is mixed and somewhat anecdotal, although *managers* felt that this was a major benefit of the reforms; 81 per cent in the NAHAT second survey of purchasers agreed that the reforms were already producing improvements in service quality for their residents (Appleby *et al.* 1992).

The early research on fundholding had concluded GPs were more effective in securing quality improvements and offering more choice to their patients. A National Audit Office survey of fundholders broadly supported this finding, but the most systematic and wide-ranging study of fundholding to date has been carried out by the Audit Commission. The Commission concluded that while the majority of fundholders had achieved some progress (see Figure 5.3) there was much room for improvement. Although a minority of leading edge fundholders were in truth 'turning the world upside-down' as purchasers, the majority were not able or willing to exploit the full range of opportunities open to them due to lack of vision, knowledge, motivation or managerial capacity.

Equity concerns were also targeted at fundholders. Worries that a two-tier service was developing, which privileged the patients of fundholders, replaced earlier concerns that fundholders would under-serve their patients to save money, concerns which did not appear to materialise (HSJ 1995; Whitehead 1994; Audit Commission 1996b). Similarly there is no evidence that 'cream skimming' – refusing to enrol potentially high-cost patients or removing them from the practice list – is occurring on a systematic basis, though individual incidences have emerged in the press (Audit Commission 1996b: 106).

However, GP fundholders were widely seen to have been treated generously in the allocation of budgets, which accounted for their ability to purchase faster or improved care for their patients (Audit Commission 1996b: 69). Budget savings made by fundholders can be retained for up to four years, and must be spent for the benefit of patients, but fundholders can still benefit personally even if savings cannot be used directly by GPs to pay themselves higher salaries. They can be used to employ more staff to provide income-paying services such as health promotion clinics, or they can be invested in the practice premises to increase its capital value when sold. Since the use of fundholder savings has generated some controversy, 77 per cent of health authorities now have written policies and 81 per cent have issued guidance on how they may be spent (Audit Commission 1996b: 72).

Are patients more satisfied with the service they receive? Discontent with the NHS reached a peak in 1989. Those dissatisfied with the NHS fell from 46 per cent in 1989 to 38 per cent in 1994 (Moore 1996). Over this period dissatisfaction with outpatient services fell from 30 per cent to 21 per cent, while dissatisfaction with inpatient services rose slightly from 15 per cent to 16 per cent, but such surveys tell us more about the current state of media coverage on the NHS and the 'gratitude factor' than they do about the quality of care.

Patients often express high levels of satisfaction with the overall level of service they have received which is belied by more specific responses on particular issues. Moore cites one of the largest interview surveys, undertaken in 36 hospitals with 5,000 patients. Although 97 per cent of patients rated their overall care as excellent, very good or good, 10 per cent had had their admissions cancelled, 11 per cent had had operations cancelled, 56 per cent received no written information about their care, 62 per cent suffered pain, and 70 per cent were not given advice on warning signs to watch out for on discharge. These are all familiar complaints, and indeed complaints to Community Health Councils have doubled (from 37,050 in 1990 to 87,184 in 1994) as have complaints to the Health Service Commissioner (from 990 in 1990–91 to 1,782 in 1994–95) (Moore 1996: 12). Does this suggest quality of care is declining, or (more probably) that people are less inclined to accept poor standards, and are encouraged not to buy the Patient's Charter?

Many theoretical predictions from the economic analysis of the quasi-market discussed earlier in the chapter were also coming true. For example, the development of a 'relational market' was a predictable response to problems of monopoly, assymetry of information, uncertainty and purchaser concern about quality of care (Propper 1993). Information deficiencies are still a major problem, although the NHS has made major strides in improving its information base, partly by spending enormous sums on computerised management information and financial systems, calculated to cost in the region of £220 million annually from 1990 to 1995 (Lock 1996). The information strategy has not been without its problems and scandals (see for instance, Independent 1996) although this is hardly surprising given the scale and complexity of the task. With more systematic epidemiological and consumer research on health needs, and larger R&D investments into clinical and cost-effectiveness of treatments, the move towards a 'knowledge-based' NHS had become more than rhetoric.

The effectiveness of DHAs as expert proxy consumers on behalf of patients is also problematic. DHAs seemed much more attuned to the wishes of GPs than local residents in spite of some interesting consumerist initiatives (Appleby *et al.* 1992; Redmayne *et al.* 1993) and, as Klein points out, faced the dilemma that they were expected both to aggregate the *demands* of local people and reflect their *needs* in their purchasing plans, yet the two may point in different directions; 'Populism and paternalism may be at odds' (Klein 1995: 238).

The transaction costs of the new system have as predicted proved to be considerable, in particular the costs associated with the annual contracting round and the administration of extra contractual referrals made by GPs. The transaction costs of fundholding seemed particularly large, since GPs tended to use more cost-per-case contracts and trusts had to deal with multiple purchasers. For 1996 the costs of dealing with each fundholding practice were estimated at £12,500 for each community trust, £8,000 for each acute trust by the NHS Trust Federation (HSJ 1996). To this must be added the £232 million received by fundholders to cover costs in staff, equipment and computers to manage fundholding by 1994–95 which were not outweighted by the efficiency gains produced (calculated to be £206 million) (Audit Commission 1996b).

Critics of the quasi-market also pointed to a rapid expansion in the number of managers (up by 10,000 between 1990 and 1993) as further evidence of high transaction costs. However, these numbers are difficult to interpret, since this was partly due to the decentralisation of management functions to trusts; in any case, the real increase was masked by changes in staffing categories and the subsequent reclassification of existing administrators or nurses as 'managers' (Appleby 1995). Even by 1994, however, managers still only accounted for 3 per cent of the total NHS workforce, but they nevertheless proved to be an easy scapegoat for the growth of bureaucratic systems which politicians had themselves introduced. In 1995 the Secretary of State, Stephen Dorrell ordered a 5 per cent cut in management costs across the board. This, together with the continuing imposition of 3 per cent annual efficiency targets, and a continual stream of interventions by the DOH which bordered at times on silliness (advice on the circumstances in which it was appropriate to offer coffee and sandwiches to those attending meetings, for example,) were an ironic counterpoint to the rhetoric of devolution and decentralisation which continued to flow in official speeches and publications.

Perhaps the most important effects of the reforms were either unintentional or only partially foreseen. First, as the balance of power shifted from hospital doctors to GPs, primary care came to occupy an ever more important place at the centre of health care delivery. Given the direction of demographic, technological and economic trends, this might have happened anyway but not at such a fast pace. Secondly, through the contracting system the NHS started to move towards a more explicit politics of rationing, in which questions of priorities began to enter the domain of public debate. Finally, the creation of trusts and GP fundholders released creative energy and a faster pace of innovation, but also created new sets of actors with vested interests to protect in an increasingly fragmented policy arena. Once greater freedoms had been enjoyed, they would be defended, and it might be difficult for any government to rein them back in future.

Note

1 The research focussed on the West Midlands RHA, which had a population of over five million people, and comprised 22 DHAs in 1989. Within the region four case study districts were selected to represent a variety of local contexts. The NAHAT project used a variety of methods and data, including nearly 150 interviews with a variety of staff in the case study districts over three years. Unless otherwise stated, all quotations from NHS managers in this chapter are taken from these interviews.

References

Appleby, J. (1995) *Testing the market: A National Survey of Clinical Services Tendering by Purchasers*, Research Paper 18, Birmingham: NAHAT.

Appleby, J., Little, V., Ranade, W., Robinson, R. and Salter, J. (1991a) *Implementing the Reforms: A Survey of District General Managers*, Monitoring Managed Competition Project, Project Paper 4, Birmingham: NAHAT.

Appleby, J., Little, V., Ranade, W., Robinson, R. and McCracken, M. (1991b) *Implementing the Reforms: A Survey of Unit General Managers in the West Midlands*, Region Project Paper 6, Birmingham: NAHAT.

Appleby, J., Little, V., Ranade, W., Robinson, R. and Smith, P. (1992) *Implementing the Reforms: A Second National Survey of District General Managers*, Project Paper 7, Birmingham: NAHAT.

Appleby, J. (1995) 'Managers in the ascendancy' *Health Service Journal*, 21 September, 105(5471): 32–3.

Appleby, J., Little, V., Ranade, W., Robinson, R. and Smith, P. (1991c) *How Do We Measure Competition?* Project Paper 2, Birmingham: NAHAT.

Audit Commission (1996a) *Fundholding Facts*, London: HMSO.

—— (1996b) *What the Doctor Ordered: A Study of GP Fundholders in England and Wales*, London: HMSO.

Baeza, J., Salt, D. and Tilley, I. (1993) 'Four Providers' Strategic Responses and the Internal Market' in I. Tilley (ed) *Managing the Internal Market*, Liverpool: Paul Chapman Publishing.

Balogh, R. (1996) 'Exploring the role of localities in health commissioning: a review of the literature' *Social Policy and Administration*, 30(2): 99–113.

Bartlett, W. (1991) 'Quasi-markets and contracts: a markets and heirarchies perspective on NHS reforms' *Public Money and Management*, Autumn, 11(3): 53–60.

Baumol, W.J. (1982) 'Contestable markets: An uprising in the theory of industrial structure', *American Economic Review*, 72(1): 1–15.

Bevan, G., Holland, W., Maynard, A. and Mays, N. (1988) *Reforming UK Health Care to Improve Health*, York: Centre for Health Economics, University of York.

Bosanquet, N. (1983) *After the New Right*, Aldershot: Dartmouth Publishing.

—— (1985) 'GPs as firms: creating an internal market for primary care' *Public Money*, 5(1): 45–8.

Boyle, S. and Darkin, A. (1994) 'Health Care Markets: Abstract Wisdom or Practical Nonsense?' in A. Harrison (ed) *Health Care UK 1993–94*, London: King's Fund Institute.

British Medical Journal (BMJ) (1996) '20% increase in four years', 26 October, 313: 103.

Buchan, J. and Seccombe, I. (1994) 'The changing role of the NHS personnel function' in R. Robinson and J. Le Grand (eds) *Evaluating the NHS Reforms*, London: King's Fund Institute.

Burke, C. and Goddard, A. (1991) 'Internal markets – the road to inefficiency?' *Public Administration*, 389–96.

Cartwright, A. and Anderson, R. (1981) *General Practice Revisited: A Second Study of Patients and their Doctors*, London: Tavistock.

Cartwright, A. and O'Brien, M. (1976) 'Social class variations in health care and in the nature of general practitioner consultations' in M. Stacey (ed) *The Sociology of the NHS*, Sociological Review Monograph Keele: University of Keele.

Casson, M. (1991) *The Economics of Business Culture*, Oxford: Clarendon Press.

Chambers, D. (1990) 'Learning from markets', in *Building the Contract Relationship*, Conference Paper 1, London: Office for Public Management.

Coulter, A. and Bradlow, J. (1993) 'Effects of NHS reforms on general practitioners' referral patterns' *British Medical Journal*, 306: 433–37.

Culyer, A.J. and Posnett, J. (1991) 'Hospital behaviour and competition' in A.J. Culyer, A. Maynard and J. Posnett (eds) (1990) *Competition in Health Care: Reforming the NHS*, London: Macmillan.

Culyer, A.J. (1988) *The Radical Reforms the NHS needs – and Doesn't*, Evidence to the Social Services Committee, House of Commons University of York (mimeo).

Department of Health (1990) *Developing Districts*, London: HMSO.
—— (1992a) *The Health of the Nation*, Cmnd. 1986 London: HMSO.
—— (1992b) *The Patient's Charter*, London: HMSO.
—— (1993) *Managing the New NHS*, London: HMSO.
—— (1994a) *Functions and Responsibilities in the New NHS*, London: HMSO.
—— (1994b) *The Review of the Wider Department of Health* (the Banks Review), London: HMSO.
—— (1994c) *Public Health in England*, London: HMSO.
—— (1994d) Department of Health and Office of Population Censuses and Surveys *Departmental Report*, London: HMSO.
Department of Health and Social Security (1983) *Inquiry into NHS Management* (The Griffiths Report), London: HMSO.
Enthoven, A. (1993) 'The history and principles of managed competition' *Health Affairs*, Supplement, 24–48.
Enthoven, A. and Kronick, R. (1989) 'A consumer-choice health plan for the 1990s' *New England J. of Medicine*, 320: 29–37 and 320: 94–101.
Ford, D. (ed) (1990) *Understanding Business Markets*, London: Academic Press.
Friedman, M. and Friedman, R. (1980) *Free to Choose*, London: Secker and Warburg.
Glennerster, H., Matsaganis, M. and Owens, P. (1992) *A Foothold for Fundholding*, Research Report 12, London: King's Fund Institute.
Glennerster, H., Matsaganis, M., Owens, P. and Hancock, S. (1994) *Implementing GP Fundholding*, Buckingham: Open University Press.
Goldsmith, M. and Willetts, D. (1988) *Managing Health Care: a New System for a Better Health Service*, London: Adam Smith Institute.
Granovetter, M. (1985) 'Economic Action and Social Structure: the Problem of Embeddedness' *American Journal of Sociology*, 91(3): 481–510.
Harrison, A. (1995) 'Creating the New NHS', in A. Harrison (ed) *Health Care UK 1994–95*, London: Kings Fund Institute.
Health Service Journal (HSJ) (1989) 'A guru vexed by his disciples', 21 September, 99(5169): 1150.
—— (1995) 'Fundholders are not putting cash before care', 105(5444): 6.
—— (1996) 'Jobs will go in drive to cut red tape', 106(5504): 3.
Higgins, J. and Girling, J. (1994) 'Purchasing for health: the development of an idea' in A. Harrison (ed) *Health Care UK 1993–94*, London: King's Fund Institute.
Independent (1996) 'NHS in £6m pay-out to doctor's company', 2nd June, p. 1.
Jones, D., Lester, C. and West, R. (1994) 'Monitoring changes in health services for older people' in R. Robinson and J. Le Grand (1994).
Klein, R. (1995) *The New Politics of the NHS*, London: Longman.
Lees, D.S. (1961) *Health Through Choice*, London: Institute of Economic Affairs, reprinted in R. Harris (ed) *Freedom or Free for All* (1965), London: IEA.
Le Grand, J. and Bartlett, W. (1993) *Quasi-Markets and Social Policy*, London: Macmillan.
Light, D. (1990) 'Learning from their mistakes' *Health Service Journal*, 14 October, 99(5148): 1–2.
—— (1994) 'Managed care: false and real solutions' *The Lancet*, 344: 1197–99.

Lock, C. (1996) 'What value do computers provide to NHS hospitals?' *British Medical Journal*, 312(7043): 1407–10.

Mawhinney, B. (1993) *Purchasing for Health: a Framework for Action*, Leeds: NHS Management Executive.

Mahon, A., Wilkin, D. and Whitehouse, C. (1994) 'Choice of hospital for elective surgery referral: GPs' and patients' views', in R. Robinson and J. Le Grand (1994).

Maynard, A. (1986) 'Performance Incentives in General Practice', in G. Teeling-Smith (ed) *Health Education and General Practice*, London: Office of Health Economics.

Miller, R.H. and Luft, H.S. (1994) 'Managed care plan performance since 1980: a literature analysis' *J. American Medical Association*, 271: 1512–19.

Moore, W. (1996) 'And how are we feeling today?' *Health Service Journal*, 106(5495): 30–2.

National Audit Office (1994) *General Practitioner Fundholding in England*, London: HMSO.

NHS Executive (1994a) *Developing NHS Purchasing and GP Fundholding: Towards a Primary Care-Led NHS.*

—— (1994b) *The Operation of the NHS Internal Market: Local Freedoms National Responsibilities (HSG(94)55).*

Paton, C. (1995) 'Contriving competition' *Health Service Journal*, 105(5446): 30–1.

Penhale, D. *et al.* (1993) 'A comparison of first-wave fundholding and non-fundholding practices' Unpublished manuscript, City University, cited in Smee (1995).

Oakley, A. (1980) *Women Confined*, Oxford: Martin Robertson.

Propper, C. (1993) 'Quasi-markets, contracts and quality in health and social care: the US experience' in Le Grand and Bartlett (eds).

—— (1995) 'Economic regulation and the NHS internal market' in A. Harrison (ed) *Health Care UK 1994–95*, London: King's Fund Institute.

Ranade, W. and Appleby, J. (1989) *To Market, To Market*, NAHA Research Paper 1, Birmingham: NAHAT.

Ranade, W. (1995) 'The theory and practice of managed competition in the National Health Service' *Public Administration*, 73(2): 241–63.

Redmayne, S., Klein, R. and Day. P. (1993) *Sharing our Resources*, Birmingham: NAHAT.

Richards, S. (1989) 'The course of cultural change', in 'Managing health in the 1990s' *Health Service Journal Supplement*, 27 April, 99(5148): 1.

Robinson, R. and Le Grand, J. (1994) *Evaluating the NHS Reforms*, London: King's Fund Institute.

—— (1995) 'Contracting and the purchaser-provider split' in R. Saltman and C. Von Otter (eds) *Implementing Planned Markets in Health Care*, Buckingham: Open University Press.

Saltmann, R. and Von Otter, C. (1992) *Planned Markets and Public Competition*, Buckingham: Open University Press.

Schapiro, J., Smith, J. and Walsh, N. (1996) 'Fluid drives' *Health Service Journal*, 106(5509): 29–31.

Seldon, A. (1981) *Whither the Welfare State?* London: Institute of Economic Affairs.

Smee, C. (1995) 'Self-governing trusts and GP fundholders: the British experience' in Saltman and Von Otter (1992).

Social Services Committee (1990) 'The government's plans for the future of the NHS' *Minutes of Evidence HC Papers 1989–90*, 148–51, London: HMSO.

Tomlinson, B. (1992) *Report of the Inquiry into London's Health Service, Medical Education and Research*, London: Department of Health.

Whitehead, M. (1994) 'Is it fair?: Evaluating the equity implications of the reforms' in Robinson and Le Grand (1993).

Williamson, O. (1975) *Markets and Hierarchies: Analysis and Antitrust Implications*, New York: The Free Press.

—— (1985) *The Economic Institutions of Capitalism*, New York: The Free Press.

CHAPTER 6

Transforming management

The job of a general manager has changed almost completely. I'm starting out now, three and a half years in, almost with a new job. That's why it's so exciting. I've got a new management team. I'm working with doctors in a different way. I'm working to new income and expenditure rules from next year. I'm thinking about marketing my services on quality and relating to customers in a way that I'd just begun to think of before but now it's come right to the front. So that's been the biggest lesson for me. Just how much things can change in a short space of time.[1]

These remarks were made by a Unit General Manager reflecting on his experience a few months after *Working for Patients* (WFP) was published. Many of his battle-weary colleagues might now regard his enthusiasm with some cynicism but most would agree with him that the nature of management in the NHS has been transformed in a relatively short space of time.

As discussed in Chapter 4, Conservative policies in the 1980s invested heavily in changing the responsibilities and style of health service management. This was part of a wider strategy throughout the public sector which was based on the simple ideological premise that the private sector had everything to teach the public sector and nothing to learn. The doctrines and principles of 'the new public management' (NPM) as it has become known rapidly became a new orthoxy, applied not only in the UK but throughout the world. Once again, as with the programmes of privatisation and marketisation in the public sector, with which NPM is closely linked, Thatcherite policies charted a course which others have followed (see for instance Osborne and Gaebler 1992).

There is no 'one right way' to manage, however: different theories or models of management spell out different approaches which are underpinned by differing theories of human motivation and organisational functioning. Their applicability may depend both on culture and context. A considerable critical literature has arisen in response to the growth of NPM, which argues that issues of context and culture have been ignored, both with regard to the factors which make the management of public services distinctive, and to the diversity of organsations within the public sector itself. At the same time the radical nature of the

Thatcherite attack has prompted fruitful re-appraisal about what is required of public management in the 21st century in the context of wider issues of governance in postmodern societies. Such a debate, of course, is rooted in the values of the participants regarding the proper place and value of government activity. This chapter looks at changes in NHS management in recent years in the context of this wider debate.

The concept of organisational culture

The wide-ranging changes which the Conservatives introduced into public administration in the 1980s placed great emphasis on changing the culture of government agencies to effect improvements in performance. Organisational culture entered the foreground of management concepts relatively recently, receiving an enormous impetus from the work of Peters and Waterman in their best-selling analysis of successful companies in the United States (Peters and Waterman 1982) (see box below).

In Search of Excellence* – a summary

In their study of 'excellent' United States companies drawn from a variety of manufacturing and service sectors. Peters and Waterman (1982) identify eight features of management practice and organisational culture which characterise successful firms.

1 A bias for action:
   - Project teams that tend to be small, fluid, ad hoc and problem/action focused.
   - High value placed on communication, learning and experimentation.
   - Tackling complex problems by shifting resources to where they are needed to encourage fluidity and action (chunking).

2 Close to the customer: Market-driven commitment to service. reliability and quality. Ability to custom-tailor a product or service to client's needs.

3 Autonomy and entrepreneurship: Commitment to innovation and experiment, decentralisation, the delegation of power and a healthy tolerance of failure.

4 Productivity through people:
   - Valuing employees as people and as a major resource, who should be trusted, respected, inspired and made 'winners'.

continued

- Organisational units should be small-scale to preserve and develop a people-oriented quality.

5 Hands-on, value-driven: Organisation has a clear sense of shared values, mission and identity, relying on inspirational leadership rather than bureaucratic control.

6 Stick to the knitting: The principle of building on one's strengths and knowledge of one's niche.

7 Simple form, lean staff: Avoid bureaucracy and complex forms of matrix organisation. Build commitments around projects or product division.

8 Simultaneous loose-tight properties: Striking a balance between central control and the need for autonomy. Core values are controlled from the centre, but autonomy is given lower down the organisation to permit action supportive of those values.

**Source*: Adapted from Morgan (1986)

It is an amorphous and difficult concept to define but powerful in its implications. In simple terms it covers the beliefs, values and assumptions which shape behaviour in organisations and are reflected (perhaps imperfectly) in structures and processes. Schein argues that these assumptions and beliefs 'define in a basic "taken-for-granted" fashion an organisation's view of itself and its environment . . . (They) are learned responses to a group's problems of survival in its external environment and its problems of internal integration' (Schein 1985: 6). For that reason a group's culture embodies to a large extent tacit, non-conscious forms of knowledge.

The determinants of an organisation's culture rest in its origins and history, technology and environment, patterns of ownership and control. But organisations are not homogenous; different departments may have different cultures reflecting their specialised tasks, professional discipline or ways of working. Management writers who emphasise the cultural properties of organisations argue that the main task of management is to integrate these subcultures into a reasonably coherent and cohesive whole, to build a corporate identity and commitment through shaping the beliefs and values which guide action.

But corporate culture is not something easily amenable to management control or manipulation. This becomes clearer if we look in greater detail at some of its underlying determinants. For example, Gordon (1991) argues that many aspects of corporate culture reflect 'industry-wide' factors which set the parameters within which the culture of any specific organisation can develop. Klein (1982) suggests that the influences which shape the environment of the health care 'industry' are:

- *Occupational complexity* – which demands the co-ordination and inter-dependence of many kinds of worker, often in teams;
- *Heterogeneity* – in the range of services provided and the technologies employed;
- *Uncertainty* – in the relationship between inputs and outputs. There is no certainty that a given input of 'health care' will produce a given output of improved health;
- *Ambiguity* – of goals and objectives and hence on the criteria of assessing success and failure;
- *Provider dominance* – the health care industry does not simply respond to consumer demands – to a large degree it creates them through the clinical decisions of professional providers about what consumers ought to have.

These features suggest some of the parameters along which corporate culture in health service organisations is likely to develop. *Complexity* gives rise to a high degree of specialisation and differentiation between different groups of staff, with relationships between them regulated by complex norms and rules of behaviour, both formal and informal. In addition, the *heterogeneity of services* provided, often under one roof, will give rise to diverse subcultures. Both of these factors suggest that the scope for conflict is high, particularly in times of change when established ways of working and the pecking order between the different health care 'tribes' is under challenge. We would expect differences of degree, however, in different types of health care organisation. These pressures will probably be more intense in the multi-speciality large acute hospital rather than in the less complex and differentiated community trust.

At the same time Harrison *et al.* (1992) remind us that the power and discretion doctors are given at the micro-level ultimately derives from the *uncertainty* and *ambiguity* inherent in the whole medical enterprise as to what works and what does not work in health care, and how the health of the population can be improved. While managers may suggest ways in which medical decision making may be improved (by the use of research evidence, comparative data, etc.) this 'puzzlement factor' ultimately sets a limit to the controls they or their political masters can exert (Harrison *et al.* 1992: 8–9). As we have seen in previous chapters, the autonomy of the medical profession and its power to commit public resources at the micro-level was also institutionalised into the design of the NHS. At a deeper level still, as the debates discussed in Chapter 2 illustrated, the dominance of medicine is manifested in the way in which health and illness have been conceptualised in Western health care systems, with the emphasis on cure rather than prevention, on the control of disease rather than the promotion of health, and the emphasis on the individual rather than populations.

There are clear links, therefore, between those factors which shape the external environment of the health care 'industry' and internal power structures and relationships, and between power and its cultural expression. The dominant cultural values and beliefs in any organisation reflect the values and interests of the dominant groups within it, and in the health service this means the medical profession. It is within this context that the development of a managerial culture should be examined.

The culture of NHS management

The overwhelming evidence from research studies into NHS decision making, summarised by Harrison (1988), demonstrates that up to the early 1980s the culture of NHS management was shaped by their relatively weak position vis-à-vis doctors. Theirs was a supportive role, smoothing the way for professionals, finding the resources to allow doctors to do their job, buying influence through performing services and favours (Haywood and Alaszewski 1980) – 'the diplomat role' in Harrison's words.

Harrison argues that three other features characterised NHS management in this period. It was *reactive*, responding to problems and issues thrust upon it day by day, rather than proactive in trying to shape the organisation's future at a strategic level. It was *incremental* in the sense that the objectives and performance of existing services and the way in which resources were used were never seriously questioned or evaluated. Planning was confined to decisions on how to use incremental additions to the budget. Improvements depended on the size of the increment, not on savings or redeployment of services.

Managerial behaviour was also *introverted*, reacting to actors and problems stemming from within the organisation instead of looking outwards to the needs and wishes of its users. Essentially this was administration rather than management, concerned with maintaining stability and the status quo rather than achieving change, with process rather than action and results. It had developed largely as a realistic response to a political environment shaped externally by the rules and conventions of public accountability to ministers and Parliament, and internally by the central position of doctors.

From consensus to general management

The managerial arrangements that Sir Roy Griffiths reviewed in 1983 had been put in place by the reorganisation of 1974. A key objective of the reorganisation was to shift service provision away from acute medicine towards the faster development of community health services for the chronically ill, and improve the 'Cinderella' status of services for the elderly, mentally ill and handicapped (DHSS 1976). To do this local authority community health services were transferred to health authorities and multiprofessional management teams were set up which tried to balance the power of acute medicine by upgrading the influence of primary care, community medicine and nursing.

Teams were appointed at regional, area and district level. Each team included a treasurer, administrator, community physician and nurse. At district level it included a part-time consultant and GP member elected by their district colleagues. The teams were to operate by consensus, each having the power to veto decisions, none with the power to impose. But the realities of medical power were relatively unaffected by putting community physicians and nurses on the management teams. Community medicine, with its basis in public health and epidemiology, had a comparatively low status in the medical pecking order of prestige, and the district post was in any case mostly advisory. By contrast, the nursing officer and administrator were the managerial heads of large numbers of staff. But although nurses had acquired heightened managerial opportunities, they were ill-equipped by tradition or training to take advantage of them and often simply managerially incompetent (Strong and Robinson 1990), an ineffective counterweight to the medical members. The co-option of general practitioners and consultants into management was largely on their own terms. Most used their power of veto to protect their members' interests and those who wanted to take a more corporate approach to district policy-making had no power to commit their colleagues.

Acute medicine retained its traditional dominance and the DHSS almost openly acknowledged its inability to make central objectives stick when it watered down its projected growth rates for the priority services in *The Way Forward*, published in 1977. The 1982 reorganisation tried to simplify some of the worst complexities of 1974 by pruning the consultative machinery, abolishing the area tiers, simplifying the planning machinery and advocating greater devolution of decision making to units of management at the level of hospitals and community services. But it did nothing to change the institutional stagnation which had been the result of consensus decision making.

The diagnosis of the management problem in the NHS by the Griffiths team was speedy and incisive, taking the form of a 23-page letter to the Secretary of State. As businesspeople and as newcomers to the NHS (apart from one, Sir Brian Bailey, who was Chairman of the Health Education Council), the team's views of the shortcomings of NHS management paralleled to a remarkable extent the findings of academic research as summarised by Harrison. The report started from the premise that the problems of managing the NHS were very similar to those in other large service organisations. The NHS did not have the profit motive but profits did not impinge on large numbers of managers in the private sector either, below board level.

> They are concerned with levels of service, quality of product, meeting budgets, cost improvement, productivity, motivating and rewarding staff, research and development and the long-term viability of the undertaking. All the things Parliament is urging on the NHS.
>
> (DHSS 1983: 10)

The reactive approach of NHS management is criticised implicitly:

> (The NHS) still lacks any real continuous evaluation of its performance against the (above) criteria . . . Rarely are precise management objectives set: there is little measurement of health output; clinical evaluation of particular practices is by no means common and economic evaluation of those practices extremely rare.
>
> (p. 10)

The insularity of managers is also sharply criticised: 'Businessmen have a keen sense of how well they are looking after their customers. Whether the NHS is meeting the needs of the patients and the community, and can prove that it is doing so, is open to question' (p. 10). Consensus management had led to 'lowest common denominator decisions and to long delays in the management process' (p. 17). Two central problems were highlighted: the difficulty of achieving any kind of change when so many groups had power of veto over decision making, and the lack of direction and leadership from the centre: 'units and the authorities are being swamped with directives without being given direction' (p. 12). The two main recommendations to meet these charges were, first to establish a Health Services Supervisory Board within the DHSS, chaired by the Secretary of State to strengthen policy direction of the NHS. A full-time multi-professional Management Board would be created to implement its policies and the link between them was the NHS Chief Executive who sat on both. The second recommendation was to create a general management function throughout the service to focus responsibility and give leadership and direction. By general management, Griffiths meant 'the responsibility drawn together in one person, at different levels of the organisation, for planning, implementation and control of performance' (p. 11). Griffiths also envisaged a new style and approach.

> The recurring themes of Griffiths' managerialism are action, effectiveness, thrust, urgency and vitality, management budgeting, sensitivity to consumer satisfaction

and an approach to management of personnel which would reward good performance and ultimately sanction poor performance with dismissal.

(Cox 1991: 94)

Coupled with the introduction of general management throughout the NHS was a real devolution of decision making down to units. Although the report was respectful of doctors, its underlying thrust was the need to assert greater managerial control over their activities, by making doctors participate in management themselves:

Their decisions largely dictate the use of all resources and they must accept the management responsibility which goes with clinical freedom. This implies active involvement in securing the most effective use and management of all resources.

(DHSS 1983: 19)

Management budgets for clinicians based on agreed workload and service targets were such 'a vital management tool' that the Inquiry had already set up demonstration projects in four districts.

The impact of Griffiths

In their evidence to the Social Services Committee on the Griffiths Report, Evans and Maxwell concluded that its most far-reaching and radical aspects were its proposals for the central management of the service, with its promise of a new relationship between the DHSS and local health authorities and the change from passive to active management (Evans and Maxwell 1984). This would not be concluded once general managers were in place but involved long-term and profound cultural change, a view which managers themselves endorsed (Strong and Robinson 1990).

Assessments about the impact of Griffiths have been mixed, hardly surprising in an organisation as large and diverse as the NHS. Best, for example, argued that changes had been immense: 'In just five years (the NHS) has been transformed from a classic example of an administered public sector bureaucracy into one that increasingly is exhibiting the qualities that reflect positive, purposeful management' (Best 1987: 4). Evidence of change lay in the increasing local diversity of management arrangements as authorities and managers used their new-found autonomy to shape structures and roles to suit themselves. This often entailed breaking down traditional professional and functional hierarchies and the creation of new 'cross-breeds' or 'clinically aware accountants and cost-conscious clinicians' (Strong and Robinson 1990). A shift towards devolving responsibilities to lower levels, the introduction of performance review for authorities and individuals, and a renewed interest in quality and the consumer are also cited. By 1987, two-thirds of management boards included a senior manager with primary responsibility for promoting service quality and consumer relations. These were often displaced nurse managers who no longer had line-management responsibilities at district level.

Above all, the new general managers appeared to be growing in confidence and authority, making decisions and taking action on issues which formerly would have been too difficult. The following interview extract vividly illustrates the perceived difference, in the eyes of one senior manager in an acute unit. He was commenting on the entrepreneurial style of his UGM, who had entered the NHS from industry in the wake of the Griffiths changes (about 100 appointments went to outsiders). This man had utilised an opportunity to integrate scattered obstetric and gynaecological services at the hospital site by building a new clinic. The anecdote is instructive for the light it throws on changing relationships with clinicians.

Manager: We sat with the clinicians and said, look we've got to identify the capital to do this properly and we drew up a clinic scheme and then we had to compromise on what they wanted and John at one stage said, 'I'm sorry, that is what you're getting. Not ifs, buts or maybes, that is what you're getting', and they moaned like hell . . . Yet they've got their own individual consulting suites, a colposcopy suite and an enormous waiting area, everything you want in a modern clinic, and yet they're still moaning . . .
Interviewer: What do you think is the reason for that?
Manager: I don't know. I'm firmly convinced that if we had been operating under the old style of management, making a consensus decision, the clinicians would have got to their clinical representative and said there's no way we want that – we want everything twice as big and gold-plated taps because patients will die, etc., and their rep would say, 'I'm sorry but it's completely unacceptable to my colleagues'. At that point the nurses would have said well, yes, we can see the reasons because we're nearly doctors as well, and the administrator would have been left high and dry. There would have been no action and there'd have been a nice plan on the table and I sincerely believe that but for general management we would have lost the opportunity to (a) have got the money, and (b) got the clinic built before people could actually realise what was happening, and there's been other instances of that.

However, other studies suggest that relationships with clinicians continued to be difficult and few general managers exerted their authority as successfully as this one did. Most consultants viewed management budgeting with suspicion, as a vehicle for cutting their budgets, and few were interested in time-consuming management posts (Harrison *et al.* 1987) while managers still had few powers of discipline or reward. By arguing that general managers would have to 'harness the best of the consensus management approach and avoid the worst of the problems it can present' (DHSS 1983: 17), Griffiths appeared to recognise the difficulties of managing a multi-professional service while seriously underestimating the power of doctors in particular to resist being managed. For that reason it was probably in those districts where consensus management had worked well that general management succeeded most.

Relations with RHAs and the Management Board also failed to live up to the Griffiths vision of giving general managers local autonomy and freedom to manage within the context of personal and corporate accountability for the attainment of agreed targets and objectives. The commitment to devolution conflicted with a stream of top-down initiatives which continued to spell out not only what managers should be doing, but how they should do it. If management is defined as 'taking responsibility for the performance of a system' (Metcalfe and Richards 1991: 37), then NHS managers were doomed to continuing frustration and disappointment.

In addition, central management failed to provide the clear leadership Griffiths had hoped for. Managers were bombarded with 47 DHSS 'priorities', many of them contradictory but all of them subservient to the overriding need to cut costs. In practice, balancing the budget dominated managerial agendas. Short-term contracts, performance review and performance-related pay for managers meant that they had little option in accepting finance driven agendas (Harrison *et al.* 1990; Strong and Robinson 1990). For many districts, Griffiths's concern with consumer research, improving quality, and evaluating effectiveness were driven to the sidelines even though Peters and Waterman's *In Search of Excellence* increasingly appeared on the bookshelves of general managers' offices.

The new public management

As mentioned earlier, the management developments taking place in the NHS were paralleled by much wider trends in public administration both in this country and many others, which are conveniently bundled together under the shorthand term of the 'new public management' (NPM). Hood (1991) argues that NPM has two strands. The first is derived from the 'new institutional economics' based on public choice, transaction cost analysis and principal-agent theory, which argues for:

- the disaggregation of public bureaucracies into decentralised units, dealing with each other on an 'arms-length' basis;
- greater competition in the public sector, through the use of contracts, competitive tendering and quasi-markets;
- greater user choice of service provider;
- discipline and parsimony in the use of resources.

The second strand is managerialism, which stresses:

- 'hands-on' professional management;
- which is given considerable autonomy and discretion (the 'right to manage');
- set clear goals and objectives;
- with rewards and the allocation of resources closely linked to the achievement of explicit standards and measures of performance.

The belief that government performance can be improved by better management is hardly new. The 1974 reorganisation of the health service was guided by similar views, and several themes of NPM can be traced back to the Fulton Report on the Civil Service in 1968. Each successive wave of managerialism is guided by the belief there can be rational, technical solutions to the complex social and moral problems of government and usually embodies currently fashionable nostrums in management theory. As Pollitt (1990) points out, at the level of ideology managerialism lays a claim to power and autonomy which is based on the assumption that the main route to social progress lies in achieving higher levels of economic growth and productivity and that management plays a crucial role in achieving these goals.

This forms the overarching 'mission statement of managerialism' (Newman and Clarke 1994: 14) but within this statement of general principles there are different theories about how the mission can be achieved, each with their own distinctive views about how organisations work and the role of managers within it. The emergence of NPM in recent years incorporates at least two models based on differing assumptions and organising principles but overlapping with each other in complex ways. The first and arguably the most influential in practice has been described by Pollitt (1990) as an updated version of 'scientific management' or neo-Taylorism. The foundations and principles of scientific management are outlined in Box 6.2. How were these updated and translated into the public services of the 1980s?

Scientific Management*

Frederick Taylor (1856–1915), one of the great pioneers of organisation theory, originally developed the concept and practice of 'scientific management' in the early years of the twentieth century. This rested on five principles:

1 Shift the responsibility for the organisation of work from the worker to the manager. Managers plan and design, workers carry it out.
2 Use scientific methods to determine the most efficient way of doing work, and design the worker's job accordingly.

continued

3 Select the best person to perform this job.
4 Train the worker to do it efficiently.
5 Monitor performance to see that tasks are done in the prescribed way, and achieve the required results.

Time and motion, work study, and organisation and methods developed as the practical consequences of scientific management, the tools for detailed assessment and measurement of every aspect of work, and designing and implementing more efficient ways of doing things. Perfect examples of this approach can be found today in the standardisation of service and product found in fast food chains like Pizza Hut or McDonalds. Every aspect of the production process has been analysed and broken down into minute components, the most efficient procedures developed and allocated to specialised staff who are trained to follow them precisely.

Taylor's methods produced startling increases in productivity in manufacturing, underpinning the assembly-line technology of car production, for example. But they also produced massive alienation from work, as workers became no more than machines themselves and gains in productivity had to be offset by higher rates of absenteeism and industrial conflict. Taylorism was as much about exerting control over the workforce as about efficient methods of production, and in the process workers were robbed of all autonomy and creativity.

Almost the entire development of management theory since has been a reaction against the mechanistic view of organisations, and the narrow approach to human motivation embodied in Taylorism. As Morgan points out, however, Taylor was probably a man before his time. Scientific management can come into its own when robots rather than human beings are doing the work.

**Source*: Adapted from Morgan (1986)

The separation of the design of work from its execution is implicit in the transition to 'management by contract' throughout the public sector. As Flynn (1994: 211) points out, contracts are often highly specific about the way in which work is to be done, not just on the results expected. This opens up the way to the standardisation and routinisation of work processes in provider organisations (a development which we noted happening in nursing and ancillary workers under contract), enhancing managerial control over labour. Flynn also points out that these developments are not necessarily the consequence of contracting *per se*, but reflect particular views about the contractual relationship and contract design.

Second, the strong emphasis on accountable management and performance measurement. Managers are to be given clear goals and objectives and held personally accountable for their achievement. In the search for economy, efficiency and effectiveness public-service managers have been set increasingly rigorous achievement targets and systems of individual performance review and performance-related pay are widespread for monitoring both their own performance and that of their subordinates. Complementing these internal systems of reward and control are the increasingly elaborate systems of external monitoring – the performance indicator 'industry' with the league tables of comparative performance in health, education or policing; the enlarged role of the National Audit Office and the Audit Commission. Performance measurement is also associated with standardisation and quantification. This has the merit of trying to make standards of performance explicit and transparent, for users of services, but also denies the validity of qualitative measures which are based on professional judgement and experience.

Underlying these moves are the Taylorist assumptions that workers respond only to extrinsic rewards such as pay, rather than intrinsic satisfactions which arise from the job itself and that they cannot be trusted to discipline themselves but must be controlled by elaborate internal and external monitoring systems.

The second, newer, model of management within NPM is derived from the 'excellence' literature which prescribes a different route for businesses trying to achieve success in a global market. Peters and Waterman (1982) align with 'total quality management' gurus like Edwards Deming (1986) in arguing that the key to success is a focus on the customer, the quality of service and the empowerment of staff to liberate the forces of enterprise and innovation and create a culture of excellence (See also Peters and Austin 1985; Peters 1988). In this model managers seek not to enforce compliance but ensure commitment, and 'human resource strategies' attain pivotal importance, the means by which an organisation seeks to meet its strategic business objectives (Salaman 1995: 12–14). Associated with the model are a package of changes advocated by the 'excellence' literature:

> Fundamental to the core characteristics of the successful companies are a number of key values: anti-bureaucracy, the breakdown of large organisational structures into separate strategic business entities, the devolution of responsibility and authority to lower organisational levels, the encouragement of 'entrepreneurship', productivity through people, quality, the dominance of market principles (even within the organisation) and flatter organisational structures.
>
> (Salaman 1995: 16)

The difference between this model and the neo-Taylorism associated with 'machine bureaucracies' (Mintzberg 1983) is described thus:

> Before management was to a great degree a question of managers' compliance with systems, procedures, regulation and authority, and ensuring the compliance of their subordinates. Management was part of, and sought to achieve, standardisation, to reduce difference, individuality and deviation. Now compliance is not enough; achieving obedience is not enough; standardisation is no longer virtuous. Now managers are responsible not for obedience but for performance and quality; managers no longer control, they empower.
>
> (p. 18)

Within this model the nature of managerial leadership changes and becomes more difficult as managers 'watch their bureaucratic power slip away' (Kantor 1989: 91). It is concerned with articulating a vision to inspire, a corporate mission and core values to guide action. The manager as commander-in-chief gives way to the facilitator, team coach, creator of cultural symbols (Senge 1990; Schein 1985). Within the public sector there is increasing evidence of some of the structural and cultural changes mentioned by Salaman, in particular:

- the break-up of multi-functional beauracracies into separable functions (e.g. Next Steps Agencies; separation of purchaser and provider functions; etc.) This is often accompanied by the elimination of management tiers (de-layering) and the restructuring of the organisation into 'business units' which operate as semi-autonomous cost centres. This has been accompanied by attempts to foster project based team-working and task groups;
- devolution of managerial authority closer to the service user (health service trusts, local management of schools, locality management/ commissioning initatives in health and local government);
- a greater focus on quality of service and customer care arising from the Citizen Charter initiatives, (e.g. 'Charter mark' awards for excellent customer service);
- the dominance of competition even internally through market testing and competitive tendering, benchmarking, etc.;
- a higher profile for the management of human resources and the personnel function.

In addition it is *de rigeur* for public agencies to have their mission statements and 'core values' – indeed the Benefits Agency has four which are taken almost word for word from *In Search of Excellence*. But perhaps the most persistent theme within the 'new' strategic management literature is the emphasis on the necessity of constant change and adaptation. Leaders must motivate their staff to 'learn to love change', and to 'thrive on chaos' (Peters 1988). The organisation of the future has to learn to be fleet-footed, wedded neither to permanent structures nor to permanent relationships, but continually renewing itself. Striking metaphors are abundant. Giant organisations must 'learn to dance' and 'build tents not palaces' (Kantor 1989). Given the torrent of changes public agencies are experiencing, and the emphasis on the role of managers as shapers of organisational culture in management theory, it is unsurprising to find that the management of change has become a key theme in NPM as well.

NPM – the critique

In this section we develop three lines of criticism of NPM. First, that the contradictions between these two models of management – the neo-Taylorist model and 'new wave' or 'excellence' models – lead in practice to impossible constraints on managers. Secondly, that transposing models of management developed in the business world *sui generis* ignores the factors which makes management in the public domain distinctive; and thirdly, that the government has in any case often chosen to draw the wrong lessons from the private sector.

The contradictions between the two models are fairly obvious. Managing by commitment rather than compliance is an attractive concept for many managers in the public sector, but is difficult to instil when workers have to compete for their own jobs through efficiency exercises like market testing. In consequence the desire to 'value all staff' has to be reconciled with the insecurity such exercises promote. At the same time, as experience in the health service amply demonstrates, if managers are driven by an endless succession of imposed targets and cost-cutting exercises, other desirable goals necessary to build a cohesive culture and quality service inevitably suffer.

Team working and group performance are undermined by performance-related pay for individuals, which fosters competition, dissension and demotivation (Flynn 1994), and it has largely been abandoned by the private sector for this very reason. The ability to articulate a strategic 'vision' for the organisation to which everyone can sign up is undermined by the fragmentation and loss of control consequent on management by contract. Devolving managerial autonomy down the line conflicts with top-down directives which constrain not only what managers do but how they do it. Government shows little willingness to abandon hierarchical means of control, and the size, scale and role of some government agencies means that bureaucracy cannot easily be abandoned. Hence, much of the 'excellence' model is implemented only in rhetoric and aspiration: employees hear the language but believe that managers don't 'walk the talk'; this is a recipe for widespread cynicism.

This leads on to our second line of criticism, which arguably reveals the root of these problems – the failure to recognise the limitations of importing private sector management models into public agencies or to understand their distinctive role, purposes and tasks (Stewart and Ranson 1988). This body of criticism has emerged largely from within the traditional study of public administration, (See, for example, Elcock 1991; Pollitt 1990; Stewart and Ranson 1988; Flynn 1997; Ranson and Stewart 1994; Pollitt and Harrison 1992; Dunleavy and Hood 1994). The differences between public and private are summarised below:

Role and purpose

Private-sector organisations have been created to serve *particular* interests and respond to individual demand in the market-place, and have as a consequence a clearer 'bottom line' – profit and the rate of return. Public organisations have been created to serve the *public* interest, and undertake collective purposes determined through the political process. Often they have been created to meet needs or express values (equity, justice, retribution) not readily met or expressed by the market.

Relations with the 'customer'

The private sector is able to define its customer base through the sale of its products. Deciding who the customer is in the public sector may be problematic. In a health authority, for example, it could mean GPs, an external organisation, patients' relatives or prospective patients as well as the present ones. In addition relations with users of services are more complex than in the private market, and may involve an element of compulsion and social control. At the same time, as we saw in the preceding chapter, notions of consumer sovereignty and powers of 'exit' are problematic in services like health and social care.

The relationship between demand, supply and revenue

If businesses generate greater demand for their products through good marketing, they can increase the supply and bring in greater revenue. The public sector manager's budget is politically determined: 'marketing' the service to generate increased demand leads only to increased costs and not (normally) to increase revenue. Even in the NHS quasi-market where money was supposed to follow the patient and reward high-performing units, some trust managers have discovered to their cost that improved efficiency is no guarantee of more money when purchasers still have fixed budgets (Kingman 1994).

Multi-valued choice

Choice and rationing therefore become inevitable in the public sector, and these choices are inescapably multi-valued, involving complex trade-offs between competing values. Choices cannot be reduced to the pursuit of the three E's – economy, efficiency and effectiveness – in response to an endless succession of single-valued targets. The social purposes of public service organisations require a broader conception of the public good and include values related to citizenship and democracy, such as equity, justice and public accountability.

Uncertainty of goals and performance measures

Hence the goals and objectives of public organisations are often multiple, conflicting and ambiguous. The political need to reconcile multiple interests, build coalitions of support, and take credit for 'success' means that goals are often specified in deliberately vague terms. In addition, as Willcocks and Harrow (1992) point out, the specificity of private interest contrasts with the indeterminateness and yet comprehensiveness of public purpose (for example, delivering 'social care' or 'educated citizens'). Together these factors make the assessment of organisational performance very difficult, or they lead to a concentration on the measurable at the expense of more intangible but nevertheless highly important aspects of service.

Accountability to elected members

The accountability of public managers to elected representatives, whether local or national, has no parallel in the private sector and has immediate implications – in particular, shorter planning timescales and difficulties of reconciling the political criteria for decisions with those of managers. One example might be the political decision taken in January 1991 that no one must wait longer than two years for an operation by April 1992, irrespective of clinical need. To meet the target, managers were forced to wastefully expend resources on the most trivial complaints. The interface between politics and management therefore becomes of paramount importance, and cannot be artificially separated, as Griffiths believed it should.

Some commentators, while accepting the force of these criticisms, believe that the differences between public and private are eroding (Metcalfe and Richards 1991; Gunn 1988) due to the changes introduced by successive Conservative governments. The boundaries between public and private are blurring, and new grey areas created. Their environments grow increasingly similar. More public agencies are being exposed to competitive pressures; private companies talk about the multiple stakeholders to whom they owe accountability and their managers experience the 'fishbowl' effect of increasingly politicised debates about, for example, the pay of their directors, or the impact of their decisions on the environment.

Metcalfe and Richards (1991) argue that the main strategic challenge for both public and private agencies in future is learning to manage for results in an increasingly uncertain and turbulent environment. Their main criticism of government policy is not that the government looked to private-sector management models, but that it drew the wrong lessons from it by implementing a neo-Taylorist model inappropriate for these new conditions, and which is being increasingly abandoned in the commercial world (Drucker 1981; Kantor 1984; Handy 1989).

Of course, within a neo-Marxist analysis of the post-Fordist restructuring of welfare and relations between capital and labour, neo-Taylorism makes a lot of sense, but, that aside, it is not clear why even contemporary strategic management prescriptions which have been devised to meet the challenges of competitive success in a global economy will be workable or appropriate for British public services. (For a case study of one hospital trust which tried and failed to implement Tom Peter's prescriptions in *Thriving on Chaos* see Harrison *et al.* (1993)). Even in the business world there is a general weariness with 'fad lag', as each successive recipe for success is found wanting. The constant delayering and downsizing that companies have undertaken in recent years is said to have led to 'corporate anorexia' and a loss of robustness (*Financial Times* 1996: 8), while the guru of 're-engineering' has had to admit that as many as 70 per cent of the firms which 're-engineered' themselves under his guidance failed to increase their market share (Jenkins 1996) while two-thirds of Peters and Waterman's 'excellent companies' were in deep trouble within five years of their book's publication. While public agencies can learn from well-managed private organisations, and have done so in recent years, they must be selective and ground that learning both in what makes public service distinctive and in the 'industry-wide' determinants that shape their own particular service, be it health care, the prison service, social security or the police.

Rethinking concepts of public management

The ultimate distinction between public and private management in the modern world lies not in their tasks or in the environment they face, but in public management's focus on structural problems and the need to manage whole systems of interdependent organisations to promote the public good (Metcalfe and Richards 1991). This emerges from the institutional features of modern govenment, and its growing loss of direct control and power in the global information economy. In a world characterised by growing uncertainty, diversity and complexity (Dunsire 1993) policy outcomes are not the product of actions by central government. Laws may be passed but thereafter what happens depends on the actions and interactions of many other players:

No single actor, public or private, has all the knowledge and information required to solve complex dynamic and diversified problems; no actor has sufficient overview to make the application of needed instruments effective, or the potential to dominate unilaterally in a particular government model.

(Kooiman 1993: 4)

At the same time interdependencies on a global scale also drain power away from the national level, shifting an increasing range of functions to higher tiers of government (the European Union) or to international institutions, and necessitate ever closer cooperation between national governments and their leaders.

The British government's response to these challenges has exacerbated their own loss of control, as services have been privatised, local government bypassed, new agencies and quangos created, and service responsibilities fragmented between a variety of public, private and voluntary providers, a process which Rhodes (1995) terms 'the hollowing out of the state'. The ability of government to coordinate and steer complex sets of organisations is reduced, although as Rhodes points out, the British government has tried to compensate for this reduction in direct hands-on control by tightening controls over financial resources and strengthening its regulatory and monitoring roles, but 'such hands-off controls may not provide sufficient leverage for the centre to steer the networks' (p. 13).

The combined effect of these complex sets of changes is to change a system of *government* to one of *governance*, which Metcalfe and Richards define as 'getting things done through other organisations' (Metcalfe and Richards 1991: 220). Governance is about managing networks of interdependent organisations in order to achieve desirable results from the perspective of the public or social good; this becomes critical when:

. . . attempts by individual organisations to pursue their own (private) aims independently of what others are doing is both self-defeating and counter-productive from the (public) point of view of the performance of the system of which they are the parts.

(Metcalfe and Richards 1993: 114)

Once again there are parallels with private-sector companies which are having to learn to 'manage through networks' (Lorenz 1991) as their relationships with suppliers and distributors becomes more complex, and when they may be cooperating with companies on certain projects, with whom they also compete in different contexts (Johnston and Lawrence 1991). The end-purpose, however, is still profit, and the interests defended are private. Public management, on the other hand, has *social* purposes and values to promote, and *collective* interests to defend. One example from the health service relates to the role of authorities in promoting the health of their local populations which requires the cooperation of a large number of agencies and groups. Yet the problem of promoting the public interest (say, in promoting better health) may conflict with the private interests of several of the key players, particularly when considerable changes in resource priorities or professional practice are required.

This discussion demonstrates the inadequacies of the neo-Taylorist model of management in NPM. First it adopts an intra-organisational focus when the problems of effective governance demand the management of inter-organisational links. It is obsessed with the achievement of narrowly defined objectives and targets when the overriding skills required of management should promote the long-term maintenance of relationships and the creation of trust. It focuses on individual performance and accountability, but in inter-dependent networks no one actor is responsible for outcomes, and accountability is hard to trace. Such a conception of the role and purposes of public management undermines even further the idea of management as control, and highlights instead the political and culture-building roles of management, along with the skills of bargaining, negotiation, the skilful use of power, building trust, creating and sustaining commitment to a shared vision (Barrett and McMahon 1990). In conclusion, the previous discussion suggests how concepts of public management need to be redefined to meet a changing environment, and indentifies the dilemmas that need to be resolved. Some key issues are:

Designing for diversity

The first step is to recognise the diversity and complexity of public organisations. They cannot all be fitted into the same rigid framework. For example, at the beginning of this chapter we saw that health care is both highly professionalised, uncertain, ambiguous and risky – all factors which suggest that professionals must be allowed a substantial measure of autonomy. Its culture tends to be 'organic', since the mode of working is through multi-disciplinary teams, yet the potential for conflict *between* different groups is also high. The vulnerability of patients and their relative powerlessness in relation to professional providers is also a special feature of health care. Within provider organisations it therefore seems important to promote values of care and service, cooperation, high trust and professional self-discipline.

Managing through networks

If managing inter-organisational dependence to achieve social results is the defining distinction between public and private management, the skills required to do this and how these may be developed are poorly understood (see, however, Snow, Miles and Coleman 1993). As pointed out above, the difficulties of 'network management' can be exacerbated by policies which increase fragmentation or by building in incentives which positively encourage non-cooperation rather than the reverse

For example, since the 1974 reorganisations of health and local government (if not before) both sides of the organisational divide have been exhorted to bridge the division between health and social care through the three 'C's – better communication, coordination and cooperation – with disappointing results. This has been due not only to structural and professional barriers but also to different budgetary cycles and accountability arrangements as well as a failure to design 'win-win' incentives for cooperation (for example, making a joint budget available to both organisations on proof of adequate joint planning and management arrangements for spending it). While the problem of appropriate incentives is increasingly acknowledged, and in some contexts is being addressed (the way in which urban regeneration grants are handled, is an example), it is clear that much greater sophistication is required if governments are to play the necessary catalytic role in 'steering change from undesirable and towards desirable ends' (Dunsire 1993). The strategic responsibilities of health authorities to improve the health of their local population and meet their needs for health care exemplifies the challenges and dilemmas of managing through networks; we will return to this theme in the final chapter.

Rethinking processes of accountability

Accountability to the public in the 'hollow state' has become increasingly problematic as non-elected quangos or private contractors take over the functions of elected bodies. The public does not know who is responsible for what, or whom to call to account when things go wrong. Many believe, for instance, that local authorities are responsible for hospitals (Stewart 1993). Processes of accountability have to take account of diversity as well. Accountability must flow downwards and outwards to users of the service, as well as upwards to councillors and ministers. New accountability processes have to grapple with the problem of legitimising managerial autonomy and discretion (to achieve results) and the need to give real rather than fictional accounts to the various stakeholders with whom the organisation interacts.

A key relationship is that with elected politicians. Management in the public sector is a highly political process, operating in the full glare of political debate and public attention. Managing the interface between the organisation and the political process is a necessary and legitimate function of senior management which requires skill and training. Trying artificially to separate politics and management, or treat the former as an illegitimate intrusion, is naive. Business people who enter the public service often have unrealistic expectations about the relationship with politicians. Victor Paige, the first Chief Executive of the NHS Management Board, resigned after 18 months complaining of 'interference'. But sometimes politicians have to be seen to respond to public concerns, if they are not to hand ammunition to their opponents. At the same time the fiction that policy and management are distinct can be used by politicians as a device to diffuse accountability (the lapses of security at Parkhurst Prison which led to the sacking of the Director of Prisons shed a fascinating insight on the behaviour of the Home Secretary in this respect (Talbot 1996)).

Being clear about the social purpose of the organisation (in management jargon, its mission and core values), and using this to clarify the nature of its relationships with users and provide an ethical system of values to guide behaviour, is a key task for managers and politicians jointly. The blurred boundaries of public and private have created many new ethical dilemmas for managers and also increased the possibilities for corruption and misuse of public funds which can only be addressed by clear working principles and codes of procedure. There is also a presumption that 'public' means just what it says: openness to scrutiny and questioning by the public, and appropriate mechanisms to ensure that is possible (Ranson and Stewart 1994: 29). Both the Audit Commission and independent researchers have argued that the secretiveness of decision making in the health service has been exacerbated since the introduction of the NHS reforms (Audit Commission 1994; Ashburner and Cairncross 1992) with fewer health-authority meetings held in public and trust boards increasingly reluctant to expose details of their work to public scrutiny.

Rewarding public service and effective management

Politicians also need to respect the motivations of those who work in the public sector. Incentive systems should be designed to promote and strengthen the social purposes and values of the organisation. Many professionals and managers choose to work in the public sector because they wish to give service or they believe in the core values of their agency. This is particularly true in the NHS: ignoring these motivations and designing performance incentives solely around financial rewards perverts those values, and leads to cynicism and demoralisation.

At the same time the quality of the management process needs to be recognised in any appraisal of effective management performance. Focusing entirely on narrowly defined targets and results can lead to 'macho management' about which there has been considerable concern in the NHS (HSJ 1994a; Maddock 1995). Achieving short-term results at the cost of the long-term demoralisation of staff or poor quality of policy outcomes is counter-productive (Gutteridge 1996). In particular the effective management of large-scale change in health service organisations has been shown to depend on aspects of management culture and process which include the quality and coherence of policy and decision-making procedures; good management–medical relations; a culture open and receptive to new ideas, which is built on shared values, effective communication and teamwork (Pettigrew *et al.* 1993; Appleby *et al.* 1994). As long ago as 1986, Gordon Best argued that managers who paid attention to developing these attributes were neither recognised nor rewarded in the accountability review process, and little seems to have changed (Audit Commission 1994; Gutteridge 1996).

Enhance creativity and flexible response

Many public managers must long for a period of stability and calm after living through years of constant upheaval, and perhaps hope to find it in a change of government. Yet that scenario is an unlikely one. In the health service we are on the cusp of even more far-reaching technological and scientific change, the consequences of which are still uncertain, and have only started the restructuring of health services which will be required to meet the demands of an ageing population. Managing in and for uncertainty will remain a reality in the health service, as it will for all organisations, whether public or private. This will need an enhanced capacity for social learning, creativity and flexible response. Ultimately creating and sustaining the 'learning organisation' (Senge 1990b; Argyris and Schon 1978; Argyris 1986), one which utilises the commitment, resources and ingenuity of all its members, may be the hardest management challenge of all.

Conclusions

In this chapter we have reviewed changes in the management of the NHS against the background of the imposition of new public management (NPM) throughout the public sector. It was argued that NPM had two components – the focus on markets, competition and the minimum state, derived from developments in economic theory (and reviewed in relation to the NHS in Chapter 5), and a version of managerialism which embodies differing models of management which overlap with each other in complex ways. It was argued that the Griffiths Report, though sophisticated and insightful in many respects, underestimated the differences between management in the public and private domains, and some of the key recommendations, particularly regarding the central management of the service, have proved problematic in practice. Nevertheless, the report was seminal in its influence. It has led to the development of a far more professional cadre of health service managers who have achieved impressive improvements in productivity, while coping with a massive change agenda in recent years.

The report also illustrates changing ideas about the relationships between four sets of actors in the public policy arena – politicians, professionals, administrators and the public. Richards (1992) argues that in the postwar Keynsian–Beveridge welfare state politicians and professionals were the most important players, with politicians drawing their legitimacy to make decisions from election, and professionals from their expert knowledge. Administrators play a mediating role reconciling the value conflicts which emerge from these two powerful domains, which in the health service accords with the 'diplomat' role so clearly described by Harrison and recognised by Griffiths. The public only enter the stage as voters or passive patients, with little voice or influence.

The Conservative crusade to cut public spending from 1979 and get better value for money from the public sector meant upsetting the established 'negotiated order' of producer interests in the name of the three Es – economy, efficiency and effectiveness. Within the 'efficiency paradigm' administrators were turned into managers and given greater power to break into and change the working practices of professionals and other groups, to deliver what the politicians demand. The Griffiths reforms started this process in the health service, but as we have seen the ability (and willingness) of general managers to enter the domain of the most powerful producer group of all, doctors, remained limited. The NHS reforms continued and strengthened the ability of managers – both as purchasers and providers – to influence and change clinical practices. However, it also marked the continuance of a more subtle strategy initiated by Griffiths – the managerialisation of professionals themselves. The new market environment facing providers reinforced the pressures for doctors and nurses to take greater responsibility for the management of resources to ensure the competitive viability of their service. Increasingly, hospitals are organised around clinical directorates, with a senior consultant responsible for the management of a speciality or group of specialities, aided by a business manager and perhaps a senior nurse. The models vary but in most cases contracts with purchasers will be negotiated at this level as well.

Finally, Richards argues that in the later stages of this managerial revolution the consumer attains greater prominence, at least in rhetoric. Championing the needs and wishes of consumers provides a powerful legitimation for political decisions but can also provide a more inspirational rationale for public managers than the narrow pursuit of the three E's. Exhorted to learn from the private sector, managers found more attractive models to copy than the neo-Taylorism of NPM, with mixed results in practice.

Recently the rise and rise of health service managers has been checked by press and Labour Party attacks. Out of expediency Conservative ministers have joined the attack on the 'men in grey suits' and there have been various purges of their numbers (see for instance HSJ 1994b; 1994c; 1995; Hancock 1994). But if a 'consumer paradigm' of public management is emerging, and consumer power a growing reality, managers would play a key integrative role between the other sets of interests – politicians, professionals and the public. As Griffiths himself pointed out in one of the last articles he wrote before his death, it seemed a debilitating paradox that those charged with the leadership of a great undertaking like the NHS 'single out for attack the very people through whom such leadership has to be expressed' (Griffiths 1994).

Notes

1 All quotations from managers and clinicians in this and later chapters have been taken from the 'Monitoring Managed Competition' (Appleby *et al.* (1991a)) case study interviews, unless otherwise stated. See footnote 1, Chapter 5.

2 Economy concentrates on inputs, efficiency on the relationship between inputs and outputs and effectiveness on the attainment of objectives or outcomes. These are discussed in more detail in the next chapter.

References

Argyris, C. (1986) *Change and Defensive Routines*, Boston, Mass: Pitman.

Argyris, C. and Schon, D. (1978) *Organisational Learning: A Theory of Action Perspective*, Reading, Mass: Addison Wesley.

Appleby, J., Smith, P., Ranade, W., Little, V. and Robinson, R. 'Monitoring managed competition', in R. Robinson and J. Le Grand (1994) *Evaluating the NHS Reports*, London: King's Fund Institute.

Ashburner, L. and Cairncross, L. (1992) 'Just trust us', *Health Service Journal*, 14th May, pp. 20–2.

Audit Commission (1994) *Aspects of Managing Hospital and Community Services*, London: HMSO.

Barrett, S. and McMahon, L. (1990) 'Public Management in uncertainty: a micro-political perspective of the Health Service in the United Kingdom' *Policy and Politics*, 18(4): 257–68.

Best, G. (1986) 'Strategic managing and organisational learning' in G. Parstons (ed) *Managers as Strategists*, London: King's Fund Institute.

—— (1987) *The Future of NHS General Management: Where Next?* Project Paper 75, London: King Edward's Hospital Fund for London.

Chandler, J.A. (1991) 'Public administration and private management: is there a difference?' *Public Administration 69*, 3: 385–91.

Cox, D. (1991) 'Health service management – a sociological view: Griffiths and the non-negotiated order of the hospital', in J. Gabe, M. Calnan and M. Bury (eds) *The Sociology of the Health Service*, London: Routledge.

Department of Health (1989) *Working for Patients*, Cmnd. 555, London: HMSO.

Department of Health and Social Security (DHSS) (1976) *Priorities for the Health and Personal Social Services in England*, London: HMSO.

—— (1977) *The Way Forward*, London: HMSO.

—— (1983) *Inquiry into NHS Management* (The Griffiths Report), London: HMSO.

Drucker, P. (1981) *Managing in Turbulent Times*, London: Pan/Heinemann.

Dunleavy, P. and Hood, C. (1994) 'From old public administration to new public management' *Public Money and Management*, 14(3): 9–16.

Dunsire, A. (1993) 'Modes of governance', in J. Kooiman (ed) *Modern Governance*, London: Sage.

Elcock, H.J. (1991) *Change and Decay? Public Administration in the 1990s*, London: Longman.

Evans, T. and Maxwell, R. (1984) *Griffiths: Challenge and Response*, Evidence to Select Committee on Social Services, London: King Edward's Hospital Fund for London.

Financial Times (1996) *'Predator that lost its habit*', 3rd February, p. 8.

Flynn, N. (1997) *Public Sector Management*, 3rd edition London: Prentice Hall Harvester Wheatsheaf.

—— (1994) 'Control, commitment and contracts' in Clarke, Cochrane and McLaughlin.

Griffiths, Sir. R. (1994) 'Grey suits are the agents of change' *Health Service Journal*, 21st April: p. 23.

Gordon, G.G. (1991) 'Industry Determinants of Organisational Culture' *Academy of Management Review*, 16(2): 396–415.

Gunn, L. (1988) 'Public management: a third approach?', *Public Money and Management*, Spring/Summer, 8(1): 21–5.

Gutteridge, D. (1996) 'Not at your disposal' *Health Service Journal*, 22nd February, 106(5491): 25.

Hancock, C. (1994) 'Managers out for the count' *Health Service Journal*, 105 (5384): 17.

Handy, C. (1989) *The Age of Unreason*, London: Business Books.

Harrison, S.H. (1988) *Managing the National Health Service: Shifting the Frontier?* London: Chapman and Hall.

Harrison, S., Hunter, D., Marnoch, G. and Pollitt, C. (1987) 'The reluctant managers: clinicians and budgets in the NHS', Paper presented to PAC/ESRC and University of York, September.

Harrison, S., Hunter, D., Marnoch, G. and Politt, C. (1992) *Just Managing: Power and Culture in the National Health Service*, Basingstoke: Macmillan.

Harrison, S.H., Hunter, D.J. and Pollitt, C. (1990) *The Dynamics of British Health Policy*, London: Unwin Hyman.

Harrison, S., Small, N. and Baker, M. (1993) 'Culture, chaos and conflict: the early days of a National Health Service Trust' Political Studies Association conference, University of Leicester, April.

Haywood, S. and Alaszewski, A. (1980) *Crisis in the Health Service*, London: Croom Helm.

Health Service Journal (1994a) 'Langlands rejects "macho" style in manifesto speech' 27th January, 104(5387): 3.

—— (1994b) 'Experts warn against lack of leadership in the NHS' 27th October, 104(5426): 5.

—— (1994c) 'The first lesson for Margaret Beckett' 3rd November, 104(5427): 15.

—— (1995) 'Redwood renews purge of NHS bureaucracy in Wales' 16th February, 105(5440): 5.

Hood, C. (1991) 'A public management for all seasons' *Public Administration*, 69: 3–19.

Jenkins, S. (1996) 'Gurus of greed are not bad for business' *The Times*, 23rd November, p. 24.

Johnson, R. and Lawrence, P. (1991) 'Beyond vertical integration – the rise of the value-adding partnership', in C. Thompson, J. Frances, R. Levacic, and J. Mitchell (eds) *Markets, Hierarchies and Networks: The Coordination of Social Life*, London: Sage.

Kantor, R.M. (1984) *The Change Masters*, London: Unwin.

—— (1989) *When Giants Learn to Dance*, London: Unwin Hyman.

Kingman, S. (1994) 'Freeman Hospital: the will to survive' *British Medical Journal*, 309: 461–4.

Klein, R. (1982) 'Performance, Evaluation and the NHS: a case study in conceptual perplexity and organisational complexity' *Public Administration 60 Winter*, pp. 355–407.

Kooiman, J. (1993) 'Findings, speculations and recommendations', in J. Kooiman (ed) *Modern Governance*, London: Sage.

Lorenz, E. (1991) 'Neither friends nor strangers: informal networks of subcontracting in French industry', in G. Thompson, J. Frances, R. Levacic, J. Mitchell (eds) *Markets, Hierarchies and Networks*, London: Sage.

Metcalfe, L. and Richards, S. (1991) *Improving Public Management*, 2nd edition London: Sage.

—— (1993) 'Evolving public management cultures' in J. Kooiman and K. Eliassen (eds) *Managing Public Organisations: Lessons from Contemporary European Experience*, 2nd edition London: Sage.

Maddock, S. (1995) 'Is macho management back?' *Health Service Journal*, 23rd February, 105(5441): 26–7.

Mintzberg, H. (1983) *Structure in Fives: Designing Effective Organisations*, Englewood Cliffs NJ: Prentice Hall.

Morgan, G. (1986) *Images of Organisation*, London: Sage.

—— (1988) *Riding the Waves of Change*, San Francisco: Jossey Bass.

NHS Executive (1995) 'Priorities and Planning Guidance for the NHS 1996–97', *EL* (95).

Newman, J. and Clarke, J. (1994) 'Going about our Business? The Managerial-

isation of Public Services' in J. Clarke, A. Cochrane and E. McLaughlin (eds) *Managing Social Policy*, London: Sage.
Osborne, T. and Gaebler, D. (1992) *Reinventing Government*, Reading, Mass: Addison Wesley.
Peters, T. (1988) *Thriving on Chaos: Handbook for a Management Revolution*, London: Pan Books.
Peters, T. and Austin (1985) *A Passion for Excellence: the Leadership Principle*, London: Collins.
Peters, T.J. and Waterman, R.H. (1982) *In Search of Excellence. Lessons from America's Best Run Companies*, New York: Harper and Row.
Pettigrew, A., Ferlie, E. and Cairncross, L. (1993) *Shaping Strategic Change in the NHS*, London: Macmillan.
Pollitt, C. (1990) *Managerialism and the Public Services: The Anglo-American Experience*, Oxford: Blackwell.
Pollitt, C. and Harrison, S. (eds) (1992) *Handbook of Public Services Management*, Oxford: Blackwell.
Ranson, S. and Stewart, J. (1994) *Management for the Public Domain*, London: Macmillan Press.
Rhodes, R.A.W. (1995) *The New Governance: governing without government*, Paper for 'The State of Britain' Seminar 2 ESRC/RSA.
Richards, S. (1992) *Who Defines the Public Good? The Consumer Paradigm in Public Management*, London: Public Management Foundation.
Salaman, G. (1995) *Managing*, Buckingham: Open University Press.
Schein, E.H. (1985) *Organisational Culture and Leadership*, San Francisco: Jossey Bass.
Senge, P.M. (1990a) 'The leader's new work' *Sloan Management Review*, 32(1): 7–23.
—— (1990b) *The Fifth Discipline: The Art and Practice of the Learning Organisation*, New York: Doubleday.
Snow, C., Miles, R. and Coteman, H. (1993) 'Managing 21st Century network organisations', in C. Mabey and B. Mayon-White (eds) *Managing Change* 2nd edn., London: Paul Chapman Publishing.
Stewart, J. and Ranson, S. (1988) 'Management in the public domain' *Public Money and Management*, Spring/Summer, 8(1): 13–19.
—— (1993) 'The renewing of public accountability', in N. Lewis and D. Longley (eds) *Accountability to the Public*, London: European Policy forum.
Strong, P.M. and Robinson, J. (1990) *The NHS: Under New Management*, Buckingham: Open University Press.
Talbot, C. (1996) 'The prison service: a framework of irresponsibility?' *Public Money and Management*, Jan–March pp. 5–7.
Willcocks, L. and Harrow. J. (eds) (1992) *Rediscovering Public Services Management*, London: McGraw Hill.

CHAPTER 7

Questions of quality

Health service reform has brought questions about the quality of health care to the forefront of political, professional and managerial attention. There are several reasons why this should be so. In part it is bound up with the trend towards 'evidence-based medicine' as a means of controlling the costs of health services. As discussed in Chapter 3, the potential for redeploying resources from less effective to more effective therapies in health care is considerable. In this case, quality and efficiency, far from being alternatives, go hand-in-hand.

Other reasons revolve around the changing demands and expectations of public services by consumers and their agents. In 1948 an austerity NHS was born in an austerity Britain and people were grateful for what they received. It is no longer an appropriate model for a generation which has developed sophisticated and discriminating consumption patterns for other goods and services. The 'Citizens Charter' and its offshoots like the Patient's Charter in the health service are an explicit acknowledgement of that fact, as well as the means by which the Major government in the 1990s sought to distance itself from the crude Thatcherite attacks on the public services which marked the 1980s. At the same time the introduction of the NHS quasi-market has forced providers to pay more explicit attention to quality issues in their efforts to compete for contracts.

But discussions about quality in health care are characterised by lack of agreement about definitions and concepts and riven by struggles for professional 'turf' (Pollitt 1992). In addition, questions of quality in the British context are particularly difficult to answer because of the complexity and range of services provided by the NHS and the wide-ranging but incomplete responsibilities health authorities have for the health of their populations. The purpose of this chapter is to try and clarify these issues by asking: (a) what is quality in health care? (b) whose quality are we talking about? (c) how can quality be turned into a reality in the new NHS? In particular, the chapter looks at the changing relationship between health care providers and users of services, considers current initiatives to empower users and the arguments surrounding different models of empowerment in a publicly funded health service.

What is quality in health care?

The literature is characterised by a bewildering range of definitions. These vary in:

- the level at which they are pitched, from the macro-level of the health care system, down to the micro-level of interventions with individual patients;
- the extent to which they incorporate consumer views;
- which aspects of the service they focus on.

A widely used definition pitched at the macro-level is Maxwell's (Maxwell *et al.* 1983), which underlay the King's Fund quality assurance initiative started in 1984. Maxwell argues that quality in health care must include elements of the following:

- *appropriateness*: the service or procedure is one that the individual or population actually needs;
- *equity*: services are fairly shared among the population who need them;
- *accessibility*: services are readily accessible and not compromised by distance or time constraints;
- *effectiveness*: the services achieve the intended benefit for the individual and for the population;
- *acceptability*: the service satisfies the reasonable expectations of patients, providers and the community;
- *efficiency*: resources are not wasted on one service or patient to the detriment of another;

But such a comprehensive definition poses contradictions between the various desirable aspects of quality and offers no criteria for making judgements on the trade-offs between them. For example, various studies have shown that the effectiveness of certain clinical interventions is increased by specialisation and this is one reason for having regional centres of expertise for more complex operations or rarer conditions to ensure clinicians see enough patients to 'keep their hand in' and efficiently ration resources. At the same time, this reduces accessibility and may be less acceptable to consumers, who would prefer more local services.

Out of Maxwell's list, Shaw insists that the key issue is one of appropriateness. All the rest depend on this being present, for if a procedure is not appropriate to a particular patient's condition it cannot be judged quality care (Shaw n.d.). However, Koch argues that acceptability drives the rest: 'the ability to provide any service which meets the patients' needs or expectations, or is seen to make stupendous efforts towards this, will be a major quality predictor of success' (Koch 1990: 132).

This already suggests that quality in health care has a 'dualist' basis: consumers of services and professional providers may have different perspectives and valuations (Morgan and Murgatroyd 1994).

When talking about quality, there is also often confusion about which aspect of a service is under consideration. Avedis Donabedian, an American pioneer of quality assurance in health care in the United States whose work has been very influential in the UK, modelled quality as a dynamic relationship between structure, process and outcomes.

- Structure refers to the inputs of tangible resources such as buildings, staff, materials, and so on, but intangibles such as staff morale could arguably be included (Judge and Knapp 1985);
- Process comprises all that is done to the patient with these resources, both clinically (diagnostic and therapeutic procedures) and nonclinically (nursing care, 'hotel' services, etc.);
- Outcome is the result of these activities and the benefits (or otherwise) to patients at the level of the individual and the population. In practice, there are big gaps in our knowledge of outcomes in terms of the effects of care on the duration and quality of life and 'intermediate' outcome measures may have to be used, such as surgical mortality rates, unplanned readmissions or prevalence of cross-infections.

The relationship between structure, process and outcome is very unclear. Although a certain minimum level of resources is clearly necessary to achieve a good quality of care similar results can be achieved with very different 'mixes' of inputs (for example, a different staffing skill mix). The key factor here, therefore, is efficiency – achieving a given output with the best technical mix of inputs at the lowest cost.

The critical elements in process are appropriateness and acceptability. The appropriateness of clinical care is assessed by expert opinion on what is 'best practice', but often no consensus exists. Wide variations in practice are partly the result of ignorance about the efficacy of many medical interventions (Black 1986, Fuchs 1984). Users of services find it easier to judge the nonclinical aspects of care which traditionally have been undervalued by providers. Part of the sociological critique of Western medicine revolved around the way patients are depersonalised in the medical system, their anxieties, discomforts and fear ignored. Much of this critique has been taken on board and many improvements made although much remains to be done (see a summary of current trends below). A growing body of research shows there are intricate relationships between these 'softer' aspects of care and treatment which seek to uphold the integrity of a patient's 'personhood', and health outcomes, either in terms of recuperation or adjustment to impairment (for a large body of references, see Williamson 1992). In particular, it is clear that well-informed patients who are enabled to feel involved in their treatment get better more quickly and are more satisfied with their health care (references cited in College of Health 1994: 1).

Changing trends in standards of nonclinical care

Environmental Provision

From:	To:
Public	Private (bathing and toilet facilities, single rooms).
Large-scale	Small-scale (normal houses for mentally handicapped group homes).
Utilitarian	Comfortable (flowers, carpets).
Fostering dependence	Fostering independence (facilities for ambulant patients to make their own coffee and tea).

Institutional routines

From:	To:
Rigid	Flexible (patients are not woken up at a set time).
Imposed conditions	Negotiated conditions (patient given choice of times for outpatient appointments and inpatient admission).
Batch	Individual (staggered appointments system for outpatients).
Closed care	Open care (access to partner or friend in childbirth; open access/overnight arrangements for parents of sick children).

Staff–patient interaction

From:	To:
Impersonal	Personal (continuing care from same practitioner in pregnancy).
Autocratic	Consultative (patient participation in drawing up care plans with nursing staff).
Inducing dependency	Supporting autonomy (fostering self-responsibility in treatment, taking own blood pressure or medication).

Finally, the critical element in outcome is effectiveness but, as already mentioned, there are still big gaps in our knowledge of the effects of many procedures both at the individual and population level. One way to bring these different aspects of quality together in a concerted way is through total quality management (TQM), discussed later in this chapter. A widely quoted definition of quality in health care which acknowledges the interests of differing 'stakeholders' and yet can underpin comprehensive strategies like TQM is given by Oretveit (1990):

> . . . we can define quality in health services as meeting customer requirements at the lowest cost, and as involving three elements: first, customer quality, which is whether the service gives customers what they want as measured by customer satisfaction and complaints; second, professional quality, which is whether the service meets customers' needs as defined by professionals, and whether the professional standards which are believed to produce the required outcome are observed; and third, 'process quality', which is the design and operation of the service process to use resources in the most effective way to meet customer requirements
>
> (Oretveit 1990: 13)

Whose quality?

Conceptual difficulties are underpinned by organisational ones. Who gets to define, measure and act on quality in the NHS is, according to Pollitt (1992), divided up along 'tribal' lines reflecting professional demarcation boundaries and struggles for control among competing groups.

Unlike a number of other countries (for example, the Netherlands, United States, Australia or Canada), Britain has no national bodies to oversee quality assurance in health care in a comprehensive way. The Health Advisory Service, originally set up in 1969, advises on standards of good practice in services for the elderly, children, people with a mental illness or learning disability, but does not have powers of enforcement, and its role is currently under review. The Audit Commission, which has been given an extended brief to audit all health service facilities under *Working for Patients* (WFP), pursues one-off enquiries usually with a value-for-money focus. Government unwillingness to establish a more powerful and comprehensive agency in Britain to set and monitor quality standards has left quality issues largely in the hands of the professionals.[2]

Managerial involvement increased after the Griffiths management reforms in the mid-1980s. One outcome was the appointment of directors of quality assurance, largely from the ranks of displaced nurse managers. These directors were usually given responsibility for all aspects of quality except medical quality, which was left to the initiatives of the Royal Colleges (see, for instance, RCGP 1985; Campling *et al.* 1990) and the voluntary efforts of local groups of doctors. WFP put further impetus behind the drive for quality, emphasising the need to make rapid service improvements in the areas of greatest public concern, and this was followed by a letter from the Chief Executive of the NHSME in June 1989 requiring districts to:

> ensure that its units develop systematic comprehensive and continuous quality review programmes . . . Within these basic frameworks health authorities will be expected to include provision to cover three particular areas mentioned in the White Paper: appointment systems, information to patients, public areas and reception arrangements, and customer satisfaction surveys.
>
> (NHSME 1989)

The government also stepped more boldly into the contentious territory of clinical standards by requiring every doctor to participate in a system of medical audit and, at the instigation of the Royal Colleges, setting up a Clinical Standards Advisory Group at central level to disseminate good practice. But early evidence of the implementation of audit and the battery of other quality initiatives in the NHS suggested that doctors, nurses, managers and other staff, not to mention patients, still stepped delicately in a ritual dance which recognised established prerogatives and power. An example of the way in which medical audit was implemented and the results used, in comparison to nursing audit provides a good illustration.

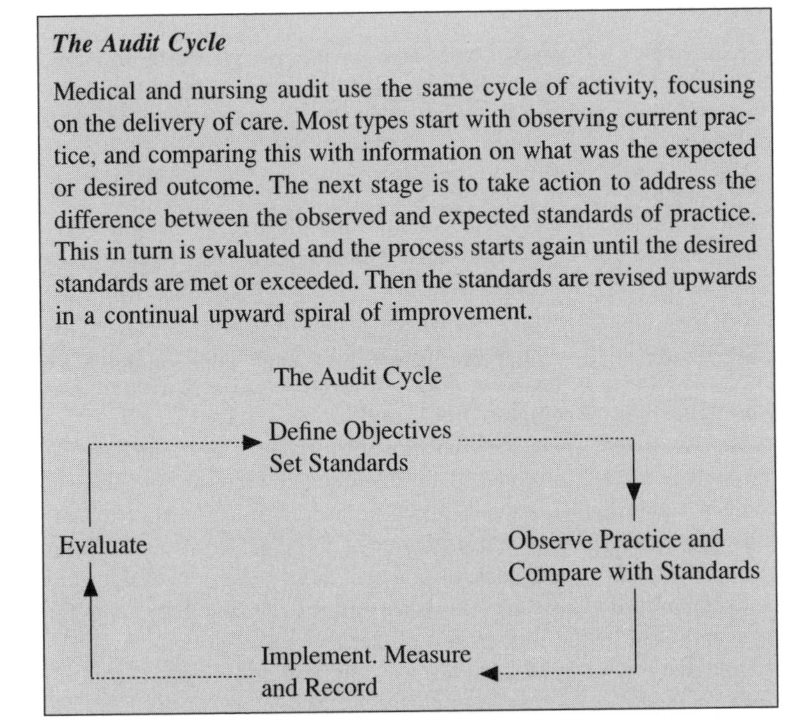

The Audit Cycle

Medical and nursing audit use the same cycle of activity, focusing on the delivery of care. Most types start with observing current practice, and comparing this with information on what was the expected or desired outcome. The next stage is to take action to address the difference between the observed and expected standards of practice. This in turn is evaluated and the process starts again until the desired standards are met or exceeded. Then the standards are revised upwards in a continual upward spiral of improvement.

Medical audit was defined in Working Paper 6 as:

> the systematic critical analysis of the quality of medical care, including the procedures used for diagnosis and treatment, the use of resources, and the resulting outcome and quality of life for the patient'
>
> (DOH 1989: 3)

Prior to 1991 medical audit was patchy in its incidence, although the Royal Colleges had been increasingly active in promoting various initiatives for some years. While this may have reflected a genuine desire to raise standards it also reflected realism about growing political and managerial pressures for increased efficiency and cost-effectiveness. As Pollitt (1992) points out, by demonstrating effective self-regulation the profession could fend off policing by others. Pollitt argues that the model of medical audit promulgated by the leaders of the profession was designed to be 'a nonthreatening activity carried out only by doctors and rigorously protected from the public gaze' (p. 4). Hence, the audit process was entirely medically controlled, participation was voluntary, standards set locally and the results kept absolutely confidential. Doctors who regularly failed to meet local standards could not be disciplined by management, only by their peers.

To a large extent this model of audit as a process of confidential medical self-management largely survived the WFP negotiations. Working Paper 6 on medical audit stated the principle of medical ownership:

> The Government's approach is based firmly on the principle that the quality of medical work can only be reviewed by a doctor's peers . . . The system should be medically led, with a local medical audit advisory committee chaired by a senior clinician.
>
> (DOH 1989: 6)

In addition the principle of voluntarism still held. Although 'every doctor should participate in medical audit' (DOH 1989: 6) the words 'compulsory' or 'mandatory' were never used and Pollitt reports that the BMA were successful in persuading the government that no new disciplinary procedures should be introduced for non-attendance, although in practice it may be the worst doctors who are least likely to audit their work (Black and Thompson 1993: 139).

Managers were given some powers of oversight. They were to agree the system of audit introduced locally, could initiate an independent audit in certain circumstances, and have access to aggregate audit results. Purchasers, too, could insist on seeing this data. However, Kerrison *et al.* (1994: 156) argue that, in practice, these powers of managerial oversight proved to be weak. This is partly due to the fact that monies for audit provided by the Department of Health were ring-fenced and distributed via regional and local audit committees under clinical control.

Ring-fencing coupled with the confidential nature of audit allowed doctors to control the topics to be studied, the method of audit, and who would have access to the results. Early studies on the actual implementation of medical audit also showed there were serious deficiencies in the process and much ignorance among doctors about how audit should be carried out (Kerrison *et al.* 1994; Black and Thompson 1993).

If managers had difficulty in gaining access to the audit process and audit results, patients were entirely excluded. The Association of Community Health Councils formally asked for CHC involvement in medical audit in 1989 and were refused by the DOH on the grounds that it was a professional exercise (Pollitt 1992). Although 46 per cent of district purchasers reported they are cooperating with their CHC on issues of quality, only 0.9 per cent included medical audit (Appleby *et al.* 1992).

Community Health Councils (CHCs)

CHCs were set up as part of the 1974 reorganisation of the health service to represent patients' interests.

Role: One for each district, to act as the public's watchdog and friend, by monitoring local health services, making recommendations for improvement and providing information to the public.

Membership: Appointed (and funded) by RHAs – half nominated by local authorities, one-third by voluntary organisations and the rest by regional authorities. 18–24 in total, with a small paid secretariat.

Powers: Limited to:

- the right to be consulted about service changes. Can oppose hospital closures, and decision must then be referred to Secretary of State;
- the right to information (could attend and speak but not vote at DHA meetings held in public);
- the right to visit health authority premises and services (but not GP practices). Since the establishment of NHS trusts this is no longer an automatic right, but must be negotiated via the purchasers contract requirements, or directly with trust management.

In contrast to medical audit, nursing audit was already well developed in the NHS by the time WFP was published, reflecting the prominent position nurses have taken in promoting quality assurance generally (Dalley and Carr-Hill 1991). More emphasis has been placed on the psychosocial care of patients, as well as the technical and physical aspects, and as a consequence there is greater acknowledgement of the need to consult patients and take account of their views.

Nursing audit has usually been introduced and run by nurse managers instead of being simply a peer group exercise. Confidentiality is therefore not such a strong theme and the results of nursing audit have always been available to managers, which, Pollitt argues, reflects the less powerful position of nursing compared to medicine. In turn this has led managers to introduce standardised and costed 'packages of care' which bring together considerations of outcome with workforce and workload planning to deploy nursing resources more efficiently.

Proctor's (1990) research illustrates the conflicts which emerge between managerial and professional perceptions of 'quality' as a result of these endeavours, with nurses arguing that high-quality care requires a continuity of staffing on wards so that staff can find out and adapt to the unique needs of each patient. Managerial systems of assessing nursing workload and skill mix on the other hand (for example, Criteria for Care, GRASP) link workload planning to assessments of patient dependency. Hence, if the dependency levels on a ward increase, extra staff can be deployed. Proctor argues that this has led to an increasingly transient workforce on the wards who are continually confronted by a different set of patients each time they come on duty, undermining attempts at individualised quality care. Dependence on standardised routines and rough-and-ready indicators of patients' needs, such as their level of mobility, is essential (Proctor 1990). Recent work by the Audit Commission confirms that this is often the case (Audit Commission 1992).

The evolution of audit

A decisive policy change in the evolution of audit was announced in July 1993 with the publication of a strategy document prepared by the Clinical Outcomes Group, *Meeting and Improving Standards in Health Care* (DOH 1993a), which was followed up by further guidance in *The Evolution of Clinical Audit* in February 1994 and various executive letters. The strategy was based on the following principles:

- a shift from uniprofessional systems to a multi-disciplinary system of clinical audit which embraces the activities of doctors, nurses, therapists and other health care staff;
- clinical audit will still be professionally led, although this may not mean by a doctor in all cases;
- a stronger focus on the patient;
- greater integration of clinical audit into mainstream contracting and wider provider quality assurance programmes, such as total quality management;

- a more active role for non-clinicians;
- audit to be linked strongly to the evaluation of clinical effectiveness and outcomes for patients.

(NHSME 1994a)

From 1994–95 funding would no longer be ring-fenced and allocated via the professional audit machinery, but distributed to health authorities in accordance with weighted capitation principles. They in turn would fund audit programmes based on agreements with clinicians and managers in the provider units on suitable topics, informed by their own medium-term health and purchasing strategies, as well as problems identified by their surveys of GP and consumer opinion. Clearly these changes have tipped the balance of power further in a managerial and purchasing direction, and suggest a more important role for other professions in relation to doctors, although the DOH is still acutely aware of the 'professional sensitivities' which have to be overcome (DOH 1994b: NHSME 1993).

Three important conclusions follow from this discussion. First, concepts of quality in health care have been determined largely by the professionals, with managers staking out an increasing role. Second, a shared view of what 'quality' means, which can underpin a commitment to organisation-wide strategies like total quality management, has often been lacking. Third, 'consumers' – that is, patients, their families, potential patients – have traditionally had least influence over the kind of service they receive. With the emergence of the 'consumer paradigm' in public management, however, the government insists that the views of consumers and those acting on their behalf should carry more weight.

Creating a user-centred approach

There are good theoretical grounds for making the user's experience central to definitions of quality in a service industry like health care. Patients judge quality by comparing the service they receive against expectations of what they should receive. Both perceptions and expectations are experiential states of mind rather than necessarily 'real'. For example, patients waiting in an outpatient department knowing that it will be 30 minutes before they are seen may be happier than those who wait half as long, not knowing how long the wait will be. In services like health care or education the experience of the user is the product being consumed. The behaviour of the 'consumer' is also an integral part of the production process. For example, the extent to which patients like or trust the doctor and nurse may affect their willingness to cooperate in their treatment.

Defining what the user expects and wants from a service, however, is complicated by the fact that perceptions change over time, according to where people are in relation to the system. They may feel differently depending on whether they are viewing the service before using it, encountering it initially, actually in receipt of the service, and, finally, viewing it in retrospect. Assessing and monitoring quality in health care will therefore require continuous interaction and feedback from users of the services at all stages of service design and delivery. There are three main ways in which the government has sought to strengthen the consumer's voice over service quality: through the contracting system; the introduction of the Patient's Charter and the promotion of quality strategies like TQM. These are discussed in turn.

Contracting for quality

The introduction of service contracts between purchasers and providers created a new mechanism for negotiating explicit quality standards and targets (often for the first time). The service specification sets out the quality standards that the purchaser expects and usually these will be at two levels: general service specifications which apply to all contracts and individual service agreements for particular specialities and services. These may be detailed blueprints for the service in question, often a statement of future aspiration rather than present reality, but serving to provide a framework for the identification of particular areas for detailed negotiation and improvement. For example, Appendix 1 sets out headings from one authority's *Service Specification for Maternity Services* in 1995–96. The specification incorporates locally determined service standards and principles within a framework of national policy for maternity services, as set out in the recommendations by the Expert Maternity Group in their report *Changing Childbirth* (DOH 1993b; NHSME 1994b), as well as Patient's Charter targets and standards. The timescales by which new or higher standards are to be introduced are also set out in the specification. As Williamson points out, over time some of the detail in service specifications may be replaced by references to sets of standards developed for a speciality or part of one by outside bodies. For example, some authorities already refer to standards for children's services developed by the National Association for the Welfare of Children in Hospitals (Williamson 1992: 125) and standards for other services are being developed by other professional and voluntary bodies.

Early advice from the DOH exhorted districts to find ways of canvassing the opinions of GPs, patients and the wider community in assessing health needs and making contract decisions (DOH 1990) but a national survey of purchasing intentions for 1992–93 revealed that districts placed more weight on GP preferences than those of patients and the public when decisions about where to place contracts were taken (Appleby *et al.* 1992). However, in 1992 an influential document from the Management Executive, *Local Voices: The Views of People in Purchasing for Health*, set out a more ambitious agenda for managers to follow. Local people's views should be heeded not only in needs assessment but:

> at other stages in the purchasing process, i.e. to help establish priorities, develop service specifications and monitor services: they represent a significant element of 'purchasing intelligence'
>
> (NHSME 1992: 3)

The reasons for this radical extension of user involvement were also clearly stated:

> If health authorities are to establish a champion of the people role, their decisions should reflect, so far as is practical, what people want, their preferences, concerns and values. Being responsive to local views will enhance the credibility of health authorities but, more importantly, is likely to result in services which are better suited to local needs and therefore more appropriate . . . Moreover as health authorities seek to bring about changes in services and make explicit decisions about priorities they are likely to be more persuasive and successful in their negotiations with providers if they secure public support
>
> (NHSME 1992b: 1)

In other words, gaining the support of local people is the way in which health authorities empower *themselves* in making what might be unpopular decisions with powerful providers. Finding methods of effective consultation and involvement is the means of establishing credibility and legitimacy. Behind 'local voices' therefore there is a strong managerialist orientation, but the radical emphasis of the document has been maintained in subsequent policy directives. For example, in the 1996–97 Priorities and Planning Guidance from the NHS Executive one of the six strategic priorities for the next three to five years is stated as:

> (giving) greater voice and influence to users of NHS services and their carers in their own care, the development and definition of standards set for NHS services locally and the development of NHS policy both locally and nationally
>
> (NHSE 1996)

To carry this out health authorities must have a system for 'systematic and continuing communication and consultation' with local people, voluntary groups, and, most importantly, Community Health Councils, and be able to demonstrate how this consultation has 'influenced the development, planning and purchasing of services'. Programmes to involve individual patients more actively in their own care and treatment choices must be backed up by higher-quality information. Finally, complaints systems should reflect the revised procedures adopted by the government in response to the recommendations of the Wilson Committee (DOH 1994b; 1995) (see below), adopted to better meet the requirement set out in the Patient's Charter that all patients' complaints must be adequately and promptly investigated and reported on.

Dealing with complaints in the NHS

Until recently the main systems for handling complaints in the NHS were:

- Service committees of FHSAs investigated complaints about breaches of contract made by GPs, dentists, opticians and pharmacists.
- The 1985 Hospital Complaints Act obliged DHAs to maintain systems for dealing with complaints in hospitals and community health services.
- The Parliamentary Commissioner for the Health Service or Ombudsman (a post set up in 1977) investigated complaints about maladministration from patients who remained dissatisfed with the local handling of their complaint, on the understanding that they will not subsequently seek legal redress.
- In cases of professional negligence or incompetence patients must seek redress from the appropriate professional body (in the case of doctors, the General Medical Council) or through the courts.

These procedures have been heavily criticised for being bureaucratic, insensitive, complex and lacking credibility with the public (Mulcahy 1995). The Wilson Committee recently reviewed NHS complaints systems to bring them in line with the principles laid down by the Complaints Task Force of the Citizen's Charter Unit (DOH 1994b). The recommendations of the Committee were accepted (DOH 1995) and are currently being implemented. They include:

- common system of complaints throughout the NHS;
- written complaints to be acknowledged within two working days;
- a three-stage approach:
  - immediate first-line response
  - investigation and/or conciliation
  - referral to an independent panel

  comprising three members and a lay majority.
  Report to be sent to complainant.

continued

Complainants still dissatisfied after stages one and two have the option of approaching the Health Service Ombudsman. All stages should be completed in three months.

An evaluation of the progress made in implementing 'local voices' was made by the NHS Executive in Spring 1994 and showed that progress had been patchy (HSJ 1995a). Twenty-one per cent of health authorities were categorised as 'good'. They had consulted widely, used this information to make tangible changes to their purchasing plans and contracts, and set up systematic arrangements for involving local people and feeding back the results of consultation. Another 57 per cent of authorities were only deemed 'acceptable' and 22 per cent 'unsatisfactory'.

The Patient's Charter

Announced in a great flurry of publicity in November 1991, the Patient's Charter announced 10 'charter rights' for patients in the NHS, as part of the Citizens Charter initiative. Seven of these simply reiterated the existing rights of NHS patients, but three were new as from April 1992. In addition, nine charter standards were announced. Authorities were also asked to produce local charters which could set more ambitious and specific targets.

The Charter's public reception was qualified. While the listing and publicising of rights was welcomed (every household in the country received a copy, at a cost of £l. 4 million to the Exchequer) there was some disappointment at the unambitious nature of the targets and the absence of enforcement mechanisms. The NHS in Scotland, for example, had already set a waiting list target of 18 months compared to the two-year target adopted for England and Wales. The Swedes, who were trying to attain a three-month maximum waiting time guarantee, were said to have 'showed disbelief that the Citizen's Charter in Britain offered a two-year guarantee' (Glennerster and Matsaganis 1992: 12). The rhetoric of rights also contrasted oddly with the failure to give more powers to Community Health Councils, and cutbacks in funding Citizens' Advice Bureaus and legal aid.

Nevertheless, ministers and the NHSME took implementation seriously and kept up the pressure on health authorities. Extra finance was forthcoming to meet the two-year waiting list target by April 1992 and Regional Health Authorities were instructed to give its achievement high priority. Though not entirely met, ministers claimed a reduction from 50,000 to 2,000 in two-year waiters within one year. From 1992–93 the target was reduced to an 18-month maximum and many districts were aiming for a year or even less.

The Patient's Charter 1995

A revised and expanded Patient's Charter was announced in January 1995. The precise contents were: With immediate effect:

- the right of a patient to know before going into hospital if s/he is/will be in a mixed-sex ward;
- national standards addressing security and cleanliness in hospitals as well as single-sex washing and toilet facilities for patients in hospital;
- the standard that children should normally be admitted to children's wards under the care of a paediatric consultant rather than adult wards.

from 1 April 1995:

- 18-month guaranteed inpatient waiting time;
- 26-week standard for first outpatient appointments and target that 90 per cent of all outpatients should be seen within 13 weeks;
- 12-month standard waiting time for coronary artery bypass grafts and associated procedures;
- 3–4 hour standard for emergency admission to hospital through A and E departments. To be strengthened to 2 hours from April 1996;
- standards addressing timeliness of community nursing visits;
- standard addressing hospital catering services.

The Charter was expanded and updated in January 1995, giving a new maximum waiting time guarantee of 18 months, one new right and a number of new national standards, referring to inpatient waiting times for some specific procedures and the introduction of maximum waiting times for first outpatient appointments

The Citizen's Charter marked a new approach to improving the quality and responsiveness of public services. Prime Minister Major's 'big idea' for the 1990s, it marked a welcome break from the grim neo-Taylorist preoccupation with economy and efficiency of the 1980s, but now 'charterism' has become a veritable growth industry. Coordinated by the Citizen's Charter Unit within the Office for Public Services and Science in the Cabinet Office, the Citizen's Charter has given birth to over 30 service-specific charters (health, education, British Rail, etc.) and in turn these have spawned countless 'local charters'. For example, each health care trust and GP practice is encouraged to develop their own model. A telephone helpline 'Charterline' has been started and 'Chartermarks' for organisations displaying measurable improvements in quality of service are awarded by the Prime Minister's Citizen's Charter Advisory Group.

Yet from the beginning this has been a centrally driven and coordinated initiative. Within the NHS the approach has been top-down, and the choice of rights and standards in the 'Patient's Charter' has been managerially inspired, not selected in consultation with the public (hence the argument for local charters). Indeed while the updated Charter explains what patients are entitled to as a right, and what is only an expectation, the plethora of rights, targets, standards and expectations it contains is extremely confusing.

This highlights Pollitt's point that there are inherent ambiguities attaching to the use of the word 'standard' in many charter documents (Pollitt 1994). Do they refer to a minimum level of acceptability, an average or best practice? Minimum standards should never be breached, whereas average standards are a norm which may not always be attained. Finally, best practice is aspirational and reflects what a service would like to achieve given time, resources, etc. Performance on these different types of standard may be diverging widely.

Some of these ambiguities are illuminated by looking at the monitoring of Patient's Charter targets by the DOH. There have been two reports so far, and from June 1994 the publication of annual hospital league tables began. Reviewing this record of performance Bayley (1994) points out that monitoring seems to be highly selective. Only five of the ten original 'rights' and three of the nine standards are mentioned in the reports, and the league tables are even more selective, covering only three standards and one right, the right to have detailed information on local health services. This is partly due to the fact that monitoring the 'softer' rights and standards – such as the right to dignity and privacy – is inherently harder to do, although the NHS Executive is currently examining ways of tackling this.

Research carried out for the Department of Health by National Opinion Polls shows that the Charter has not captured the public's imagination, and that there is widespread scepticism and cynicism about it (and the publication of the league tables) which seems to to be linked with current disaffection with politics and politicians (McIver and Martin 1996). At the same time patient organisations and the Association of Community Health Councils have concluded that the original rights of NHS patients codified in the charter had not been strengthened, and only one new right, the two-year waiting guarantee, unambiguously achieved. Two more – the right to detailed information on local services and to have complaints properly investigated – were linked to specific NHS initiatives which still have to prove their worth (ACHEW 1995).

However, the most telling criticism of the charter movement in Britain is that it has little to do with notions of 'citizenship' at all, which must be based on a conception of the rights and duties of persons acquired by virtue of their membership of a particular state. As Pollitt

(1994: 12) points out, although concepts of citizenship are 'notoriously underdeveloped in British constitutional and administrative law, relative to the sophisticated formulations of some of our continental European partners', the implicit notion of citizenship within the Citizen's Charter seems to be particularly stunted. Civil or political rights are simply ignored and instead the citizen is repackaged as a consumer and taxpayer, concerned with economic and market-based rights only. Even these prove insubstantial in practice, for there are no legal powers of redress or compensation when they are broken.

This contrasts with the approach to patient's rights in Finland, which are now set out in law (Calnan 1995: 22). This covers the patient's rights to good health and medical treatment; access to care and information; self-determination; emergency treatment; the status of minor patients and the right to competent care. Patients are supported in upholding their rights by locally nominated health care ombudsmen who have an important role in providing practical advice and support in all matters relating to the law, including claims for compensation.

Total quality management

Total quality management (TQM) is a strategic organisation-wide approach to quality improvement in the health service, adopted from the lessons of Japanese industry and the exhortations of management gurus like Tom Peters. Its key tenets are:

1 *The customer comes first*: the first and most important characteristic of total quality is the search continually to meet, and even exceed, the customer's demands and expectations;
2 *Corporate commitment and planning*: TQM requires a particular kind of strategic leadership which can provide the vision and commitment, plan for change and see that it is implemented (Peters and Austin 1985). Peters talks of the obsession with quality which characterised many leaders in the 'excellent company' research;
3 *Everyone participates in TQM*: Quality must become everyone's business, not just that of top management or quality specialists. Everyone has customers, even though these may be internal to the organisation, and many quality defects can only be dealt with on an inter-departmental basis. Indeed, TQM partly evolved from the realisation that improvements can only be achieved if professional and departmental barriers are broken down, people stop blaming each other for defects and constructively work together to solve them;
4 *Valuing all staff*: Because TQM emphasises each link in the internal quality chain, all staff, even those traditionally seen as of low status or unimportant, have a contribution to make;

5 *Quality measurement is essential*: 'Quality measurements for each area of activity must be established where they don't exist and reviewed where they do' (Crosby 1979: 132);
6 Corporate systems must be aligned to support TQM: Two of the great pioneers of total quality management, J. Edwards Deming and J.H. Juran, whose work had great influence on Japanese companies after the Second World War, discovered that quality problems were usually built into the design of production processes and could not be attributed to the ill-will or incompetence of workers. It was primarily management's responsibility to help workers to do their jobs in a high-quality way ('doing it right first time'), by identifying the sources of error and planning the production process to prevent their occurrence;
7 *Constant striving for improvement*: TQM is a neverending struggle for an unattainable goal. 'Improve constantly and forever the system of production and service, to improve quality and productivity and thus constantly decrease costs' (Deming 1986: 23).

Many health authorities claim to have adopted a TQM approach to quality improvement, and the DOH funded 17 pilot sites from 1989 with more added later. However, none fully meet the tenets of TQM. Criticisms made by an independent evaluation team included:

1 The failure to carry out any organisational audit before implementing TQM to establish quality benchmarks. It was therefore difficult to tell how much progress had been made;
2 Failure to develop a corporate-wide approach to quality which would align the relevant information and management systems and processes. TQM often seemed like 'just another initiative' to be tacked on to countless others. In particular the links and potential of resource management in supporting TQM were not exploited;
3 Tensions between a corporate approach to quality like TQM with monoprofessional systems of audit and quality assurance. This was particularly apparent among the doctors, who rarely participated fully in TQM initiatives, pursuing their own system of medical audit (Joss and Kogan 1995). (See, however, recent developments in audit which may help to meet these criticisms, discussed on pp. 148–9.)

There are, however, real difficulties in transposing a model of TQM developed to meet the needs of private-sector manufacturing industry to a public-sector welfare service like the NHS. For example, in manufacturing TQM is primarily designed to reduce variation in standards and eliminate waste – to 'do it right first time'. In some service-sector industries, reduction of variation may also be important (for example, fast-food restaurant chains) but highly professionalised personal services, such as health care or education, may be more concerned with *increasing* variation if staff are to respond appropriately to the needs and demands of individual users. In addition, as mentioned earlier, there is little tangible 'product' from a personal service encounter which can be evaluated and monitored. Instead the service is 'consumed as it is constructed', and assessing the quality of that staff–customer encounter requires continual feedback from service users (Joss and Kogan 1995: 28).

Public services like the NHS may also have broader goals than their private-sector counterparts, such as improving access and equity, or empowering the user (Pfeffer and Coote 1991) which TQM manufacturing models were not designed to meet. For these reasons, the translation of TQM concepts into health care has to be adapted to the different culture and working environment with sensitivity.

Morgan and Murgatroyd (1994) argue that the main focus of TQM development in health care, both in Britain and North America, has been on customer audits and customer satisfaction, with the development of service standards a close second. Relatively little work has been done on improving systems, although the potential for reducing the costs of error and waste by redesigning the production process and achieving improvements in patient care at the same time is considerable. In effect, this reverses the normal priorities inherent in manufacturing models of TQM (Joss and Kogan 1995)

Morgan and Murgatroyd defend this sequence of priorities by arguing that:

> . . . customer audit is the logical starting point for TQM in a professional public sector setting such as health . . . What customers (both external and internal) reveal are the key indicators of quality within the total detail of processes which go to make up health care . . . these can (then) be measured and the data used as part of the totality of factors used in discussion by professionals to produce a service standard.'
>
> (1994: 78)

A service standard is defined as 'a customer-driven agreed level of performance appropriate to the population addressed, which is observable, achievable, measurable and desirable' (Morgan and Murgatroyd 1994: 79). These serve both as a yardstick against which current performance can be compared, and as targets to be achieved by methodical planning of services. In this way, considerations of structure, process and outcome can be brought together. What is useful and important in this approach to TQM in health care is the emphasis given to understanding the staff–customer encounter from the customer's perspective, and the reasons why both sides may have differing perceptions.

If these differences are acknowledged and understood, staff can begin the cultural journey away from 'professional paternalism' to a

Figure 7.1 **Features of the provider and customer service experience**

Provider's experience	*User's experience*
Their job	Distraction from normal life
Familiar • setting • language • people • conventions	Strange • setting • language • people • conventions
Feel confident	Feel anxious
Not in pain	In pain
Knowledgeable	Limited lay knowledge
In control of events	Limited or no control

(*Source*: Morgan and Murgatroyd op. cit. p. 84). Reproduced by kind permission of Open University Press, Buckingham.

more equal partnership with their patients. The potential of TQM initiatives to empower patients is demonstrated by an example from one of the West Midlands case study districts in the 'Monitoring Managed Competition' research, who are themselves a national TQM demonstration project. The hospital had a commitment to shared care with the patient and patient's relatives and care plans were drawn up in full consultation with both. This was based on an explicit philosophy of preserving the dignity and independence of patients. The Director of Quality Assurance explained:

Far too long, for the last 40 years, you go into hospital and you lose everything. You lose control of your life. For the first time you lose control of your own fate. What we are saying is, the patient ought to be able to determine at any stage of their illness what care they receive, and they ought to know what is coming next.

Doing things to patients which they were capable of doing for themselves was also wasteful of resources:

Why should we bath someone when they are capable of bathing themselves? Why should we give their medication when they are capable of taking it themselves? Why do we need two nurses going round with a medicine tray? You take your medicine at home, why not here? If in pain control, you were in control of your own pain, you have less than if it were a set wait every four hours for us to come and give you a tablet.

Having well-informed patients who have more control over their care, and who are helped to retain independence is good for quality and is also cost-effective.

Whether it be aspirin or 10 mg of morphine, a trained nurse has got to do both. Roughly 30 per cent of the patients in our hospital, shall we say, are just on antibiotics; they can take it themselves. That should give us at least half a whole time equivalent nurse on every ward. If you multiply that up, that is £250,000 worth of money that could then be given to alternative developments.

TQM is not the only strategic approach to quality improvement, and there is current interest in two other approaches, patient-centred care and 'whole hospital re-engineering'. Both involve radical restructuring of hospitals systems and processes from a patient-centred perspective, and attempt to facilitate a more coordinated and seamless pattern of care as well as eliminating waste and duplication of effort. The potential for improvement can be quite dramatic as the example below demonstrates.

The Byzantine complexity of the typical hospital*

To demonstrate the benefits of reorganising hospital processes along patient-centred lines. Andersen Consulting undertook a survey of 10 hospitals. The results were startling:

1 Junior doctors walked on average seven miles a day on each shift, consuming up to three hours of their productive time and adding substantially to the exhaustion they experienced. Porters were covering up to 20 miles a day.
2 A common pathology test took on average 10 people and 18 hours to carry out, and 80 per cent of all tests requested comprised a few simple procedures which could be easily carried out by nurses on the ward.
3 The typical patient came into contact with 47 care providers in the course of a five-day spell in hospital.
4 Hospitals in the survey averaged 201 job classifications.

The consultants' approach, which was being implemented in London's Central Middlesex Hospital, is to organise patient care with multi-skilled teams of staff who can meet most of the patient's needs on the spot. Responsibility for planning, implementing and auditing care becomes team-based, and existing demarcation boundaries on who does what are broken down. The system is claimed to produce improved quality of care, staff morale and job satisfaction and cost savings in the order of 10–15 per cent.

**Source*: Andersen Consulting 'Patient-centred care: reinventing the hospital': see also *Financial Times*, 24th June 1992

'Whole hospital re-engineering' is currently being piloted by the NHS Executive with Leicester Royal Infirmary and King's Healthcare

Trust in London and promises to overtake TQM as the most fashionable approach to quality improvement. Specially selected teams of staff, including clerks, clinicians, porters and managers, pool their knowledge, experience and ideas to 'map' various processes and look at how these can be redesigned to improve patient care. In Leicester, one of the first processes to be mapped was the outpatient or day surgery visit, right from referral by a GP back to the return of the patient to the GP's care. The teams discovered that a relatively standard outpatient clinic visit involved 122 separate activities of which only half were necessary, simply making work for staff and irritation for patients (HSJ 1995b).

In the end a commitment to excellence may be more important than the precise techniques used to attain it. To be successful all these approaches require an appropriate culture and style, one characterised by a fluid approach to multi-disciplinary working, openness to innovation, and creativity in problem-solving, as discussed in the previous chapter.

Conclusions

Questions of quality are now high on the agenda of health service managers, professionals and politicians, but conceptual confusion and lack of agreement on objectives still bedevil progress. What should quality mean in a publicly funded health service like the NHS? Should the debate be about minimum, average or optimal standards? This links to the question of resources and how quality improvements will be funded. As we have seen, TQM and other strategic approaches to quality improvement in health care have the potential to achieve considerable savings. Joss and Kogan (1995: 104), for example, report that their evaluation of the TQM pilot projects in Britain suggested that 'the average acute unit or community service might well be able to save around 15 to 38 per cent of costs found in other studies'. At the same time, improving quality also demands considerable investment, notably in training to achieve behavioural change. The successful implementation of TQM requires particularly intensive training strategies for all staff and this may have been a factor in the limited success of the health service TQM pilots. Joss and Kogan report that very little training was carried out at most sites, and the resourcing of TQM generally was about one-third of what is spent on typical programmes in the commercial sector. Even this was reduced after the Department of Health grants ran out (Joss and Kogan 1994: 103–4).

An even more fundamental and unresolved question in the quality debate concerns the relationship with the user of services. The plethora of terms in current use – patient, customer, consumer, citizen – are used as substitutes for each other, yet they imply quite different models. Two broad approaches are discernible, according to Hoggett and Hambleton (1987); consumerism, which focuses on the responsiveness of public services (broadly the approach of the Major government); and collective responses which emphasise the democratisation of services. Consumerism is a response to the critique of inward-looking public service organisations which fail to put the customer first, articulated by the Griffiths Report in relation to the NHS. The preferred solutions draw heavily on the lessons of the 'excellence' literature, but also derive from Conservative beliefs in market mechanisms in facilitating consumer choice and empowerment. However, our discussion in previous chapters showed that concepts of the 'customer' or the 'consumer' with regard to public services are problematic for various reasons, and particularly so in health care. The age of the deferential patient may be declining, replaced by one where a more educated and assertive public expect higher standards and more information, but inevitably the gap between the professional and the patient in knowledge and expertise is real. There are also big differences between groups as to how far they are able or willing to act as 'good consumers'. For example, Shackley and Ryan (1995) point out that the idea of 'shopping around' for one's GP is anathema to many, and particularly to the elderly who, because of their greater vulnerability, need to be more trusting of their doctor. It is also unclear whether encouraging the public to act as 'consumers' is desirable in a resource-limited environment. Fuelling public demands for 'free' services through initiatives like the Patient's Charter simply leads to higher levels of dissatisfaction when expectations cannot be met.

Consumerism is concerned with empowering individuals in relation to the services they receive; collectivists go further than this, stressing the differences which exist in the nature of consumption and accountability in the public and private sectors. Users of services are citizens and taxpayers too, and part of the social purpose of public management may be to enhance democratic mechanisms of accountability and diffuse participation in decision making to wider sections of society. In other words, can we go beyond the consumer paradigm in public management, and what might that mean in relation to the NHS? We return to this important question in the final chapter.

Notes

1 Source: NAHA/NHS Training Authority (1988) See also Williamson 1992: 123.

2 Since the introduction of the NHS reforms there have been growing signs that more formal and comprehensive systems of quality accreditation may be

introduced in Britain. Accreditation refers to the process of setting explicit standards of good practice and checks by external agencies to see that these are met by health care providers. In 1993 the Department of Health commissioned research into different forms of accreditation and the benefits it could bring to the NHS (Scriven 1995) and different systems of 'whole hospital' accreditation are already being developed, the best known of which is the organisational audit system developed by the King's Fund.

References

Association of Community Health Councils in England and Wales (ACHEW) (1995) *Health Perspectives: the New Patient's Charter*, London: Association of Community Health Councils.

Appleby, J., Little, V., Ranade, W., Robinson, R. and Smith, P. (1992) *Implementing the Reforms: A Survey of District General Managers,* Monitoring Managed Competition Project (1992), Project paper 4, Birmingham NAHAT.

Audit Commission (1992) *The Virtue of Patients: Making Best Use of Ward Nursing Resources*, London: HMSO.

Bayley, H. (1994) 'Charter challenge' *Health Service Journal*, 104(5418): 22–3.

Black, A.D. (1986) *An Anthology of Fake Antitheses*, Rock Carling Monograph, London: Nuffield Provincial Hospitals Trust.

Black, N. and Thompson, E. (1993) 'Obstacles to medical audit: British doctors speak' *Social Science in Medicine*, 36(7): 849–56.

College of Health (1994) *Consumer Audit Guidelines*, London: College of Health

Calnan, M. (1995) 'Citizens' views on health care' *J. of Management in Medicine*, 9(4): 17–23.

Campling, E.A., Devlin, H.B. and Lunn, J.N. (1990) *Report of the National Confidential Enquiry into Perioperative Deaths 1989*, London: Royal College of Surgeons/Royal College of Anaesthetists.

Crosby, P. (1979) *Quality is Free*, New York: McGraw Hill.

Dalley, G. and Carr-Hill, R. (1991) *Pathways to Quality: A Study of Quality Management Initiatives in the NHS: A Guide for Managers*, York: University of York, Centre for Health Economics.

Deming, W.E. (1986) *Out of the Crisis*, Cambridge, Mass: Massachusetts Institute of Technology.

Department of Health (DOH) (1989) *Working for Patients: Medical Audit, Working Paper 6*, London: HMSO.

—— (1990) *Contracts for Health Services: Operational principles*, London: HMSO.

—— (1993a) *Clinical Audit: Meeting and Improving standards in Health Care*, London: HMSO.

—— (1993b) *Changing Childbirth*, London: HMSO.

—— (1994a) *The Evolution of Clinical Audit*, London: HMSO.

—— (1994b) *Being Heard: the Report of a Review Committee on NHS Complaints Procedures*, London: HMSO.

—— (1995) *Acting on Complaints: the government's proposals in response to Being Heard*, London: HMSO.

Fuchs, V. (1984) 'Rationing health care' *New England Journal of Medicine*, December 18.

Glennerster, H., Matsaganis, M. and Owens, P. (1992) *A Foothold for Fundholding*, Research Report 12, London: Kings Fund Institute.

Health Service Journal (1995a) 'The listening blank', 21st September, 105(5471): 22–4.

—— (1995b) 'Time machine', 105(5449): 11.

Hoggett, P. and Hambleton, R. (1987) *Decentralisation and Democracy: Localising Public Services*, Bristol: School of Advanced Urban Studies, University of Bristol.

Joss, R. and Kogan, M. (1995) *Advancing Quality: Total Quality Management in the Health Service*, Buckingham: Open University Press.

Judge, K. and Knapp, M. (1985) 'Efficiency in the production of welfare: the public and private sectors compared' in R. Klein and M. O'Higgins (eds) *The Future of Welfare*, Oxford: Blackwell.

Kerrison, S., Packwood, T. and Buxton, M. (1994) 'Monitoring Medical Audit' in R. Robinson and J. Le Grand (eds) *Evaluating the NHS Reforms*, London: King's Fund Institute.

Koch, H. (1990) 'The changing face of the National Health Service in the 1990s', in P. Spurgeon (ed), London: Longman.

McIver, S. and Martin, G. (1996) 'Unchartered territory' *Health Service Journal*, 106(5521): 24–6.

Maxwell, R. *et al.* (1983) 'Seeking quality' *The Lancet* January 1/8(8314–5): 45–8.

Morgan, C. and Murgatroyd, S. (1994) *Total Quality Management in the Public Sector*, Buckingham: Open University Press.

Mulcahy, L. (1995) *Redress in the Public Sector*, London: National Consumer Council.

NAHA/NHS Training Authority (1988) *A Manual for Health Authority Chairmen and Members*, Birmingham: National Association of Health Authorities.

NHS Executive (1996) (NHSE) *Priorities and Planning Guidance for the NHS 1996–97.*

NHS Management Executive (NHSME) (1989) 'Quality', Letter to Regional and District General Managers, 22.6.1989.

—— (1992a) 'Implementing the Patient's Charter' Health Service Guidelines HSG(92)4. January.

—— (1992b) *Local Voices: The Views of Local People in Purchasing for Health*, EL(92)1. January.

—— (1993) *Clinical Audit in HCHS: Allocation of Funds 1993–94* EL(93)34, 23.4.1993.

—— (1994a) *Clinical Audit: 1994/95 and Beyond* EL(94)20 28.2.1994.

—— (1994b) *Woman-centred Maternity Services* EL(94)9 Oretveit, J. (1990) 'What is quality in health services?' *Health Services Management* June: 132–3.

Peters, T. and Austin, N. (1985) *A Passion for Excellence: the Leadership Difference*, London: Collins.

Pfeffer, N. and Coote, A. (1991) *Is Quality Good for You?* Social Policy Paper 5 London: Institute for Public Policy Research.

Pollitt, C. (1990) 'Capturing quality? The quality issue in British and American health policies' *Journal of Public Policy*, 7(1): 71–92.

—— (1992) 'The struggle for quality: the case of the NHS', Paper given to UK Political Studies Association Conference, Queen's University Belfast, April.

—— (1994) 'The Citizen's Charter: a preliminary analysis' *Public Money and Management*, April–June: 9–13.

Proctor, S. (1990) 'Accountability and nursing' *Nursing Review*, 8(3/4): 15–21.

Royal College of General Practitioners (RCGP) (1985) *What Sort of Doctor? Assessing Quality of Care in General Practice*, London: RCGP.

Royal College of Nursing (1989) *A Framework for Quality: A Patient-centred Approach to Quality Assurance in Health Care*, London: Royal College of Nursing.

Scrivens, E. (1995) *Accreditation: Protecting the Professional or the Consumer?* Buckingham: Open University Press.

Shackley, P. and Ryan, M. (1995) 'What is the role of the consumer in health care?' *Social Policy and Administration*, 29(2): 517–41.

Shaw, C.D. (n.d.) *Introducing Quality Assurance*, Project Paper 64, London: King's Fund College.

Williamson, C. (1992) *Whose Standards? Consumer and Professional Standards in Health Care*, Buckingham: Open University Press.

CHAPTER 8

Health for all?

Working for Patients (DOH 1989) was a policy document with a hole at its heart, lacking any vision or strategic direction for the NHS to take. It said a great deal about how to deliver health care, but very little about what kind of health care should be delivered. Given its neo-liberal provenance and Mrs Thatcher's contempt for strategic planning and the 'nanny state' this is hardly surprising. What is more surprising is the apparent change of direction that has taken place under the Major government with the publication of the first national health strategy document, *Health of the Nation* (DOH 1992). This set targets for achieving improvements in health in five key areas and followed a year of consultation on a first draft. In addition, health authorities are urged to make 'health gain' the focus for commissioning and purchasing decisions. 'Health gain' is the current jargon for achieving reductions in mortality and morbidity or improvements in quality of life. In the more memorable language of the World Health Organisation, it is 'adding years to life and life to years'.

This chapter will discuss these policies in the context of three questions: What are the principal health problems faced in Britain? What are the components of an effective national strategy for improvement? To what extent does present government policy meet these criteria?

Health and ill-health in Britain

On many measures, the health of the British population has improved greatly over the last 60 years. Life expectancy has steadily increased to 73.7 for males and 79.1 for females. Infant mortality has declined from 74 per 1,000 births in 1929 to 6.2 per 1,000 in 1993. Maternal mortality is negligible, although in the 1930s over 2,500 women died annually in childbirth. Infectious diseases like tuberculosis, poliomyelitis and diptheria were brought under control in the first half of the century (although recently there has been a worldwide increase in these diseases again, see Chapter 9, p. 202) and since the introduction of the combined measles, mumps and rubella vaccine in 1988, these diseases have declined dramatically as well.

Figure 8.1 ***Distribution of total deaths by cause and age: 1931 and 1988***

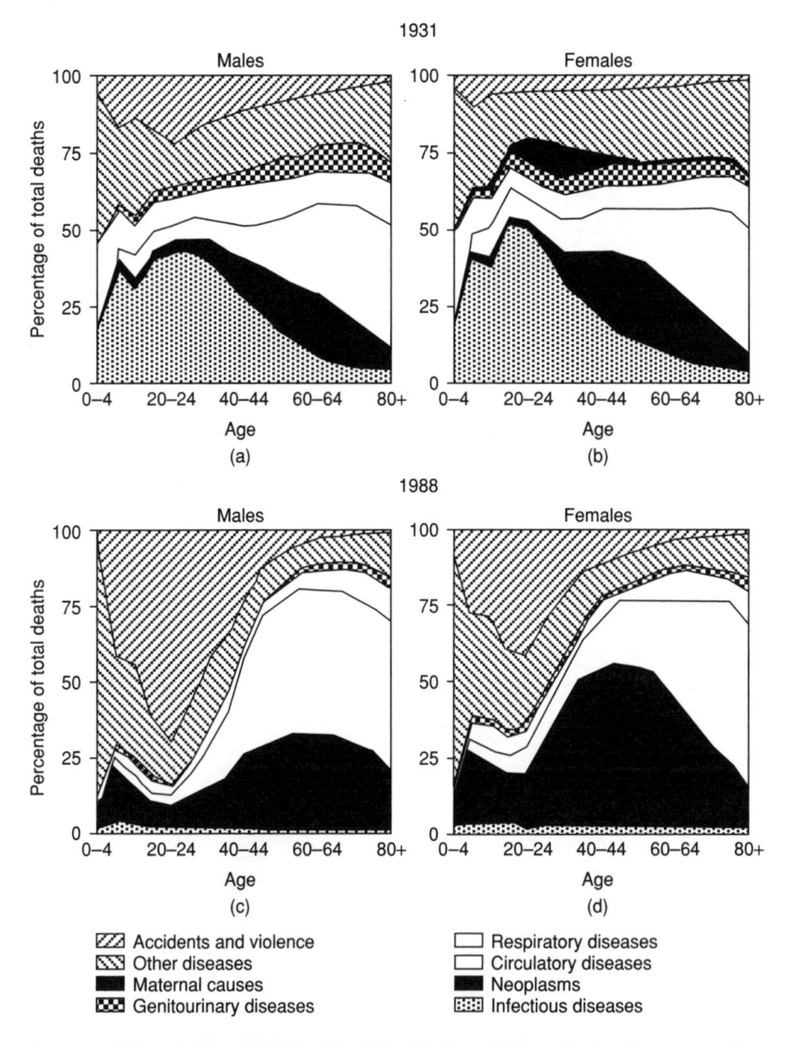

Source: Adapted from *The Health of the Nation: A Consultative Document for Health in England*, Cmnd. 1523, DH (1991). Crown ©. Reproduced with the permission of the controller of Her Majesty's Stationery Office.

Changes in the distribution of mortality mean that today the major causes of death are heart disease, cerebrovascular disease (stroke) and cancers, particularly lung and breast cancer. Figure 8.1 documents the changes in the distribution of total deaths from all causes by sex and age between 1931 and 1988. Figure 8.2 shows the years of life lost up to age 65. This gives more weight to deaths at younger age-groups,

Figure 8.2 **Distribution of years of life lost up to age 65 by cause: 1988**

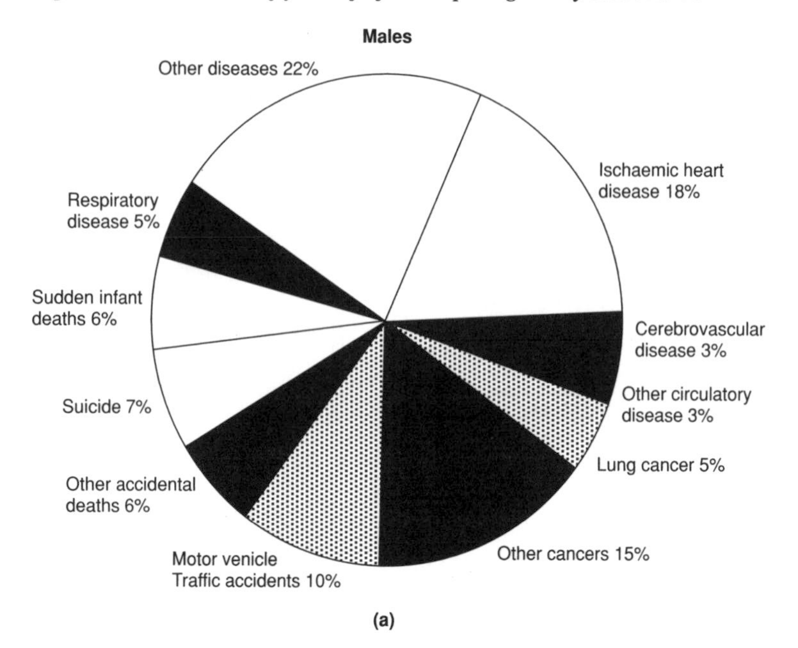

(a)

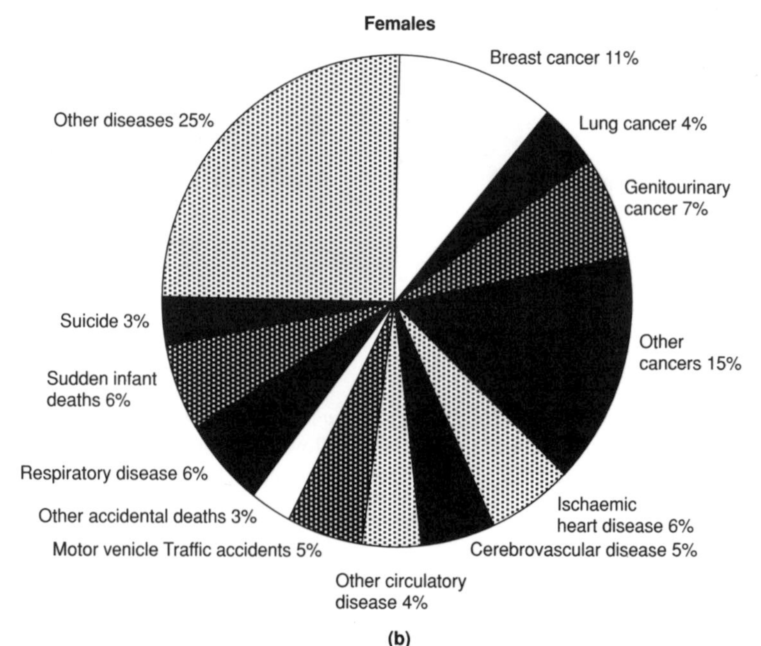

(b)

Source: Adapted from *The Health of the Nation: A Consultative Document for Health in England*, Cmnd. 1523, DH (1991). Crown ©. Reproduced with the permission of the controller of Her Majesty's Stationery Office.

since a death at 15 would count as 50 years lost, in contrast to a death at 60 which would count as five. On this kind of analysis, deaths from accident become a more important source of years of life lost for males since it is the principal cause of mortality between the ages of 5 and 35. In females, cancer, particularly of the breast, cervix, uterus and ovary, is a major contributor to years of life lost.

In the past it was more difficult to document changes in morbidity not related to death because of the paucity of reliable sources, but these are improving steadily in quantity and quality. The regular source of information on morbidity is the General Household Survey (now published as *Living in Britain*) which surveys 25,000 people annually, and includes questions on self-reported longstanding illness. The number of people reporting longstanding illness, disability or infirmity was 34 per cent in 1993, an increase of 2 per cent over the previous year.

Assessing the burden of morbidity is complicated by the different meanings attributable to 'health', and in particular the differences apparent between lay and biomedical definitions. In an important national study of the health and lifestyles of 9,000 people undertaken in 1984–5, Mildred Blaxter and her colleagues tried to capture four different dimensions of health.

1 *Fitness/unfitness*: this was based on physiological measurements of blood pressure, lung function and measures of height/weight by a nurse and hence represented the most objective biological measure.
2 *Presence/absence of disease and impairment*: medical definitions of health rest on the presence or absence of pathological symptoms, ascertained normally by clinical examination. In this study the researchers had to rely on self-report, using similar questions to the General Household Survey, for example, 'Do you have any long-standing illness, disability or infirmity?' (If yes) 'What is the matter with you?' (followed by questions on the functional effects of the condition).
3 *Experienced illness/freedom from illness*: many people under-report symptoms of disease and impairment, either because they dismiss their significance or because they are undiagnosed and untreated. The researchers tested for this by asking respondents if they had experienced 16 common illness symptoms ranging from back pain to headaches 'in the past month'.
4 *Psychosocial malaise or wellbeing*: this was tested by asking questions on the experience of depression, worry, stress, feelings of strain, and so forth.

Unfortunately it is not possible to do justice here to the rich and fascinating data produced by the survey, and the intriguing patterns which occur on scores for the four dimensions of health by social group. The authors do, however, try to produce a summary index score

Table 8.1 **Distribution of combined health categories by age and gender (per cent)**

8.1(a) Males

Health category	*Age* 18–29	*30–44*	*45–59*	*60–69*	*70+*
Excellent	19	11	5	4	2
Good	34	33	23	18	16
Good but unfit	7	11	17	16	18
Good but poor psycho-social health	14	10	7	3	3
High illness without disease	7	9	7	7	8
'Silent' disease*	7	9	15	15	12
Poor, non-limiting disease	5	8	10	13	16
Very poor, limiting disease	6	7	17	23	24
(N=100%)	(738)	(986)	(72)	(452)	(361)

8.1(b) Females

Health category	*Age* 18–29	*30–44*	*45–59*	*60–69*	*70+*
Excellent	10	9	5	3	3
Good	31	31	20	15	10
Good but unfit	6	8	10	14	13
Good but poor psycho-social health	21	14	10	8	4
High illness without disease	17	13	14	12	12
'Silent' disease*	4	6	6	9	8
Poor, non-limiting disease	6	9	14	17	18
Very poor, limiting disease	5	9	18	23	32
(N=100%)	(879)	(1,318)	(926)	(562)	(414)

Note: 'Silent' disease refers to a disease without any functional consequences or high rate of illness symptoms. This included some people with sight or hearing problems, skin disease, or orthopaedic problems which did not impair mobility.
Source: Blaxter (1990).

on all four dimensions which distinguishes between different health categories. The results are shown by age-group and sex in Table 8.1. Table 8.2 shows the proportion taking prescribed drugs in the three major health categories.

Table 8.2 ***Proportions taking prescribed drugs in different health categories (per cent)***

	Males			Females		
Health category	*Age* *18–39*	*40–59*	*60+*	*19–39*	*40–59*	*60+*
Excellent	2	7	19	9	9	29
Good	5	12	26	14	18	23
Very poor	42	73	87	58	74	88

Source: Blaxter (1990).

Aggregate figures conceal large variations in the health experience of different groups. Age, gender, ethnic and socio-economic status, occupation, place of residence: all affect objective and subjective measures of health in ways which are not completely understood. Mortality rates from coronary heart disease, for example, which accounts for 26 per cent of all deaths, vary considerably within each country and region of the United Kingdom, with Scotland and Northern Ireland having the dubious distinction of heading the world league table.

National and regional differences disguise even more marked local variation. For example, although the North East of England and the city of Newcastle-upon-Tyne in particular has some of the highest coronary heart disease death rates in the the UK there are considerable small area differences. For instance, the risk of dying from coronary heart disease in the electoral ward of West City is four times higher than in South Gosforth, the ward with the lowest rates, for persons under 65, and nearly two and a half times higher for persons aged 65–74 (Newcastle Health Authority 1995). Not surprisingly, West City is one of the poorest wards in the city as measured by the Townsend Deprivation Index (see details see discussion on pp. 173–4), while South Gosforth is the most affluent.

Health inequalities and social class: the evidence

The association between social position and health status is one of the best documented findings in social science, and Britain has a long and honourable tradition of such research, going back to the enquiries of Farr and Chadwick in the 19th century. More recently, the work of the Black Working Party on social class inequalities in health triggered enormous research interest among the academic community in spite of the cool reception it received from government. Summarising the evidence of a further decade of work in 1987, Margaret Whitehead concluded:

> Whether social position is measured by occupational class, or by assets such as house- and car-ownership, or by employment status, a similar picture emerges. Those at the bottom of the social scale have much higher death rates than those at the top. This applies at every stage of life from birth, through to adulthood and well into old age.
>
> (Whitehead 1987: 1)

This was true for almost every indicator of health status: death rates from all the major killer diseases, chronic sickness and disability, low birth weight, height and weight of children. Blaxter's work confirmed this picture. On all four dimensions of health in the study and at each age group 'there was a tendency for experience to be poorer as social class declined' (Blaxter 1990: 66). The gap between manual and non-manual groups was particularly marked in the middle years of life. More recent evidence, notably the OPCS Longitudinal Study (Smith 1995) developed over the last 20 years, but also including a follow-up *Health and Lifestyles* survey which traced 5,352 of the original 9,000 respondents seven years later (Cox *et al.* 1992), confirms the continuing existence and even widening of mortality differentials. (See Table 8.3 below, also Marmot and McDowall 1986; Phillimore *et al.* 1994 and

Table 8.3 ***Trends in male mortality[1] by social class, 1970–89 England and Wales***

	1971–75	*1976–81*	*1981–85*	*1986–89*
Social class in 1971:				
I Higher managerial administrative or professional	80	69	61	67
II Intermediate, managerial, admin, or professional	80	78	78	80
III N Supervisory, clerical, junior managerial, admin or professional	92	103	98	85
III M Skilled manual workers	90	95	101	102
IV Semi-skilled and unskilled manual workers.	97	109	113	112
V State pensioners, widows, (no other earners); casual or lowest grade workers, or long-term unemployed.	115	124	136	153
All social classes	100	100	100	100

[1]Aged 15–64
Source: Derived from Smith 1995: 19.

for Scotland, McLoone and Boddy 1994). Translated into average life expectancy, those in Class 1 can expect to live on average eight years longer than those in Class V (DOH 1996a: 9).

It is important to be clear about what is being asserted. Although death rates for all classes have declined since the 1930s, the rate of progress has been greatest among the better off and this gap continues to widen. However, in socially deprived areas death rates are actually beginning to rise again in absolute terms for some age groups, notably young unskilled men, reflecting the high incidence of deaths from violence and accidents (Blane *et al.* 1990).

Research on health and inequality has provoked much academic debate and political dissension, in particular the claim that social class inequalities have widened and that poverty is the root cause rather than cultural or personal lifestyle factors. The claim that health inequalities widened between 1951 and 1972, originally made in the Black Report (Black 1980), was subject to a good deal of methodological criticism (Wilkinson 1986; Illsley 1986; Illsley and Le Grand 1987; see also Klein 1988). In particular it was argued that the changing size and composition of classes made historical comparisons problematic, or the findings could be due to differential social mobility (poor health causes low social status, rather than the reverse). Since then a number of important studies have painstakingly tried to overcome these difficulties with results that largely reinforce the Black Report's findings (Townsend 1990a, 1990b; see also Whitehead 1987, Benzeval *et al.* 1995).

Since 1979 Conservative governments have a sorry record of trying to dismiss or suppress evidence of widening health inequalities, which bordered at times on the ludicrous (Thunhurst 1991). Where the evidence was incontrovertible, the second line of attack was to dispute the primary cause. The Black Report attributed the worse health records of the lower social classes to lower incomes, poorer working and living conditions, higher exposure to risk and insecurity; in other words the material conditions of life they experience which are socially and economically structured. An alternative explanation, largely reflected in government policy, put more emphasis on the lifestyles and health choices that individuals make. The poorer social classes smoke and drink more, eat less healthy diets, take less exercise and appear to put less value on future health as assessed, for example, by the take-up of preventive health care.

In a major study of health inequalities in 678 local authority wards in the Northern region, Townsend and his colleagues (Townsend *et al.* 1987) took the argument further by trying to relate health status to direct measures of material deprivation. Health status was assessed by three measures combined into a single index: standardised mortality; percentage of low-birth-weight babies; percentage of chronically ill and disabled. The four indicators of material deprivation were percentage unemployed, house and car ownership and household overcrowding.

The results largely supported the Black Report's conclusions, with material deprivation accounting for 65 per cent of the variance in health status between wards. In spite of this impressive evidence, Edwina Currie, then Junior Health Minister, visiting the Northern region on the day the report was released, commented: 'I honestly don't think (health) has anything to do with poverty. The problem very often for many people is just ignorance . . . and failing to realise they do have some control over their own lives' (quoted in Townsend 1990b: 383).

This of course is the central point, the extent to which people do have control over the forces which shape their lives and are capable of making the changes necessary for a healthier lifestyle. One well-founded theory of behavioural change asserts that if people believe they can achieve what they want through their own actions (internal locus of control), they are more likely to change their attitudes and behaviour in the desired directions. If people believe their lives are shaped by forces beyond their control (external locus of control) there is less incentive to make changes. But these attitudes and perceptions are influenced and shaped by material circumstances as well as cultural beliefs. As Graham points out in her discussion of family health:

> Health choices are shaped by material as well as mental structures. The barriers to change are represented by the limits of time, energy and income available to parents. In such circumstances health choices are more accurately seen as health compromises which, repeated day after day, become the routines which keep the family going.
>
> (Graham 1984: 94)

Choosing a healthy diet

A brief look at some of the evidence on dietary patterns illustrates Graham's point. Basic knowledge about what constitutes a 'healthy' diet is now fairly widespread, through government health education messages, women's magazines and food advertising. Several studies have shown that even low-income groups are well-informed about the need for more fruit and fresh vegetables more fibre and less fat in the diet (Jones 1992, MacDonald and Hanes 1988; HEA 1989; 1995) and express a desire to eat more of these foods if they could afford them. Income is also not a barrier to healthy food choices over a broad range of incomes (Wilson 1987, Blaxter 1990), the exceptions being low-income families and families where men keep tight control over patterns of spending, including food expenditure. Blaxter (1990) concluded that income, education and region were the best predictors of a healthy diet, with education having the strongest effect except for women between the ages of 40 and 59 where income remained the most important variable (pp. 125–6).

In low-income families the constraints on healthy diets are severe. At Income Support levels families would need to spend 50 per cent of their incomes on food to attain the nutritional standards recommended by the government's advisory body (NACNE 1983, MacDonald and Hanes 1988). A recent research report on diet among low-income mothers in the North East of England shows that in practice many are spending this proportion of their income on food, leaving very little for all the other necessities of life (Jones 1992). The 62 women in the sample all had at least one child under five. Average gross household incomes ranged from £60 to £100 per week, and 71 per cent spent more than 30 per cent of their income on food, with one in five spending more than 50 per cent. Analysis of food diaries kept by the women showed that, in spite of this, diets were seriously imbalanced, high in fat and low in fibre, and provided less than the total energy requirements recommended by the government. There were serious deficiencies of many vitamins and essential minerals through shortages of fresh vegetables and fruit. The availability of 'healthy' foods like wholemeal bread, low-fat spreads and semi-skimmed milk locally was limited and even when it was available, the price difference with less healthy alternatives – whole milk, white bread and economy margarines – was greater than in more affluent areas of the city.

Menus were also affected by the availability of facilities for food preparation and storage. As income increased so did facilities, as did the preparation and cooking of food from raw materials, although cooking skills generally were poorer in the younger age groups. There was another logic to the greater use of convenience foods by the poorest women, however, which was that they eliminated waste, rendering precise measurement possible. 'Junk' foods are also a cheaper source of calories: according to the London Food Survey they are cheaper than the cheapest form of healthy diet (Lang and Cole-Hamilton 1986).

Wilson argues that poverty reinforces conservative food choices, since women cannot afford to experiment with foods which husbands or children may reject. Indeed the food preferences of the family are a major constraint in changing towards healthier diets across all income levels as long as the preparation and serving of food is so intimately bound up with the gendered nature of the marriage contract and the association of food with love and comfort. For this reason, women often cook separate things for different members of the family, and in general are turning more to convenience foods to save work, particularly when cooking for children (Wilson 1989).

In terms of gender differences, women eat less and have healthier food preferences than men (Whichelow 1987, Newby 1983, Wilson 1987), although this is also affected by education. Large appetites and 'proper meals' which contained meat appear to be part of the construction of masculinity among some social groups (the 'real men don't eat quiche' syndrome). Obesity among both sexes is a growing problem, however: the second *Health and Lifestyles* survey found that 53 per cent of men and 57 per cent of women over 25 were obese, compared to 47 per cent and 50 per cent respectively seven years earlier. (Cox *et al.* 1992). This may be related to low levels of participation in physical exercise, particularly for women (DOH 1996: 49).

To sum up, the evidence suggests that health education messages about healthy diets have been fairly successful: most people know what they should do to eat well, but cultural and structural constraints prevent them from doing so. Low income is the most severe barrier of all. As Wilson points out health education is simply irrelevant as a guide to action in poor families.

> In these households it is more important to avoid waste than to try and convert an overstressed family to foods it does not know. Health education has to be seen as an investment for better times. Its immediate effect can only be to increase worry rather than lead to action.
>
> (Wilson 1989: 183)

Income and not ignorance is the main determinant of the diet of low-income families, although education, culture and gender relations within the family exert complex effects. The evidence on dietary patterns also shows the growing reliance of all income groups on processed and semiprocessed foods, and hence on the policies of the agricultural, food processing and retail distribution industries and the government departments which regulate them. The food scares of recent years – salmonella in eggs, listeria in cheese, and most explosively of all 'mad cow disease' (BSE) incurred through infected animal feed, and now linked to Creutzfeldt-Jakob disease in humans – demonstrates how little control individuals have over the safety and quality of food that appears in the shops as a result of the production methods of agribusiness. The enormous public alarm and economic consequences of the BSE and CJD scare may in fact signal a turning point in attitudes to food production in Britain, and much greater questioning of the 'cheap food' policies that have dominated the industry since the war, both on grounds of health and taste. Another food 'scare' with even wider ramifications than BSE is currently brewing – the use of genetically engineered foods, notably soya beans and maize, in many different products when the health consequences are simply unknown.

At the same time, health education messages from the DOH are contradicted by the policies of other departments. Until the late 1980s the Milk Marketing Board ensured that only full-fat milk appeared on our doorsteps in an effort not to increase the European butter mountain by skimming the fat off (Robbins 1991). Through the illogic of the Common Agricultural Policy (CAP) farmers received a premium on producing full-fat milk, and the growing of sugar beet and even tobacco is still subsidised under CAP. Policies to ensure a healthier British diet would have to tackle these issues as well as a raft of others: food labelling, the link between additives and allergies or other illnesses, the targeting of 'unhealthy' products at children and teenagers, the pricing and distribution policies of the retail chains. Individuals do have choices to make but within the context set by government and industry who can either make the healthy choice the easy choice or not.

A strategy for health: Health for All 2000

A successful strategy for health must tackle its socio-economic and environmental determinants and replace the existing dominant biomedical model of health with a social model. The World Health Organisation's (WHO) *Health for All 2000* (HFA) has been particularly influential and some of its policy offshoots, notably Healthy Cities and the concept of 'healthy public policy', have excited imagination and inspired national and local action in many countries.

Central to the development of HFA has been the emergence of what has become known as the New Public Health. Ashton dates its birth to McKeown's work in the early 1970s and the sociological and feminist attack on medicine discussed in Chapter 2 (Ashton and Seymour 1988). In policy terms its beginnings are often traced to the Lalonde Report produced by the Canadian federal health minister, Marc Lalonde in 1974. The report argued along McKeown lines that further improvements in the health of Canadians depended far more on environmental and lifestyle change than on improvements in health care and medical science.

The Lalonde Report triggered renewed interest in public health and prevention in many other countries, coinciding as it did with growing disillusion about the costs and limits of therapeutic medicine. This growing momentum found expression in WHO's *Global Strategy for Health for All by the Year 2000* (WHO 1981) and the resolution that:

> the main social target of governments and WHO in the coming decades should be the attainment by all citizens of the world by the year 2000 of a level of health that will permit them to lead a socially and economically productive life.

The European Regional Committee of WHO then produced a European strategy for health as the framework for accomplishing HFA, which was later developed into 38 targets, endorsed by all the member states in 1985. These were subsequently updated in 1991 (WHO 1991). Six major themes underlie the targets and the whole HFA strategy, which is also based on the definition of health adopted by WHO as 'a state of complete physical, social and mental well-being and not merely the absence of disease or infirmity' (WHO 1946). The themes are:

- *Equity in health*: By reducing disparities in health status between countries and between groups within countries;
- *Health promotion and prevention of disease*: The aim is to develop health in the positive sense of a resource for life, so that people can make best use of their capacities. The emphasis should therefore be on health promotion and prevention of disease;
- *Community participation*: Health for all can only be attained with the active participation of the whole community. This means giving people the skills and knowledge to empower them to take control of their own health, and implies a different relationship between professional workers and the community – summed up by the phrase 'professionals on tap, not on top';
- *Multi-sectoral cooperation*: The multi-dimensional determinants of health require cooperation between the different levels and departments of government, business, academia, voluntary and community organisations;
- *Primary health care*: The focus of the health care system should be on meeting basic health needs of the community as fully as possible through easily accessible primary health care services;
- *International cooperation*: Many health problems transcend national frontiers, for example, AIDS, pollution, traffic in health-damaging goods, and solutions require international cooperation.

The concept of health promotion

Health promotion was the backbone of the new public health and a key concept in the strategy of HFA. Tannahill (1987) defines it as encompassing three overlapping types of activity: health education, prevention and health protection. The first two can be seen as the more traditional roles of the health promoter but activities which fall under the rubric of health protection extend the remit more widely to include advocacy and campaigning for policy change in all spheres affecting health (what David Player, former Director of the Health Education Authority, has termed 'trouble making for health').

In the context of HFA, the Ottawa Charter of Health Promotion in 1986 (WHO 1986) fleshed out the concept and potential for action as:

- building healthy public policy;
- creating supportive environments;
- strengthening community action;
- developing personal skills;
- reorienting health services.

All are interlinked. Building healthy public policy involves putting health on the agenda of public policy-makers in all sectors and at all levels, identifying barriers to health-promoting policies and ways of removing them. Creating supportive environments means developing the social and physical environments which establish the conditions for health and healthy behaviour, and accepting as a guiding principle of social life 'reciprocal maintenance – to take care of each other, our communities and our natural environment' (WHO 1986). Strengthening the capacity for community action means developing social networks and support systems, and helping people develop the skills and knowledge they need to take greater control of their own health. (Figure 8.3 shows the ways of doing this at the local level.) Reorienting health services means moving beyond the traditional provision of curative and clinical services. Recognising that most of the causes of ill-health lie outside the direct influence of the medical sector, health professionals must be willing to work with those who can influence those causes.

The new public health therefore is challenged to move radically beyond its old frontiers and develop renewed links with social justice, social change and reform. It is also closely linked with the Green movement: societies that pollute and destroy their natural environment reap a bitter harvest of sickness and disease.

Think globally, act locally: the Healthy Cities movement

The Healthy Cities movement has provided an important testbed and learning network for implementing HFA at the local level. The project itself started in 1985. The original intention was for WHO to work with a small number of cities to develop ways of giving practical expression to HFA principles and to develop innovative examples of the new health promotion in practice, developing models from which others could learn. Cities were an appropriate level to test out the concepts. Although responsibilities vary in each country, most cities administer a large number of services that impact on health, and possess their own political mandate and sense of civic identity. In addition, over 75 per cent of Europeans and a majority of the world's people will live in cities

Figure 8.3 **Community action for health at city level**

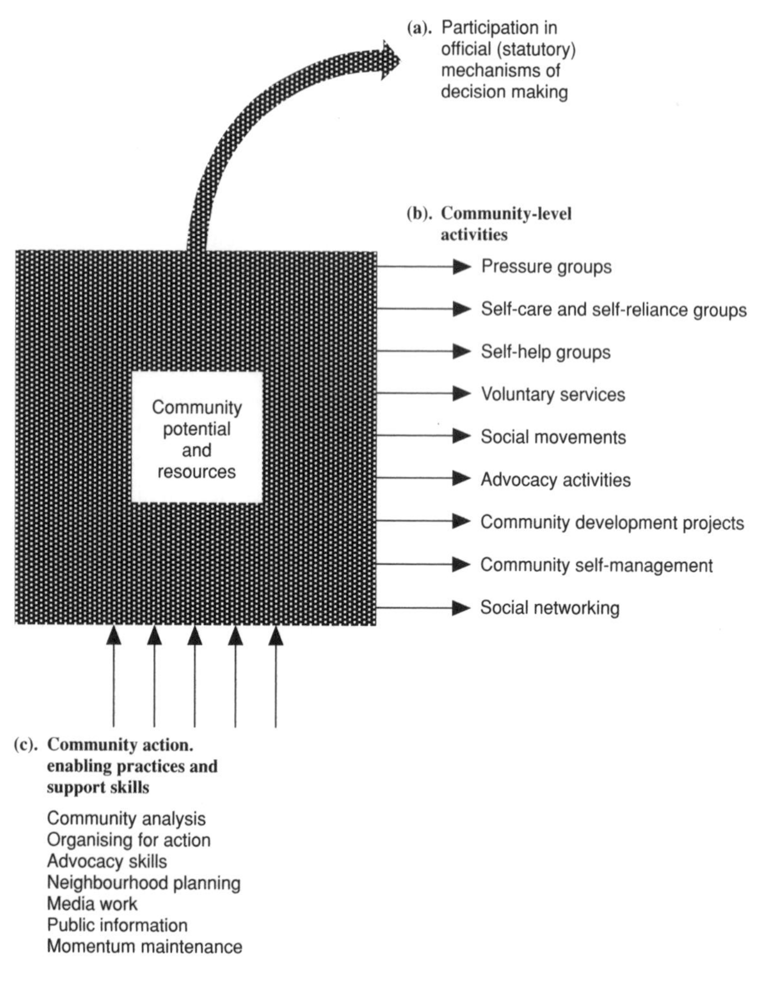

Source: Adapted, by permission, from Tsouros, A. (ed) *WHO Healthy Cities Project: A Project Becomes a Movement*, Copenhagen, WHO Regional office for Europe, 1991.

or large towns by the year 2000. Cities are often very unhealthy places to live, particularly for the poor, just as their 19th-century predecessors were. It was fitting that the new public health blazed a trail in the cities just as the old public health, based on the sanitary revolution, did before it.

WHO's Healthy City planning group intended a modest project involving five to eight cities, but by 1992 the project had developed into a major public health movement in response to the enormous interest it provoked. 500 cities within Europe are involved, networked nationally and internationally (with the formation of the European Association of National Healthy Cities Networks or Euronet Association) in 1994, with 300 further cities in other parts of the world.

In the first phase of the project WHO's Regional Office for Europe worked directly with 35 European cities, and supported the creation of the national networks linked into these. The project cities undertook:

1 To increase the visibility of health issues and the factors influencing health at the local level;
2 To move health high on the political and social agenda of the city and develop healthy public policies at the municipal level;
3 To change the way organisations and agencies work in order to encourage cooperation between departments and sectors, and strengthen community action;
4 To create innovative action for health that emphasises the interaction between people, environments, lifestyles and health. Inevitably the priorities and entry points for action would depend on the cities' social and economic status and priorities, from major environmental actions to programmes to support individual lifestyle change.

In trying to meet these challenges, the project cities as well as the hundreds of other cities linked in the Healthy City networks developed a wealth of innovatory initiatives but, perhaps of greater importance still, they began tackling the political and institutional barriers which impede a holistic approach to health problems. Changing the way organisations work with others, how professionals work with other disciplines, and how 'experts' work with local communities has been the most significant and far-reaching accomplishment, the essential precondition for more integrated approaches to health. This progress is reflected in the second phase of the Healthy City project, which began in 1993 with 33 cities, chosen partly for the organisational development they have already made. The aim now is to develop city-wide health profiles and health strategies to improve equity, sustainable development and accountability for health.

Already in the UK many members of the Healthy City network are working along these lines. For example, Newcastle Healthy City has brought together over 40 agencies and parent groups working on a child accident prevention strategy for the city which is setting itself increasingly ambitious targets, including a comprehensive city-wide scheme for the provision of home safety equipment to all low-income families. Glasgow Healthy City has developed a city health plan and is currently setting up an ambitious city-wide Children's Forum to bring together information and a strategic focus to improving the health of the city's children (Sherwood 1996). Sheffield has pulled together local authority departments, health authorities, business groups, environmentalists and transport authorities to agree a policy document on transport (Carlisle 1996). Specific events have also been used by other member cities to heighten awareness of health issues. Barcelona used the 1992 Olympic Games to begin a city-wide fitness campaign and made the entire games no-smoking. Thereafter, several European cities linked together to pursue the goal of a tobacco-free city. Multi-city 'issue-based' networks have also developed to work on other issues as well, such as AIDS, environmental health, women's health, disability issues or child safety; one offshoot of these has been the 'health-promoting hospital' project involving 20 pilot hospitals (Tsouros 1994).

Another important international development has been a growing recognition of the common ground that exists between HFA and Healthy Cities and other organisations in the health and environmental fields. For instance, the Earth Summit in Rio de Janiero in 1992 agreed 27 principles for sustainable development in the 21st century (defined as 'development that meets the needs of the present without compromising the ability of future generations to meet their own needs' UN 1993), and all governments signed Agenda 21, an action plan specifying what was needed to achieve this. Stemming from this were developments like the OECD's 'ecological city' initiative (the first joint conference between the OECD and the Healthy City project was held in Madrid in 1995), and the Sustainable Cities campaign that was launched by the European Union. This convergence is paralleled at a local level, with closer links being forged between health, the environment and urban regeneration. Local Agenda 21 mandates local authorities to begin the implementation of Agenda 21 by involving the entire local community in agreeing a new sustainable approach to environmental management, producing plans for their own areas by the end of 1996. Actively supported by the Local Government Management Board, and internationally legitimated by the United Nations, Local Agenda 21 is based on an almost identical set of principles to HFA, a parallel commitment to developing local action within a global strategy, and a holistic vision of the future which, like HFA, provides the framework for integrating public policy across social, economic and environmental spheres.

At the same time, urban regeneration initiatives like City Challenge also require innovative and holistic approaches to the problems of deprived local areas, which do not compartmentalise health issues and separate them from those of economic decline, poverty, racism, crime and lack of social support. Some of the most successful City Challenge projects (for example, Tipton Challenge Partnership in Sandwell), have made the improvement of health and quality of life the key to regeneration, often in response to the declared priorities of local residents themselves. In terms of both philosophy, working principles and organisation, therefore, these three strands of urban policy are converging, often under the umbrella of politically powerful multi-sectoral committees representing the city's main stakeholders.

Charting progress

What achievements does HFA have to its credit? Altenstetter (1989) argues that its successes lie in changing political and social attitudes to health, and internationalising the debate. Each member state is required to monitor and report progress at regular intervals and the HFA Regional Office for Europe has done much good work clarifying concepts and the indicators to be used, which has led to considerable improvements in the routine information available for monitoring health trends on a comparative basis, exposing political and professional elites in many countries to unfavourable evidence about the health status of their populations and the fact that for some groups or regions this was declining. The World Health Organisation has succeeded in internationalising the terms of the health debate among policy planners and health experts and there is now widespread acceptance of the basic philosophy and tenets underpinning HFA. In concrete terms it has led to the reorientation of health policy in many countries. By 1988:

> 18 countries either have finished or are in the process of making their own national HFA policy, following the framework of the target document; four finished this process during the last 12 months, five have started the process, and the other nine all made major advances in their work. The remaining countries are those where prevailing conditions were more difficult, e.g. countries with more federal structure and weaker planning mandates, or countries where pressure groups were initially sceptical . . . By now there seems no longer to be an organised resistance to the application of the European HFA targets in any country in Europe.
>
> (WHO 1988)

A paradigm shift of this nature is a real achievement. In terms of health outcomes, good progress has been made in Europe in achieving many of the targets set, but widening distributional inequalities in several countries means that the central target – reducing inequity in health by 25 per cent by the year 2000 – will not be achieved. In the developing world the position is much bleaker. Many of the basic prerequisites of health – security, peace, access to clean water, food – have not been met and the gap between the world's rich and poor has become a chasm. Between 1960 and 1991 the share of the world's wealth held by the richest 20 per cent of citizens rose from 70 per cent to 85 per cent, while that of the poorest 20 per cent declined from 2.3 per cent to 1.4 per cent (UN 1996).

But the importance of HFA and Healthy Cities lies in the process and not just the goals. WHO Europe states that the main aim of the Healthy City project was 'to change how individuals, communities, and private and voluntary organisations and local governments throughout Europe think about, understand and make decisions about health' (Tsouros 1991: 39). This is change of a fundamental nature, but the battle of ideas, at least in some European countries, is being won. In ways of working, too, Healthy City activists are pioneers in the methods and skills required for 'effective governance' in the 21st century, as discussed in the previous chapter. They are developing new styles of action which cuts across traditional functional and agency boundaries, creating coalitions and partnerships for health between the powerful and powerless, in surprising and unexpected combinations, showing how 'network management' can be successful in practice. They are working with local communities in ways which give them a credibility with disadvantaged people that local officials (and politicians) might envy. As a result they are developing exactly the kind of facilitation, brokerage and political skills that public-sector managers need, and increasingly they find a receptive audience for their message in local government and health authorities.

Above all, HFA has succeeded in inspiring thousands of political and public activists as well as ordinary people with an alternative social vision, which has at its heart an enriched understanding of health, not as 'complete wellbeing' which is both a static and utopian concept, but as 'wholeness' – in individuals and societies, mental, physical and spiritual. Where it will go in future is uncertain. As Dooris (1995) points out, the agenda is moving on and HFA needs to keep its radical edge. The focus on the environment and sustainability has given it a new powerful impetus and way forward. It may be reincarnated in a different form and with a different language, one that can successfully mobilise a new generation of activitists, perhaps towards the goals of 'sustainability' or 'quality of life' rather than 'health'. The language matters less than the vision of a cooperative community, which channels its energy and resources to achieve a healthy and sustainable future.

Constraints and opportunities: the British perspective

The British government has not been at the forefront of the new public health. WHO requires each member state to evaluate its progress on meeting HFA goals and targets at periodic intervals. The 1985 British report was marked by complacency and self-satisfaction (Dooris 1987).

Britain resisted translating HFA into a meaningful national policy and strategy, and its report was highly selective, ignoring the issues of community participation, equity and intersectoral working and focusing entirely on the role of the NHS. By contrast, HFA stimulated a good deal of activity and interest from other organisations at national and local level. By the late 1980s, the Healthy Cities movement, in particular, had stimulated many local and health authorities into action, and its combination of vision and pragmatism had great appeal. But the prospects for local action were constrained by the government's lack of political commitment to, or even understanding of, HFA's principles and prerequisites. Indeed the thrust of public policy and the ideology of Thatcherism were antithetical to these principles: growing centralisation, sustained attacks on the autonomy and powers of local government, the subordination of social goals for macroeconomic ones and the disparagement of collective values created a hostile environment.

The NHS reforms, however, created a new opportunity for public health through the separation of purchasing and providing functions, and the new strategic role given to health authorities. It was NHS managers and professionals themselves who seized the opportunity of shaping that role in a public health direction and influencing the direction of policy, in the working parties established by the NHSME after the White Paper's publication.

Health authorities had already been required to appoint Directors of Public Health following the recommendations of the Acheson Report (DOH 1988) in 1989 and to produce annual reports on the local population's health. These started appearing in 1990 and had the potential of becoming an important focus for local debates on priorities, providing over time more incisive analyses of health needs to inform commissioning and contracting. Several commentators (including this writer) hoped that in their new role visionary health authorities, acting within an HFA framework, could lead and coordinate imaginative strategies for health, act as catalysts for change and advocates for healthy public policy, starting to transform the NHS into a health service for the first time in its history (see, for example, Alderslade and Hunter 1994; Hunter 1991; Parston 1991). Another important stimulus to this development was the publication of the White Paper, *Health of the Nation*, in 1992 (DOH 1992), the first real attempt to adopt a national strategy for health.

Health of the nation: a new direction?

In April 1991, John Major called his Cabinet to a seminar on health with a number of health experts. The outcome was a consultative document on a national health strategy in June 1991. The paper (DOH 1991) discussed a number of key areas which could be selected as national health priorities. The criteria for selection were threefold:

1 It should be a major cause of premature death or avoidable ill-health;
2 Effective interventions are possible, offering significant scope for improvement;
3 It should be possible to set quantified targets for improvement and monitor progress through specific indicators.

Sixteen possible candidates for inclusion were then discussed. The document was seen as a considerable step forward for several reasons. It gave firm support to the importance of health promotion as a central part of the 'mission' of the NHS, there was greater acknowledgement of the multi-dimensional determinants of health, and the Department planned to put in place some of the essential research and monitoring arrangements to support a health strategy. But the document, though acknowledging its debt to WHO's HFA strategy and targets, fell far short of its principles. There was no serious discussion of health inequalities and their causes. Equity in health, the centrepiece of HFA, is banished to a bald comment in an appendix that differences in health status between manual and non-manual workers were unlikely to be reduced by the year 2000 (DOH 1991: 105).

The consultation period produced an enormous response, with over 2,000 organisations and individuals responding (DOH 1992), and dozens of conferences and seminars. But enthusiasm within the Cabinet seems to have waned in that time and the new Health Secretary, Virginia Bottomley, had difficulty in pushing her White Paper through. Once again, it seems to have been pressure from the top of the NHSME and from the Chief Medical Officer, Kenneth Calman, which helped to tip the balance. Significantly the price for acceptance was Mrs Bottomley's agreement to drop the DOH's support for a ban on tobacco advertising, a poor augury for the success of the new health strategy (HSJ 1992).

The White Paper *Health of the Nation* (HoN) appeared in July 1992. Five initial priority areas which met the criteria for selection out of the 16 originally discussed were chosen, and sharper implementation arrangements were identified. A Ministerial Cabinet committee covering 11 government departments was established to oversee the implementation of the English strategy and coordinate UK-wide health policy issues, while a number of top-level Departmental Working Groups, already established when the consultation paper was published, continued to plan specific aspects of the strategy in England. (The Scottish and Welsh Offices are responsible for the arrangements for Scotland and Wales.)

Health of the Nation – *a summary of key areas and main targets:*

1 Coronary heart disease and stroke – by the year 2000
- to reduce deaths from CHD in under-65s by at least 40 per cent;
- to reduce deaths from CHD in 65–74s by at least 30 per cent and deaths from stroke by 40 per cent.

2 Cancer – by the year 2000
- to reduce deaths from breast cancer in the screened population by at least 25 per cent*;
- to reduce cervical cancer by at least 20 per cent;
- to reduce deaths from lung cancer in under-75s by at least 30 per cent in men and 15 per cent in women;
- to halt deaths from skin cancer by the year 2005.

3 Mentally ill people – to improve significantly the health of mentally ill people and by the year 2000
- to reduce suicides by at least 15 per cent;
- to reduce suicides among severely mentally ill people by at least 33 per cent.

4 HIV/AIDS and sexual health
- to reduce gonorrhoea by at least 20 per cent by 1995;
- to reduce conceptions by under-16s by at least 50 per cent by 2000**.

5 Accidents – by the year 2005
- to reduce deaths from accident among children under 15 by at at least 33 per cent;
- to reduce accidental deaths among 15–24s by at least 25 per cent; and among over-65s by at least 33 per cent.

(All baselines 1990 except *1986 and **1989)

Risk factors reduction: Targets have been set for reductions in smoking, alcohol consumption, mean blood pressure in adults, obesity and consumption of saturated fats. A 10 per cent reduction in the numbers of injecting drug users who share equipment has also been set.

The White Paper discussed the role of local authorities, the voluntary sector, the Health Education Authority, the media and others in the strategy. Support for Healthy Cities was promised; indeed the government's enthusiasm for healthy environments seemed to know no bounds: the paper talks of promoting 'healthy workplaces', 'healthy hospitals', 'healthy schools', 'healthy homes', even 'healthy prisons'!

On more familiar ground HoN spelt out in detail the role and responsibilities of the NHS in implementing the strategy and the organisational arrangements the Department was putting in place. The targets for health improvement set by HoN in the five key areas were in future to form the core overall objectives for the NHS: 'Increasingly NHS authorities' performance will be measured against the efficient use of resources and working with others, to achieve improvements in the health of the people' (DOH 1992: 34). Coordinators would be appointed to take a lead at regional level, and local targets and goals would be agreed with health authorities and written into their annual corporate contracts.

Finally, a strengthened information and research capability was an essential component of the strategy. Expanded or new health surveys and epidemiological overviews to improve baseline data on the health of the population would be undertaken. A Central Health Outcomes Unit would lead on developing and coordinating work on the assessment of health outcomes. Information systems which enabled adequate monitoring and review would be developed including a Public Health Information Strategy.

Appraising the strategy

The White Paper was broadly welcomed as the first coherent attempt yet undertaken to give the NHS a positive health direction and work out a detailed strategy for implementation, but the analysis was still fundamentally flawed by the government's ideological inability to accept the centrality of poverty and social deprivation as causes of ill-health or to take responsibility for policies which had widened the numbers caught in its trap. Since 1979, when the Conservatives took office, the number of people living on incomes below half the national average (the nearest thing to an official poverty line) has increased from five million to 13.9 million in 1991–92 (DSS 1994), of which 7.9 million have incomes lower than 40 per cent of the national average. The UK now has the second highest level of distributional inequality among industrialised nations, with a ten-fold difference in the earnings of the richest 20 per cent compared to the poorest 20 per cent (UN 1996: 17). This is an even higher rate than that of the United States where the difference is nine times as great. Ideology is also responsible for measures which prevent local authorities using their capital receipts from council house sales to build new homes to combat the growth of homelessness and to replace inadequate housing stock. Almost half of Britain's housing stock was built before 1939, and well over 2.5 million homes suffer severe dampness, making the inhabitants prone to a range of respiratory and other diseases (*Observer* 1996; Best 1995) as well as making heating costs a major slice of low incomes, which could be better spent on adequate nutrition.

Even the choice of targets had an ideological flavour. For example, asthma was one of the original sixteen considered in the consultation paper, but dropped in the final selection, although it affects one in ten children, and accounted for 10,000 hospital admissions in 1990, a two-and-a-half-fold increase in ten years (BMJ 1994). In spite of overwhelming evidence that these increases are intimately linked to the growth of road traffic (Parliamentary Office of Science and Technology 1994: HSJ 1996), the government has postponed taking stronger government action by calling instead for even more research on the precise nature of the links, announcing a £2.5 million research programme in 1996.

To this example can be added others. The tobacco advertising fiasco, and the refusal to countenance a more comprehensive approach to tackling smoking (see below), the recent relaxation of 'safe' alcohol limits by the Secretary of State against the main body of medical advice (Edwards 1996) not to mention the handling of the BSE crisis – all these induce scepticism about the government's strength of commitment to health promotion and its ability to face down powerful lobbies among its friends and backers. They also speak volumes about the failure of the interdepartmental coordinating committee to enable the DOH to have much influence on other government departments.

Banning tobacco advertising

Smoking is responsible for half a million deaths in Europe annually, and three million worldwide. Unless current smoking patterns change this will rise to 10 million deaths by 2025 (BMJ 1994). In the UK half of all British smokers will be killed by their habit (Doll *et al.* 1994). To make up for these lost consumers the tobacco industry has to recruit 300 new smokers every day. Inevitably these must be children and young people. There is sound evidence to show that cigarette advertising does get through to children, reinforces the smoking habit among those who already smoke, and encourages others to start. 'Brand stretching', associating cigarettes with other products like luxury goods or holidays, and tobacco sponsorship of sports and the arts, also works well with children (Hastings 1991).

In 1991 the European Commission drafted proposals which would have:

1 Ended all tobacco advertising and promotion except in specialist tobacconists' shops.

continued

2 Banned the promotion of tobacco through sponsorship of sport and the arts.
3 Stopped 'brand stretching'.

There was widespread lobbying in favour of a 'yes' vote by health authorities, and professional and voluntary organisations like Action on Smoking and Health. Two-thirds of the British public already supported such a ban in 1987 (Roberts and Smith 1987). The British government's support was vital in turning the proposal into legislation. It voted against on the grounds that 'the Government remains to be convinced that a total ban will produce a significant reduction in smoking' (letter from Baroness Hooper, Under Secretary of State for Health, Dec. 2nd, 1991).

Yet the evidence from countries like Norway (which introduced a ban in 1975) and Australia (complete ban attained by 1990) is quite clear. In Australia the ban is part of a comprehensive and effective package of anti-smoking measures which has seen sharp falls in all age groups and classes in tobacco consumption (Powles and Gifford 1993; Musk *et al.* 1994). Norway's ban has had a marked effect on the level of smoking among 13–15 year olds.

Nevertheless the government has moved a long way from the Thatcher era and continues to do so. HoN has been energetically implemented by the DOH and NHS Executive and progress has been made, information has improved, and the HFA principle of 'healthy alliances' has been repeatedly emphasised as essential in achieving the health targets (for instance there are 'Health Alliance' awards for particularly impressive examples).

Two further milestones were the Metter Report on Variations in Health ('inequalities' is still a taboo word) and the proposed extension of health targets to the environment. The Metter Report is the product of the HoN Variations Sub-Group, and probably owes much, once again, to the influence of the Chief Medical Officer. It summarises the main evidence on the extent and causes of 'variations' in health by social class, gender, ethnicity and region, and suggests criteria to guide priorities for action and research (DOH 1995).

The extension of HoN's remit to the links between the environment and health was announced on the fourth anniversary of the programme, with a consultation paper promised by Autumn 1996, suggesting possible environmental target areas – for example, relating to air quality, radon, noise or drinking water. At the same time the publication of the UK's National Environmental Health Action Plan was announced, Europe's first, and a model for use by WHO in the rest of Europe (DOH 1996b).

What of the outcomes? Is the strategy helping to deliver a healthier population? Good progress has been made in achieving 11 of the 27 targets set, although in some cases (for example, coronary heart disease, stroke, and lung and breast cancer) these may have been achieved without HoN, since death rates were already on a downward slope. Insufficient or inadequate data mean that several targets, for instance those relating to mental health, cannot be monitored properly yet. Others – obesity, smoking by children and female alcohol consumption – are moving in the wrong direction. Smoking among 11–15 year olds is particularly worrying, jumping from 8 per cent of the age group in 1988 to 12 per cent in 1994, twice the level it was targeted to be (National Audit Office 1996; DOH 1995).

Conclusion

Whatever the flaws of HoN as a strategy to improve the nation's health, its publication marked a decisive break with the past, and it created an opportunity to build an infrastructure to tackle health inequalities in future. Four years later the policy is still being actively pursued and has not, as some argued it would, become simply a form of 'symbolic policy making'. However, in relative terms, progress only seems great when compared with the government's previous record, not in comparison with the scale of the task or with the more comprehensive and systematic approaches taken by some other countries such as the Netherlands or Sweden (Whitehead 1995).

The brutally plain fact remains that under the Conservatives inequalities of health have widened as a consequence of widening inequalities in income and wealth. Jacobson and her colleagues (1991) liken the total excess deaths in the most disadvantaged half of the population to the equivalent of a major air crash or shipwreck each day; but just as important as death rates are the burdens of chronic illness and disability, which bear most heavily on the lower social classes (Breeze *et al.* 1991). Much of this is avoidable and could be addressed by interventions of known practical effectiveness if the political will was evident (for a wealth of suggestions see Benzeval *et al.* 1991).

But even if a future government was willing to take this agenda on board, is the NHS the right agency to lead the strategy for health in the first place? Some critics have argued that the NHS will never sufficiently free itself from medical definitions of health and from medically driven priorities. One proposal is to transfer the whole budget for health commissioning to local government, in the interests of a wider health strategy, integration of health and social care and democratic accountability (Hunter 1995; AMA 1994). Clearly the argument is broadening to a wider look into the future. We consider the possible options in the final chapter.

References

Alderslade, R. and Hunter, D. (1994) 'Commissioning and Public Health' *J. of Management in Medicine*, 8(6): 20–31.

Altenstetter, C. (1989) 'Europe beyond 1992: implications for health and health policy', Paper prepared for European Community Studies Association Conference, May 24–25.

Ashton, J. (ed) (1992) *Healthy Cities*, Milton Keynes: Open University Press.

Ashton, J. and Seymour, H. (1988) *The New Public Health*, Milton Keynes: Open University Press.

Association of Metropolitan Authorities (AMA) (1994) *Local Authorities and Health Services: the Future role of Local Authorities in the Provision of Health Services*, Birmingham: AMA.

Benzeval, M., Judge, K. and Whitehead, M. (1995) *Tackling Inequalities in Health: An Agenda for Action*, London: King's Fund Institute.

Best, R. (1995) 'The housing dimension' in M. Benzeval, K. Judge and M. Whitehead (eds) *Tackling Inequalities in Health*, London: King's Fund Institute.

Black, Sir Douglas (1980) *Inequalities in Health: Report of a Research Working Group*, London: DHSS.

Blane, D., Davey-Smith, G. and Bartley M. (1990) 'Social class differences in years of potential life lost: size, trends and principal causes' *British Medical Journal*, 301: 429–32.

Blaxter, M. (1990) *Health and Lifestyles*, London: Tavistock/Routledge.

British Medical Journal (1994) 'Slowing the march of the Marlboro man', Editorial, 309: 889–90.

Breeze, E., Trevor, G. and Wilmot, A. (1991) *General Household Survey 1989*, OPCS Series GHS Nol 20 London: HMSO.

Carlisle, D. (1996) 'All or nothing?' *Health Service Journal*, 106(5524): 16.

Cox, B. *et al.* (1992) *The Health and Lifestyle Survey: Seven Years On*, Dartmouth Publishing.

Davey-Smith, G. and Morris, J. (1994) 'Increasing inequalities in the health of the nation' *British Medical Journal*, 309: 1453–4.

Department of Health (1988) *Public Health in England: The Report of the Committee of Inquiry into the Future Development of the Public Health Function* (The Acheson Report), Cmnd. 289, London: HMSO.

—— (1989) *Working for Patients*, Cmnd. 555, London: HMSO.

—— (1991) *The Health of the Nation, A Consultative Document for Health in England*, Cmnd. 1523, London: HMSO.

—— (1992) *The Health of the Nation*, Cmnd. 1986, London: HMSO.

—— (1995a) *Variations in Health: What can the Department of Health and the NHS Do?* (The Metters Report) London: HMSO.

—— (1995b) *Fit for the Future: Second Progress Report on the Health of the Nation*, London: HMSO.
—— (1996a) *Health Related Behaviour: An epidemiological Overview*, London: HMSO.
—— (1996b) 'A Healthier Environment,' *Target*, Issue 18, July.
Department of Social Security (DSS) (1994) *Households Below Average Income 1979–1991–2: A Statistical Analysis*, London: HMSO.
Doll, R., Peto, R., Wheatley, K., Gray, R. and Sutherland, L. (1994) 'Mortality in relation to smoking: 40 years observations on male British doctors' *British Medical Journal*, 309: 911–18.
Dooris, M. (1987) 'Health for All by the Year 2000 in the United Kingdom', Unpublished dissertation for Diploma in Health Education, South Bank Polytechnic, London.
—— (1995) 'Health and Sustainability: the new agenda for Health for All' *Health for All News* Faculty of Public Health Medicine, 32: 4–6.
Draper, P. and Harrison, S. (1991) 'Prospects for healthy public policy', in P. Draper (ed) *Health through Public Policy*, London: Merlin Press.
Edwards, G. (1996) 'Sensible drinking' *British Medical Journal*, 312: 1.
Graham, H. (1984) *Women, Health and the Family*, Brighton: Wheatsheaf.
Hastings, G. (1991) 'The hard evidence against tobacco advertising', *Times Health Supplement*, Dec: 7–8.
Health Education Authority (HEA) (1989) *Diet, Nutrition and Healthy Eating in Low Income Groups*, London: Health Education Authority.
—— (1995) *Health in England 1995: What People Know; What People Think, What People Do*, London: Office for National Statistics/Health Education Authority.
Health Service Journal (1992) 'Smoking row looms as White Paper rises from the ashes', 30 April: 5.
—— (1996) 'Collision course' 1st August: 14.
Hunter, D. (1991) 'Breaking down barriers', *Health Service Journal*, 3 Oct, 101(5272): 19.
—— (1995) 'The case for closer cooperation between local authorities and the NHS' *British Medical Journal*, 310: 1587–9.
Illsley, R. (1986) 'Occupational class, selection and the production of inequalities in health', *Quarterly Journal of Social Affairs*, 2(2): 151–65.
Illsley, R. and Le Grand, J. (1987) 'The measurement of inequality in health' in A. Williams (ed) *Economics and Health*, London: Macmillan.
Jacobson, B., Smith, A. and Whitehead, M. (1991) *The Nation's Health: a Strategy for the 1990s*, London: King Edward's Hospital Fund for London.
Jones, I.A. (1992) 'An investigation into the factors affecting the diet of low income groups', Unpublished Dissertation for B.Sc. Hons. in Applied Consumer Science, University of Northumbria.
Klein, R. (1988) 'Acceptable inequalities' in D. Green (ed) *Acceptable Inequalities? Essays on the Pursuit of Equality in Healthcare*, London: Institute of Economic Affairs.
Lalonde, M. (1974) *A New Perspective on the Health of Canadians*, Ottawa: Government of Canada.

Lang, T. and Cole-Hamilton, I. (1986) *Tightening Belts: A Report on the Impact of Poverty on Food*, 2nd edn, London: London Food Commission.

McLoone, P. and Boddy, F.A. (1994) 'Deprivation and mortality in Scotland 1981 and 1991' *British Medical Journal*, 308: 1465–70.

MacDonald, A. and Hanes, F.A. (1988) 'Can I afford the diet?', *Journal of Human Nutrition and Dietetics*: 389–96.

Marmot, M.G. and McDowall, M.E. (1986) 'Mortality decline and widening social inequalities', *The Lancet*, 2: 274–6.

Musk, A., Shearn, R., Walker, N. and Swanson, M. (1994) 'Progress on smoking control in Western Australia' *British Medical Journal*, 308: 395–8.

National Advisory Council for Nutrition Education (1983) *A Discussion Paper for Proposals for Nutrition Guidelines for Health Education in Britain*, London: Health Education Council.

National Audit Office (1996) *Health of the Nation: a Progress Report*, London: HMSO.

Newby, H. (1983) 'Living from hand to mouth: the farmworker, food and agribusiness' in A. Murcott (ed) *The Sociology of Food and Eating*, Aldershot: Gower.

Newcastle Health Authority (1995) *Health Profiles by Locality*, Directorate of Public Health.

The Observer (1996) 'Thousands die of "home sickness"' 2nd June, p. 8.

Parston, G. (1991) 'Intentions and possibilities in the commissioning process' in *Beyond the Contract Relationship*, London: Institute of Health Service Management.

Phillimore, P., Beattie, A. and Townsend, P. (1994) 'Widening inequality of health in Northern England 1981–1991' *British Medical Journal*, 308: 1125–8.

Parliamentary Office of Science and Technology (1994) *Breathing in our Cities*, London: House of Commons.

Powles, J.W. and Gifford, S. (1993) 'Health of Nations: lessons from Victoria, Australia' *British Medical Journal*, 306: 125–7.

Robbins, C. (1991) 'Our manufactured diet' in P. Draper (ed) *Health through Public Policy*, London: Merlin Press.

Roberts, J. and Smith, C. (1987) 'Public health promoted', *Health Service Journal*, 22 Sept: 1230–1.

Sherwood, L. (1996) 'The BIG idea' *UK Health for All Network News*, Summer pp. 10–11, Liverpool: Health for All Network Ltd.

Smith, J. (1995) 'The OPCS Longitudinal Survey' *Social Trends* 26, p. 19 London: HMSO.

Tannahill, A. (1987) 'Regional health promotion planning and monitoring', *Health Education Journal*, 46(3): 125–7.

Townsend, P., Phillimore, P. and Beattie, A. (1987) *Health and Deprivation: Inequality and the North*, London: Croom Helm.

Townsend, P. (1990a) 'Widening inequalities of health in Britain: A rejoinder to Rudolf Klein', *International Journal of Health Services*, 20(3): 363–72.

—— (1990b) 'Individual or social responsibility for premature death? The current controversies in the British debate about health', *International Journal of Health Services*, 20(3): 373–92.

Thunhurst, C. (1991) 'Information and Public Health' in P. Draper (ed) *Health Through Public Policy*, London: Merlin Press.

Tsouros, A. (ed) (1991) *WHO Healthy Cities Project: A Project Becomes a Movement*, Copenhagen: WHO Regional Office for Europe.

—— (1994) *The WHO Healthy Cities Project: State of the Art and Future Plans*, Copenhagen: WHO Regional Office for Europe.

United Nations (1993) *Fair principles For Sustainable Development*: Essays on Sustainable Development Aldershot: Edward Elgar.

—— (1996) U.N. Human Development Report 1996, Oxford: Oxford University Press.

Whichelow, M.J. (1987) *The Health and Lifestyle Survey*, London: Health Promotion Research Trust.

Whitehead, M. (1987) *The Health Divide*, London: Health Education Council.

—— (1995) 'Tackling health inequalities: a review of policy initiatives' in M. Benzeval, K. Judge and M. Whitehead (1995).

Wilkinson, R.G. (1986) 'Occupational class, selection and inequalities in health: a reply to Raymond Illsley', *Quarterly Journal of Social Affairs*, 2(4): 415–22.

—— (1989) 'Class mortality differentials, income distribution and trends in poverty 1921–1981' *Journal of Social Policy*, 18(3): 307–37.

Wilkinson, T. (1992) 'Smoke signals', *Health Service Journal*, 30 April: 28–9.

Wilson, G. (1989) 'Family food systems, preventive health and dietary change: a policy to increase the health divide' *Journal of Social Policy*, 18(2): 167–85, Cambridge University Press.

—— (1987) *Money in the Family: Financial Organisation and Women's Responsibility*, Aldershot: Avebury.

World Health Organisation WHO (1946) *Constitution* Geneva: WHO.

—— (1981) *Global Strategy for Health for All by the Year 2000* ('Health for All' Series No. 3), Geneva: WHO.

—— (1985) *Targets for Health for All*, Copenhagen: WHO Regional Office for Europe.

—— (1986) *Ottawa Charter for Health Promotion*, Copenhagen: WHO.

—— (1988) *The Work of WHO in the European Region 1987, Annual Report of the Regional Director*, Copenhagen: WHO Regional Office for Europe.

—— (1991) *Targets for health for all: the health policy for Europe*, Copenhagen: WHO.

CHAPTER 9

Future directions

The NHS reforms have run their course for six years. Much has changed, yet the terms of the debate about the NHS and it's problems continue to sound depressingly familiar. In 1995–96 a parsimonious budget (an increase of 1.1 per cent in real terms) coincided with growing demands on emergency care, shortages of acute beds, and rising waiting times. Warnings of 'crisis' and charges of 'underfunding' were once again being sounded (see for instance NAHAT 1996; HSJ 1996a; *Independent* 1996).

A parable which health promotion professionals are fond of quoting helps to explain why we face the same set of problems six years on. The health care system is likened to a river: upstream people are falling in through the hazards and accidents of modern life – poverty, stress, unemployment, pollution – and by their own health-damaging behaviours. Downstream the health care workers work harder and harder trying to pull them out. Until we swim upstream – against all the currents and impediments – and prevent so many people falling into the river in the first place we will never solve the problems of health care systems. Often we know very well what is required, yet there are tremendous forces to overcome: 'battling for the new public health can seem like taking on the world' (Draper and Harrison (1991: 257).

In the struggle for the new public health, Hancock (1991) argues that in practice we must 'muddle through to Utopia' – firm in vision and purpose, flexible in tactics, recognising there will be retreats and sidesteps on the way. But this still requires a strategic analysis of the major trends driving change and shaping the context of health policy, which present differing opportunities and threats for those trying to work towards a healthier and sustainable future.

Consequently this chapter begins by reviewing some of the major trends shaping the context of health care policy in the UK and other advanced capitalist societies as we approach the 21st century (some of which have been explored in earlier chapters). It continues by assessing the current state of the NHS and community care reforms and the most recent Conservative proposals for the future, and concludes with a critical assessment of Labour Party proposals for health and health care.

A strategic overview

The economic context

The impact of economic pressures on health care policy and health care systems is both complex and contradictory. Health care can be viewed both as a central and (expensive) welfare responsibility of government and as an industry which by the mid-1970s had become the world's biggest (Jencks and Schieber 1991), playing an increasingly vital role in strategies of national competitiveness in the global context.

As an industry, Moran (1997) shows how the struggle for world markets by multinationals in the pharmaceutical and medical devices industries involves substantial research and development, much of it funded by the state, the centrality of the micro-electronics revolution to this innovation, and the way in which technological advances in health care sprang from developments in other fields, in particular from military research. Leading defence contractors have been at the forefront of adapting this research to the medical field, diversifying their activities as defence contracts have declined in recent years. At a national level, states have not only financed research, but shaped and regulated the market by their purchasing power.

But if innovation and investment in R&D are the sources of competitive advantage in world markets for multinational companies in health care (and this is a field where Britain is home to some of the world leaders), curbing the appetite for their products is the key to cost containment at home. As the discussion in Chapter 3 made clear, the restructuring of welfare states which has been underway since the late 1970s is driven by the need to improve the structural competitiveness of national economies in the struggle for markets and inward investment. Health care policy has thus been driven by the need for cost containment, yet this poses the dilemma that:

> In trying to manage the consequences of successful technological innovation in health care, states are attempting to manage forces in two different geographical spheres: one sphere is the global, where markets are organised; the other is the national, where health care systems are organised. The most rational strategy for a state, but one which is virtually impossible to pursue, is to promote successful innovation in its medical goods industries, but export all the results of that innovation.
>
> (Moran 1997)

Additional complexities are caused by the importance to the national economy of the health care industry as an employer. In the UK the NHS employs nearly a million people directly, but in addition many thousands in the private sector are dependent on it, including the 50,000 self-employed practitioners in the family health services who work under contract with the NHS. Griffith *et al.* (1987) argue that from its inception the NHS was never the monopolistic state-run system it was depicted to be, but a heterogenous set of interests and activities – part public, part private – brought together by government. On the private side this included general practitioners, dentists, high-street pharmacies, opthalmic services, pharmaceutical manufacturers and the hospital supply industries. From the routine statistics provided by the DOH, Salter (1995) concludes that, in 1993 52 per cent of NHS expenditure was undertaken in the private sector. To this list should be added the massive IT contracts of recent years, the rapid rise in the use of private management consultants, contracted-out services which now cover clinical as well as non-clinical areas and the effects of the Private Finance Initiative (see box) on capital development.

The Private Finance Initiative

The PFI, which was inaugurated in 1992, requires all public-sector capital schemes to be tested for private finance before public funding is considered, with tenders awarded by open competition.

In the NHS facilities developed by private capital in conjunction with an NHS partner are owned by the contractor, and leased back to the NHS. Since only the lease payments count as public spending, not the full value of the assets, the government can claim credit for short-term reductions in public expenditure, while capital facilities are still provided for the NHS. In some of the bigger schemes, like a new hospital development, the private contractor may design, build, maintain and operate all the services in the hospital except clinical services. By August 1996 there were 57 PFI projects in various stages of development worth about £500 million (the NHS capital programme is currently about £2 billion pounds) but most projects are comparatively small (below £15 million) and few big developments have yet to come to fruition.

Critics of PFI argue that:

- in the long term, public expenditure will not be reduced since the ongoing costs of providing and maintaining the services and repaying the capital costs comes out of public funds;
- the transfer of risk to the private sector is not total, and this has been acknowledged through recent legislation. If a trust is dissolved before the end of a leasing contract the Secretary of State, through the NHS (Residual Liabilities) Bill can take on the debts and liabilities.
- lease arrangements are being entered into which will commit tax revenues for 20 or 30 years, building a degree of inflexibility into

continued

the provision of services, and long-term funding commitments which may be difficult or costly to break.

- many schemes depend for their viability in selling services to non-NHS purchasers and setting up private patient facilities. NHS trusts, denied access to public funds, are forced to stimulate demand from private patients and use the profits to fund new facilities for NHS patients. This tortuous process is not the most cost-effective way of financing services for NHS patients, and may produce a range of undesirable side-effects.
- the costs of preparing options are extremely high with no guarantee of success, both for the private contractor and the NHS partner. In large schemes, consultancy costs may be as high as £2 million.
- 'design, build and operate' schemes could lead to privatisation by the back door. If more services are run by private contractors (extending to clinical services) the NHS loses expertise in areas crucial to its business, with a progressive loss of control to the private sector.

So far PFI has not lived up to the government's ambitions: less than half the £300 million cut in Treasury funding for NHS capital has been made up by private capital since 1995.

Sources: Terry (1996) Dawson and Maynard (1996) Appleby (1996) HSJ (1996d)

Cost-containment strategies had to take account of this economic role and, in addition, for a government ideologically committed to private enterprise, do as little damage as possible to private economic interests. Hence the attraction of market-based solutions which opened up the NHS to further opportunities for market penetration by private providers of goods and services, and of 'managed competition', which promised the efficiency incentives of markets without their equity consequences. It has also led both here and in many other countries to a transfer of social costs to individuals, by imposing higher charges and restricting user entitlements.

In the UK this has been done sometimes by stealth, sometimes by default. For example, the virtual privatisation of dentistry as dentists, dissatisfied with their contracts, withdraw from the NHS; the growing list of deregistered drugs which can no longer be dispensed or paid for by the NHS, usually because they are cheaper than the official prescription charge which in 1996 stood at £5.50 per item. In effect this privatises the cost of medicines for those ineligible for exemptions (Earl-Slater 1996). Most important of all is the transfer of responsibility for long-stay nursing care for the elderly from the NHS, where it is free, to local authority social service departments, where it is means-tested (see p. 205–8) and mainly provided by the private sector. How far governments can continue down this road depends, as Moran points out, on the workings of democratic politics. Paradoxically many of the policy changes the government has initiated, such as the Patient's Charter, may simply have helped to fuel higher expectations of what the NHS should provide, and made it more difficult for governments to square the economic circle.

The elderly have been the chief victims of cost containment in health systems, and in some case the scapegoats as well. The argument that a tax-funded NHS cannot 'afford' the costs of growing numbers of very elderly people is often used to justify privatised solutions, in which individuals who can do so make their own private provision, or pay higher charges (see, for instance, Healthcare 2000 1995).

Recently these claims have been subjected to greater critical scrutiny and a shift in the policy climate. Further confirmation that there is little link between an ageing population and health care costs internationally is provided by a report from the Institute of Public Policy Research, which also confirms that the current gap between demand and resources in the NHS is no greater than it has ever been, and does not justify radical changes in the funding regime which are neither equitable or efficient (Wordsworth *et al.* 1996). (This view is also reflected in a recent government White Paper, see p. 203) The report does support the view, expressed in Chapter 3, that preventive measures targeted at the middle-aged and elderly would be highly cost-effective, since healthy elderly people make few demands on the health service.

Health in old age, however, depends crucially on adequate social and economic security in youth and middle age. To the extent that this is missing then more problems are being created for the future. The economic restructuring which has taken place in recent years has had marked effects on health as well as health care. These include: the insecurities and stresses caused by post-Fordist labour market strategies; the impact of technology on the manufacture of goods and services, improving productivity at the expense of jobs; and growing social and economic inequality. All of these damage health and lead to much preventable morbidity and premature mortality (Whitehead 1995; Milio 1995). Ironically, the people who have to deal with the casualities of this system – health workers themselves – are some of the worst affected by social change. Recent research commissioned for the DOH found that sickness absence rates in the NHS are higher than the average in the private sector (4.8 per cent average compared to 3.4. per cent). Particularly significant are the high levels of stress, with 27 per cent reporting minor psychiatric disorders serious enough to benefit from professional help. This rises to an alarming 41 per cent among female health service managers, and 36 per cent of female doctors (Moore 1996).

A changing intellectual paradigm: the battle of ideas

Is the heyday of the therapeutic era and the medical model of health drawing to a close, or simply taking a new direction in the 21st century? Socio-ecological concepts of health and illness have exerted a powerful intellectual challenge in recent years, underpinning a renewed and expanded public health movement, but the importance of health care as an industry, the conjunction of medicine and its commercial exploitation by powerful world players in the international market place, as well as the revolutionary implications of scientific and technological development in health care, point to a Herculean struggle.

All our futures?

Future predictions in health care are more than usually hazardous, as the last six years have shown, but that does not stop the futurologists. In a recent article looking at developments up to the year 2020 it was predicted that:

- daily health checks at home by computer and the use of artificial intelligence-based support devices for elderly and handicapped people are perfectly feasible with today's technology;
- before 2005 sensors directly stimulating nerve endings to act as artificial senses will be in development; within 10 years it should be possible to connect them directly to sensory nerves;
- before 2005 the widespread use of robots at home and in hospitals;
- by 2020 the development of artificial eyes and peripheral nerves will be in development, and direct computer-brain links will be emerging from the research stage.
- the storage of living bodies by hibernation and attempts to explain the logical reasoning mechanism in the brain may also be moving from the research stage to development by then.
- the mapping of the entire human genome within ten years.

The revolution in biological sciences 'will have a greater impact than the industrial or atomic revolutions' with profound consequences for the study of ageing, the control of the immune system, and new classes of diagnostic and therapeutic agents.

Source: Crail and Cross (1995).

Yet there are counter-forces which also have important economic effects – the collapse of the British beef industry in the wake of the BSE crisis, estimated to cost the taxpayer a minimum of £3.3 billion pounds over four years, is a case in point (*Financial Times* 1996). This example also shows how rapid change can be when it is driven from below – in this case the collapse of consumer confidence in the safety of British beef, and the consequent banning of the meat throughout the world (but not, significantly, in Britain). Another is the remarkable recent successes of the American anti-smoking lobby in the wake of a successful court case against a subsidiary of British Allied Tobacco Industries. Similar successes have been won in the environmental field by grass-roots action and concern.

The most vaunted successes of medicine can also seem fragile. The growth of drug-resistant bacteria has led to the return of diseases which seemed to have been vanquished. Tuberculosis, pneumonia and malaria, which could be cured by anti-biotics a decade ago, once again claim millions of lives worldwide (BMJ 1994). Concern about the harmful side-effects or ineffectiveness of orthodox medicine, particularly for some chronic and degenerative illnesses, has led to a consumer-driven explosion in the popularity of alternative therapies, which are based on more holistic models of health and which, Saks argues, also have a significant self-help component. Saks reports that one in seven people used alternative practitioners by 1991, and this has almost certainly increased since (Saks 1994: 85). The growth is all the more remarkable when the competitive disadvantage and marginal status of alternative practitioners is taken into account.

At the same time, the search for cost containment has forced governments throughout the Western world to begin evaluating the benefits and costs of medical interventions and technologies more systematically and to renew interest in both prevention and health promotion. Though critics rightly argue this has largely taken an individualistic victim-blaming stance to date, the weight of evidence supporting a socio-ecological model of health is now becoming so overwhelming that governments of different ideological persuasions, albeit at different speeds and with differing degrees of reluctance, are having to accept its validity and policy implications.

Changing the focus of health care delivery

Changing technologies will impact on the way health care services are organised and delivered, changes which we can broadly summarise under the headings of decentralisation and diversity. In general the expansion of day surgery and improved techniques of managing conditions like cystic fibrosis, diabetes and asthma will further increase the importance of ambulatory and domiciliary care at the expense of acute hospitals. The primary-care revolution will continue but there will be far more diversity in the way services are offered (already signposted by the recent primary care White Paper, discussed below).

The number, size and functions of hospitals will also change, although not in easily predictable ways. Commissioners' interest in outcomes and effectiveness as well as changes in medical training will put great pressure on the traditional multi-speciality District General Hospital, and will kill off small specialities in such hospitals which cannot meet the training and quality standards expected. Newchurch and Company (1995) predicts that only a few large multi-specialist hospitals will survive, some focusing on trauma and major surgery, others on specialist diagnosis and treatment of complex diseases serving a large population. Most hospitals will be smaller, either highly specialised units or local hospitals offering a range of general, often continuing, health and social care services to a limited local community.

These changes will have immense consequences for health care staff – Newchurch predicts that the reshaping of the acute sector will require about one-quarter of the health care workforce to change their jobs over the next five to ten years. But the content of those jobs will also change, and with it will come changes in power and status for different groups. Old demarcation barriers between professions and sub-professions will be dissolved and new ones created.

The political and ideological context

A key change since 1992 is the repositioning of the Labour Party by its leader, Tony Blair, as a centre-left social democratic party ('New Labour'), to appeal to a broader social spectrum and acknowledge the socio-economic shifts that have taken place in recent years. In doing so it has jettisoned much ideological baggage, including its instinctive hostility to the market, and accepted a great deal of Conservative policy, for example, on trade union reform, the welfare state and management of the economy. This is true also of the health reforms, and it is fascinating to map the change in Labour Party attitudes since 1992. The reforms have moved so far, so fast, that they are difficult to reverse.

The Conservatives, too, have been careful to distance themselves from aggressive marketspeak and dogmatic prescriptions. In a recent White Paper they have also repudiated the view that an ageing population makes a tax-funded health service unaffordable in future and reaffirmed its commitment to the NHS (DOH 1996a). The retreat from ideology is nowhere better signalled than in another White Paper which pushes forward the revolution in primary care (DOH 1996b). In utter contrast to *Working for Patients* in 1989, this White Paper is based on months of consultation and all its proposals are for piloting and evaluation first. Evolution and pragmatism appear to have replaced revolution and ideology as the basis for health policy-making at present, perhaps reflecting a more considered view of the sheer complexity of health care systems and the unintended consequences of even minor policy change.

As far as funding is concerned, New Labour is so keen to distance itself from its previous 'tax and spend' image that we have the irony of a Labour Party whose Iron (Shadow) Chancellor will make no financial promises, short of paying for 100,000 extra operations by cutting 'bureaucracy', while at the same time the Conservatives boast of their spending record. In his 1996 Budget speech the Chancellor claimed that spending on the NHS had increased in real terms by 79 per cent since 1979, and he pledged to spend more than the level of inflation every year for the next five years (Clarke 1996). It is true that far from cutting back public spending as a proportion of GDP as the Conservatives intended, it is still roughly the same (at 42 per cent) as it was 17 years ago, and the three big programmes of the welfare state – social security, health and education – make up an increasing proportion (61 per cent in 1996–97 compared with 49 per cent in 1978–79) (Timmins 1996)). In this respect, the realities of democratic politics have outweighed ideology again – voters of all parties have never wavered in their support for a tax-funded health service and more support it today than in the past (Taylor-Gooby 1995: 4).

Conservative munificence to the health service looks less generous, however, when exposed to more detailed scrutiny. The 1997–98 settlement promises a cash uplift of £1.6 billion in cash terms, or a 2.9 per cent increase in real terms given an estimated inflation rate of 2 per cent. However, NHS inflation is always higher than general price inflation, and will probably be nearer to 3 per cent next year. More will be eaten up by the accumulated deficit of 1996–97 (estimated at £200 million), while some of the NHS increase has been at the expense of cuts in the personal social service budget, which is bound to have knock-on effects. Increases in revenue are also balanced by further cuts in the capital budget, totalling one third in two years. The Private Finance Initiative is supposed to make up the difference, but given that only £65 million was realised last year from a planned total of £165 million this seems grossly unrealistic. If this is the best the NHS can hope for in an election year, it would seem unrealistic to think that either party will do what the public – in opinion polls at least – wants them to do – tax and spend more on the NHS.

The NHS and community care reforms: the current state of play

Primary care

A White Paper published in November 1996 carries the primary care revolution further by proposing legislation to break the monopoly status of GPs as sole providers of general medical services. Restrictions on commissioning and providing pharmaceutical and dental services are also eased (DOH 1996a). New providers are encouraged to pilot and test different ways of offering services, freed from current financial and regulatory restrictions. Favoured options are:

- salaried service for GPs, either within existing partnerships or with other organisations, such as NHS trusts and other bodies. This would allow community or acute trusts to employ GPs to extend their services either horizontally (a coordinated package of primary and community health services) or vertically (coordination between hospital and primary care). Private providers (pharmacy or supermarket chains) could also enter the field, although the Labour Party say this is something it would reverse. Salaried service could prove attractive to GPs in inner cities, already facing severe pressures of overwork, poor facilities and lack of security, and may address the recruitment problems experienced in many socially deprived areas.
- contracts made with practices (rather than with individual general practitioners) which could potentially raise the influence of nurses and other primary care professionals, who could at last become full partners in a multidisciplinary primary health care team (Hancock 1996).
- allowing fundholders and total purchasers to use their budgets more flexibly by pooling the funds they receive for general medical services and hospital and community services. This would allow them to experiment with more cost-effective ways of delivering services (e.g. the more extensive use of nurses and nurse practitioners).

Although caution and evaluation are the watchwords of this White Paper it could have as radical consequences as that former experiment, GP fundholding. Some observers believe it could develop into fully fledged Health Maintenance Organisations, led by GPs, who contract with the health authority to deliver a comprehensive package of services according to tight performance and cost standards, for a fixed period (Light 1994: Maynard 1996).

Community care: boundary and whole systems issues

The primary-care White Paper begins to address one set of barriers impeding the integrated commissioning and delivery of primary and secondary care, but another set of barriers, between health and social care, remain formidable.

Local authority social service departments have been occupied with their own revolution since the passing of the NHS and Community Care Act in 1990, and with the transfer of financial responsibilities for residential and nursing-home care from the social security budget to local authorities from April 1993. This has involved separating the purchasing and providing sides of the organisation; stimulating the market in social care; implementing needs assessment and care management; supporting and developing their own providers to become more autonomous and capable of competing with the independent sector; and moving to a system of contractual relationships with providers and seeking ways of improving choice and independence for users and carers.

As in the early stages of the NHS reforms, the main preoccupation of the DOH was to secure a smooth transition and ensure no disasters (Foster and Laming 1992). Early monitoring exercises showed that authorities had managed this transition relatively smoothly and that by the second year, users and carers were reporting some service improvements (Henwood 1995). (For a full discussion and references see Henwood *et al.* 1996; Harrison 1995.) In spite of this satisfactory progress longer-term problems were already emerging in relation to the adequacy of resources and boundary issues with the health service, on which we concentrate here.

The organisational divide between health and social care is not paralleled by the needs of individuals, and it is often difficult if not impossible to define precisely the line between the two. Historically, social care provided by local authorities has always been means-tested under the National Assistance Act 1948, in contrast to NHS 'free' care, but the issue has achieved much greater significance since 1993 in relation to the funding of long-stay care. This has received most publicity in relation to the elderly, but similar issues apply to other groups with complex health and social needs.

Even before the NHS and Community Care Act 1990 health authorities had started to define the long-stay care of elderly people as 'not part of our core business' (Ranade and Appleby 1989: 19), and were shifting the costs onto the social security budget by transferring such patients into the voluntary or private sector. By 1993–94, the number of NHS geriatric beds had fallen by 22 per cent from 1989–90 (Wistow 1995: 80). With the transfer of financial responsibility to local authorities in 1993, old people who needed residential or nursing home places could only obtain a 'free' place if they had assets less than £3,000 pounds, and had to pay in full if they possessed assets greater than £8,000. (These limits were increased in 1995 to £10,000 and £16,000.) Elderly people were now at risk of losing their lifetime savings and even their homes to fund long-stay care, disinheriting their children and causing much political embarrassment to John Major's government, who had boasted of creating a property-owning democracy with wealth 'cascading down the generations'.

A related boundary problem occurred with discharge arrangements. It was unclear to what extent people admitted to hospital as an emergency could refuse to be discharged to a nursing or residential home for which they would have to pay in part or in full. Growing demand pressures (for instance the Patient's Charter waiting time targets) coupled with fewer numbers of beds in total, meant that trusts were often desperate to discharge patients quickly to prevent them 'blocking' beds needed for other patients.

Cost-shunting was another problem. Trusts began withdrawing services, such as domiciliary nursing or mental health services, perceived to be on the borderline of health and social care, shunting costs onto social service departments and GPs. Local authorities in turn starting shifting more of the costs onto users. Nine out of ten authorities were charging for domiciliary care by 1994, and though charges still represented a small proportion of overall costs, they were rising rapidly (Harrison 1995: 10). Variations in service levels and eligibility criteria between different local areas were causing major inequities for users and their families.

In 1994 a highly critical report by the Health Service Commissioner and growing public and media outrage prompted the government to clarify many of these boundary issues through a definitive set of guidelines, published in 1995 (DOH 1995). These included:

- a statement of health service responsibilities for providing a full range of services and an explicit commitment to continuing health care as 'an integral part of the NHS' (para.1);
- the requirement that purchasers should invest in such services where they are currently failing to do so;
- a timetabled action plan for bringing these changes into effect by lst April 1995;
- the establishment of independent lay panels to review individual cases where there is dispute.

The importance attached to implementation was reflected in the fact that this was one of only six national priorities for the NHS over a three- to five-year period outlined by the NHS Executive in its *Priorities and Planning Guidance 1996–97*. Implicitly the guidelines acknowledge that the boundary between health and social care has shifted too far, and seeks to pull it back in the health service's direction, by setting out a comprehensive list of NHS responsibilities.

This may reduce the scope for anomalies and inequities (and some progress seems to be have made in establishing more coherent joint policies since the publication of the guidance, see Henwood 1996), but is unlikely to abolish them altogether. Professionals will still have to make fine distinctions entitling some people to free nursing or other health services for which others have to pay, which users are bound to find unjust. (A partial solution would be to make all nursing care free irrespective of where it is delivered – see Hancock 1996, Health Select Committee 1996.)

Genuine joint planning and commissioning between health and local authorities, with a pooled budget to support them, would dissolve these definitional problems. Where this has been achieved it is normally due to determined individuals and fortuitous circumstances (Duggan 1995). More often, established differences in organisational culture and perspectives are compounded by different trajectories of change between the two authorities which create a mismatch in the patterns of decision making and budgetary control. For example, in some authorities there may be substantial devolution of budgets to GPs, which is not paralleled by devolution to the roughly equivalent level of care managers in Social Service Departments (SSDs) (Charlesworth *et al.* 1996). In other parts of the country the reverse may be true (Duggan 1995). The task of cementing relationships, both at strategic and operational level, is also made more difficult by continuous organisational upheaval within the NHS, and the impact of local government restructuring on SSDs in some parts of the country.

The discussion on the effects of the 'new public management' (NPM) in Chapter 7 is also relevant here. Some aspects of the NHS and community care reforms have made it easier to develop new ways of providing services that emphasise the inter-relationships between agencies and different kinds of provider, and have begun to break down what seemed to be impenetrable service boundaries. But managing these relationships is infinitely more complex when they are both competitive and complementary at the same time. Devolving budgets down the line may increase a sense of ownership and autonomy, but it can also lead to defensive and proprietorial stances, particularly if coupled to tightly specified contracts or performance targets, introducing new sources of inflexibility.

Health authorities and trusts: expectations and realities

Early visions of health authorities adopting a public health approach to health improvement and acting as the champions of a wider health strategy have been slow to materialise. The reasons why become more obvious if we look at what is entailed, and how far it departs from current practice.

Alderslade and Hunter (1994: 22) advocate a model of commissioning based on 'public health management'; which would entail:

- a description of the health needs and experience of the local population, based both on epidemiological data and extensive consultation;

- defining health programmes, 'a programme being a coherent set of promotion, prevention, therapy and rehabilitation services directed towards an identifiable health problem' (p. 22). These could embrace services for a client group (mental illness) or disease entities (coronary heart disease);
- exposing each element of the programme to the tests of effectiveness, efficiency, acceptability and appropriateness, to see which options maximise health improvement from the resources designated for the programme. This stage of 'health policy analysis' is, the authors argue, the intellectual core of commissioning;
- the translation of these decisions into the more conventional activity of deciding how much and where to purchase services, drawing up service specifications, and contracts.

The authors admit that such a model of commissioning does not yet exist anywhere else in the world, hence the intellectual, political and managerial challenges it poses are immense, though the benefits could be great. Some authorities are beginning to introduce health programmes for one or two disease entities, but in general this is not usual, and progress is beset by difficulties. For example:

- the present contracting system still reflects present service boundaries and specialities rather than health programmes, and the difficulties of apportioning costs in a different way are considerable;
- many authorities are still working with incomplete and unreliable data on what they buy and what each service element costs (Roberts 1996);
- the programme approach is not supported by appropriate performance targets which would concentrate on effectiveness and outcomes, rather than, as at present, input costs and activity measures (Appleby and Little 1993; Appleby *et al.* 1993; Coote and Hunter 1996).

None of these problems are insurmountable given sufficient political and managerial will to make progress. Of greater concern are the overloaded agendas of health authorities which means that energies are increasingly taken up with issues surrounding the rationing and cost-effectiveness of health care, the reshaping of acute services and the development of primary care. Organisational fragmentation and marketised relationships make the task of developing a wider health strategy harder. Contracts themselves often bear little relationship to the needs assessment process (Watt *et al.* 1994), and the timeconsuming nature of the annual contracting round drives out the capacity for creative thinking.

On the provider side, it was expected that the quasi-market would provide the right incentives to improve efficiency, innovation and quality of service, but many trusts have been disappointed to find that good performance does not always bring its own reward (Kingman 1994). Much depends on the resource position of local purchasers, their degree of market power, or the extent of fundholding. Efficiency savings averaging 3 per cent a year still have to be found, and hospitals may find themselves treating more patients for less money, just as they did before the reforms.

Trusts have also been criticised for excessive secrecy (Ashburner and Cairncross 1992), poor communication, failure to involve clinicians in management and poor personnel practices (Audit Commission 1994). As always in such a huge enterprise as the NHS, generalisations are difficult to make and there are many examples of management excellence, too.

At a systemic level 'complexity and interdependence makes it hard to see if policies are consistent with each other. The impact of a policy initiative in one part of the health sector may be transmitted or 'shunted' to another' (Harrison 1995: 73), often with perverse effects. We have already seen how this applies at the boundaries of health and social care. Another example is the pressure on acute hospitals to treat more patients, do more day surgery and cut waiting times. Not only is this difficult to reconcile with the 'strategic shift' of resources to primary care, it also creates spillover effects in other parts of the system. For example, GP workloads increase by having to deal with more patients discharged from hospital 'quicker and sicker'. They, in turn, appear to be reacting by a narrower interpretation of their contract, cutting down desirable activities for which they are not specificially paid, and admitting more patients to hospitals as emergencies. Workload pressures are once again thrust back onto hospitals, who find it hard to balance the twin demands of emergency and elective cases. Pulling together the 'tangled webs' (Charlesworth *et al.* 1996) of health and community care is the strategic responsibility of health authorities and local government jointly but to be successful this requires more integrated policies at national level, and the development of more sophisticated 'systems models' which can predict how changes in one part of the system affect the rest.

The quest for efficiency

In the last two decades European health systems have been preoccupied by the goal of efficiency. In the 1980s cost containment or macro-efficiency goals were pre-eminent; in the 1990s attention turned to micro-efficiency issues at the institutional and clinical level. Market-based incentives figured prominently in these experiments but, as Saltman (1996) points out, market instruments can be applied in a number of different ways. For example, competition can be introduced into the financing of health care, one or more subsets of production (hospitals, primary care, long-stay care, physicians, pharmaceuticals) or the way resources are allocated to providers. Once again there are a range of possibilities – expanding consumer choice, negotiated contracts, open bidding.

How and where market instruments have been applied depend greatly on existing institutional and ideological contexts. The UK's route to efficiency has been through professionalising management, competition on the supply side, and negotiated contracts. The reforms have been used to alter the balance of power between managers and clinicians, purchasers and providers; however, the real, rather than rhetorical, power of the users – whether viewed as consumers in a market or citizens in the polity – has not fundamentally changed.

By contrast, in Sweden quasi-market structures have been used to strengthen consumer choice and local democratic control (Saltman 1997). Saltman also claims that Sweden has achieved efficiency gains both at the micro and macro-level. In the UK the evidence of efficiency gains at the micro-level is not so clear cut, as our evidence in Chapter 5 illustrated, while at the macro-level health spending as a percentage of GDP drifted up from 6 per cent in 1989 to 7.1 per cent in 1993 (OECD 1995). (In Sweden the percentage declined from 9.4% to 7.4% over the same period.)

Ironically some of the perverse incentives of the old NHS, given as one of the main reasons for reform, have not disappeared and the quasi-market has added others (new forms of cost shifting, gaming on contracts, 'cream-skimming') coupled with much higher transaction costs. We cannot romanticise the past and in many ways the reforms have had a catalytic effect, breaking open the immutable institutions and rigid routines of a decade ago, creating an era of unparalleled innovation. But the downside of flexibility and diversity is loss of direction and new sources of inequity. Above all managerialism and marketspeak – 'privatising from within' – have had an insidious effect on the NHS culture, demoralising staff and alienating the public. We need a revaluing process which is rooted in the day-to-day experience of those receiving and giving care in all its varied settings, and which recognises their needs, in order to restore trust and confidence. It is time for the pendulum to turn, to restore the values of solidarity, caring, cooperation, and coordination. Efficiency is not the only god, though it will always be an important one.

Which way forward?

On the 1st May 1997 the Labour Party was swept back into power after eighteen years in opposition, with a landslide majority of 179 seats, far surpassing its own private estimates. The new Labour MPs brought with them a totally different set of ideas, values and experience to Parliament from their previous Conservative counterparts, as an independent survey of candidates makes clear (reported in The Observer 1997). Before the election the party's health proposals were fairly modest, but with such a decisive mandate for change the party in office may be readier to contemplate more radical alternatives over time.

The fullest statement of Labour Party policy was published in 1995 in *Renewing the NHS*, which was fleshed out further in a speech by the Shadow Secretary of State for Health, Chris Smith in November 1996. The main points of his speech are summarised below.

Labour health policy: a summary

Four key aims:

- Responsive health services
- Achieve greatest possible improvement in nation's health
- Reduce health inequalities.
- Raise standards and quality of care.

Eight guiding objectives:

- equitable resource distribution
- improving quality of care through evaluation of health outcomes and continuation of 'evidence-based medicine'
- cut transaction costs
- NHS-funded services delivered by NHS providers. No further extensions of private companies operating services under the Private Finance Initiative, or employing GPs as allowed under the proposed primary care legislation (DOH 1996a).
- national priority-setting framework
- separation of health commissioning from delivery of services (the purchaser–provider split).
- a voice for all GPs and primary health care staff in shaping health services.
- greater accountability and transparency of decision making.

Key proposals:

- Trusts remain – renamed 'local health services'
- Trust boards remain – renamed 'governing bodies'
- Primary-care led commissioning by 'local commissioning groups' (LCGs) led by GPs.
- Individual fundholding abolished, unless LCG agrees to further delegate budgets down to individual practices.

continued

- Contracts remain – renamed 'local health care agreements' and shift towards longer term agreements (three to five years) and programme approach to commissioning.
- Health authority role – strategic planning (needs assessment, public health, primary care development), information clearing-house, resource allocation and performance monitoring.
- Principle of contestability remains, where commissioners dissatisfied with a provider's performance.
- Strengthened arrangements for public health.

Mr Smith's speech was significant in clearing up uncertainty on the future of fundholding and the quasi-market. Individual practice-based fundholding is abolished in favour of commissioning by Local Commissioning Groups led by GPs. The format is flexible but will probably be geographically based, with five to 15 groups within present health authority boundaries. The groups could adopt a variety of organisational models, based on existing GP and locality commissioning schemes, discussed in Chapter 5, and even decide to devolve a portion of their budget further to individual practices. Each group would commission most of the services it needed from its delegated share of the health authority's budget, apart from emergency and high-cost specialist care. Deciding where to place contracts would be based on 'cooperation not competition' and involve health authority staff, trust managers and clinicians, and other primary care personnel in the discussions. However, a Local Commissioning Group, backed by the health authority, could move a contract from a provider who failed to provide a reasonable quality service over a specified period – in other words an element of contestability remains.

As with any set of broad policy proposals, the devil is in the details, which still have to be filled in. The accountability arrangements of the commissioning groups to the health authority and the way disagreements and conflicts will be handled will be crucial. GPs have not in the past been noted for cooperation and consultation, either with each other or with anyone else, and while there have been great improvements in some parts of the country through successful multifund initiatives, or total purchasing consortia, has the professional culture changed sufficiently to make GP-led commissioning a viable national model? Whether the substitution of individual fundholding with local commissioning groups will reduce transaction and administrative costs is also problematic, although the Labour Party's private costing exercises suggest that it will (personal communication). There are also hopes of moving towards longer-term contracts (already signalled by the present administration), and the setting out of 'a default set of national terms and conditions governing agreements between local groups and providers' to reduce transaction costs further (Smith 1996: 15).

Turning to other proposals, we assess them in the light of four key questions:

- would they promote the public's health, in accordance with the principles of Health for All 2000?
- would they strengthen democratic accountability and citizen participation?
- what approach would they take to rationing and priority setting?
- would they restore public and staff confidence in the future of the NHS?

Promoting the public's health

On the first question, the Labour Party appears to embrace the philosophy of HFA 2000 more enthusiastically than the Conservatives, and reducing health inequalities is a key objective. Policies like a minimum wage, reducing long-term unemployment, protections for workers under the Social Chapter, the progressive release of local authority housing receipts to finance house improvement and new building, tighter controls on air quality and banning tobacco advertising – these all support the wider health strategy if successfully implemented.

At central level, leadership and coordination should be improved by the appointment of a senior Minister for Public Health, a more independent role for the Chief Medical Officer, and a revamped and more powerful Health Education Authority. The requirement that each government department undertakes a health audit of its policies and publishes annual health impact statements should encourage greater appreciation of the wider health strategy among civil servants and the public, if it is taken seriously. Setting up a food standards agency independent of the Ministry of Agriculture is an overdue response to conflicts of interest between consumers and farmers which have arisen in recent years.

The continuing development of primary care, and the lead role given to all GPs in commissioning, seems to accord with the WHO emphasis on primary health care as the cornerstone of services. Nevertheless, there is a difference between primary *medical* care – which is based on the diagnosis and treatment of illness – and primary *health* care, as envisaged by WHO, which has as its key aim the maintenance and promotion of health in partnership with individuals and communities. Duggan defines it as care which is 'accessible, holistic, continuing and personalised' (Duggan 1995: 64) and argues it is more likely to be practised by nurses and other primary health care staff than doctors, because of differences in their training and professional philosophy.

The Labour Party's faith in medical 'experts' (which featured in the original design of the NHS) counterpoints the exaggerated distrust and attacks on professionals which were a feature of Thatcherism, but they could go too far. It would be ironic if, in trying to find a formula to persuade GPs to give up fundholding by giving them the lead role in commissioning, a Labour government perpetuated a medical model of health. Power would simply be transferred from one set of doctors (in hospitals) to another in primary care (although in practice non-medical managers will still do most of the day-to-day work of commissioning and setting contracts).

It is also difficult to tell whether the devolution of commissioning will allow health authority staff, in particular Directors of Public Health and their colleagues, to put more effort into the wider health strategy, and cultivate 'healthy alliances' or whether, in practice, there will be just as much work in supporting GP-commissioning as there was before.

Strengthening democracy and accountability

On the second question, it was argued in Chapter 7 that Conservative rhetoric of 'consumer choice' and consumer rights may have heightened user expectations but had not been backed by real choices or enforceable rights. At the same time, democratic accountability, always weak in the NHS, has been weakened further. The partisan and secretive nature of appointments in the 'quango state'; growing fragmentation of responsibilities at local level, so that people do not know whom to call to account when things go wrong; growing secretiveness of decision making; and rising levels of detected fraud have all caused concern (see, for example, Stewart 1993; Ashburner and Cairncross 1992; Limb 1996; Audit Commission 1996).

In response New Labour proposes to make appointment procedures to trusts and health authority boards to follow the standards laid down by the Nolan Committee on Standards in Public Life, to satisfy criteria of openness and equal opportunities. It also proposes to widen membership to include social service and staff representatives, and, on trusts, representatives from the local community. There are a number of proposals to strengthen the quality and quantity of information made available to the public (and the Party has also promised to introduce a Freedom of Information Bill), and the representative role of Community Health Councils (renamed Local Health Advocates) would be strengthened, with new powers and wider recruitment, but these are not spelt out in any detail. In addition the independence and powers of the Audit Commission would be further enlarged.

Do these arrangements go far enough to strengthen either representative or direct democracy in the NHS? Wall (1997) argues that the Party's proposals about widening health authority and trust membership suggest muddled thinking about the nature of representation and accountability in the NHS, and a throwback to the unsatisfactory arrangements prior to 1991. Up till then health authority members were either appointed by the RHA or nominees of local councils, medical and nursing organisations, trade unions and universities. Their role was confused, part managerial, part representative, and in practice they did neither well. Nominated members were particularly likely to act as representatives of special interests or the local authority, making a corporate approach hard to achieve. As a result, authorities were manipulated by the full-time officers, and members largely rubber-stamped decisions made elsewhere. Since 1991 smaller, more tightly knit boards of executive and non-executive members seem to work more corporately, and have been managerially more effective, but are even less accountable to local people.

As Wall points out, true representation is possible only under an electoral process when people are able to sack those whose record they deem unsatisfactory. Direct democracy means that people speak for themselves, and participate directly in the decisions that effect them. The possibility of strengthening representative democracy through transferring health commissioning to local authorities has been advocated by Coote and Hunter (1996: 92–4) on a pilot basis, and this could be combined with experiments in direct democracy by building on some of the more radical locality initiatives organised on community development lines. A small number of local authorities which had already demonstrated a strong commitment to devolved decision making and joint working with the health authority could be chosen to pilot an integrated approach to commissioning within a locally democratic framework. This would break down the boundaries between health and social care, and public and environmental health. The pilots could be used to explicitly push forward and give prominence to the Healthy Cities model of working and the principles of HFA, and they would be set targets to meet, much as the Healthy City project cities were, as outlined in Chapter 8. But such a proposal seems too radical for New Labour at present.

Approaches to rationing

A more open and accountable approach to issues surrounding health care rationing is also needed. Rationing decisions are made at several levels by different people – politicians, civil servants, managers and professionals. At the macro-level political decisions on levels of taxation and public spending, and how the overall public spending will be allocated among competing priorities, determines the global budget available for the health service. New Labour has already signalled its opposition to higher taxes even for the better off and there is little prospect of growth monies for the NHS greater than the rate of inflation, so resource pressures will continue to be intense. Whether Labour's position on taxation will be sustainable is arguable, although if priorities have to be made, proponents of a social model of health would argue that measures such as tackling low pay and unemployment would deliver more 'health gain' than spending more on the NHS.

The next stage of rationing occurs through the method chosen to allocate resources geographically, which determines what is available to meet the health care needs of people in each region and health authority area. Since 1976 the resource allocation formula has been based on the principle of trying to secure equal access to services for people in equal need, but in spite of its seeming objectivity the formula has always contained debatable value judgements. The current formula is based on population, weighted for the costs of treating patients in different age bands, a health needs factor and the higher costs incurred by authorities in the South East. The formula was reviewed for the DOH in 1994 by a team of health economists at York University, based on the updated 1991 census data and more discriminating indicators of health needs (incorporating, for example, unemployment). The revised formula would have redistributed millions of pounds to deprived authorities, particularly to those in the North, and away from London and the South East, but ministerial concern about the political consequences led to two changes to the groups' recommendations. 24 per cent of the total budget was left unweighted for health needs, and a 'Market Forces Factor' was introduced to take greater account of geographical price variations, which considerably lessened the scale of redistribution. The DOH has promised to rectify the first distortion to improve equity of access, following critical scrutiny from the Health Select Committee, but not the second. Hacking (1996) argues that the two main beneficiaries from the Market Forces Factor are North and South Thames regions. The worst losers are those with the worst health statistics and the highest needs – Northern and Yorkshire, and the North West. The Labour Party is committed to reassessing the fomula on the grounds that the current one 'raises serious questions about its impartiality and fairness, and we cannot have a system of resource allocation that is open to criticism of party advantage' (Smith 1996: 6).

Further stages in the rationing chain occur when health authorities decide how resources will be distributed between services and make their purchasing decisions (what we might call meso-level rationing) and professionals make decisions at the micro-level about individual patients. Traditionally rationing at the meso-level was based on historical patterns, short-term pressures and clinical shroud-waving and not on explicit principles or priorities. At the micro-level rationing was carried out by 'deterrence, diversion, dilution and delay' (Ruddle 1991): deterrence through inconvenience, unpleasantness, the imposition of time or travel costs; diversion by shifting patients onto other budgets, for example, social service departments; dilution through reducing the intensity of treatment, prescribing cheaper drugs, doing fewer tests; and delay by making people queue for treatment on the waiting list. Clinicians took decisions about individual patients on largely implicit criteria which could be both arbitrary and discriminatory (for example, against the elderly).

Setting priorities at the meso-level is now (in theory at least) a more focused activity, as managers in purchasing authorities decide what to purchase and in what quantity according to their assessments of local needs, consultation with the public and users, and judgements about cost-effectiveness. Clinicians in provider units will have to argue their case for funding before they can introduce new treatments or services. But as Klein demonstrates from two national surveys of purchasing plans for the years 1992–93 and 1993–94, in the early stages of the reforms historical patterns of provision still prevailed, with purchasers making few changes (Klein 1994). The challenges of explictly defining health care packages based on needs and effectiveness were daunting and remain so, but purchasers are becoming more confident. In 1994–95, explicit rationing measures – making some treatments not available on the NHS altogether – were on the increase (NAHAT 1995). Excluded treatments were usually restricted to marginal activities (tattoo removal, cosmetic surgery, and more controversially, *in vitro* fertilisation). Even these have been contested and DOH guidance is that nothing should be removed completely although it may be designated very low priority – a euphemism for saying it will be exceptionally difficult for patients to access. However, the methods purchasers adopt to make their decisions, and the weight they place on different factors varies greatly, while the criteria used is often not openly debated or made clear. Inequities in access to services have always been a feature of the NHS, and the courts have never upheld the view that the principle of 'comprehensiveness' implies any *substantive* rights to a specific treatment or service. The difference now is that inequities are the outcome of explicit decisions, and access to some services depends on where one lives. In one area all pregnant women over 30 may be offered the choice of screening for Down's Syndrome, in others only those over 35 are eligible. Fertility treatment may not be provided at all in some areas; criteria for using expensive drugs like beta interferon for multiple sclerosis can also vary widely. Meanwhile, managers who refuse treatments for children with serious illnesses even if they are unlikely to work, stand in the media firing line while politicians dodge the flak.

The Labour Party approach is to create a 'clearer national framework for service priorities' based on 'epidemiological and demographic evidence of the need for health care and on clinical evidence of the effectiveness of treatment. We need to marry the bottom-up approach that derives decision making close to the patient, with the national approach that sets out goals, guidelines and priorities' (Smith 1996: 8). This still leaves plenty of room for debate about how this might be done (see, for instance, New and Le Grand 1996; Lenaghan 1996; Health Select Committee 1994; Honigsbaum *et al.* 1995; Klein 1995) and it will be important to learn from countries like Sweden, New Zealand and Holland who are going down the same route; nevertheless promises to restore a national framework and clearer rules of entitlement are a step in the right direction.

Restoring confidence

This leads us to the final question: will the Labour Party be able to restore public and staff confidence in the NHS and its future? Trust in politicians has reached a low ebb (Curtice and Jowell 1996: 148). Many voters believe that former promises of 'cradle-to-grave' care by the NHS have been broken and expectations breached. To the extent that if this continues they will feel compelled to turn to private insurance out of fear, although this cannot be an efficient, effective or equitable alternative to the NHS, as US experience shows.

The Labour Party starts with the advantage that as the creator of the NHS it is always trusted more with its governance than the Conservatives. The measures it proposes to restore cohesion and the sense of a national service which is provided to all on the same terms and conditions should also help to restore confidence. In addition, although there appear to be few differences in the substance of policy between New Labour and the present administration, it is clear there are real value differences informing its policies and goals for the NHS, which seem more in line with the original purposes of the NHS and which are broadly supported.

Sceptical policy analysts would argue, however, that while values and political choices are always important, policy outcomes depend on the flux and flow of many forces, and there can be a big gap between intention and result. Many party leaders have presided over policies which they had staunchly opposed at the start of their reign, or were unable to prevent what they most feared. As in the past, the NHS will be strongly affected by external pressures – both national and international – and health care itself is entering an era of even more unpredictable change. The Party has acknowledged it does not have all the answers (as to how long-term care should be funded, for example).

Inevitably there will be complex and difficult decisions to take, but if 'evidence-based medicine' can be matched by 'evidence-based policy-making', a commitment to social learning and open honest debate, then we may be able to build a future for the NHS which we can all support, and which allows it to enter the 21st century with renewed confidence and hope.

References

Alderslade, R. and Hunter, D. (1994) 'Commissioning and public health' *J. of Management in Medicine*, 8(6): 20–31.

Appleby, J. (1996) 'PFI: RIP?' *Health Service Journal*, 8th August, 106(5506): 32–33.

Appleby, J. and Little, V. (1993) 'Health and efficiency' *Health Service Journal*, 3rd June, 103(5351): 20–22.

Appleby, J, Sheldon, T. and Clarke, A. (1993) 'Run for your *money*' *Health Service Journal*, 23rd June, pp. 22–4.

Ashburner, L. and Cairncross, L. (1992) 'Just trust us' *Health Service Journal*, 14th May, 102(5302): 20–2.

Audit Commission (1994) *Aspects of Managing Hospital and Community Services*, London: HMSO.

Audit Commission (1996) *Fraud Bulletin. Protecting the Public Purse: Ensuring. Probity in the NHS – 1996 Update*, London: Audit Commission.

British Medical Journal (1994) 'Drug resistance is a worldwide threat, warns report' 26th October, 309: 1109.

Charlesworth, J., Clarke, J. and Cochrane, A. (1996) 'Tangled Webs? Managing local mixed economies of care' *Public Administration*, 74 Spring, pp. 67–88.

Clarke, K. (1996) Budget Speech *Financial Times*, 27th November, pp. 17–19.

Coote, A. and Hunter, D. (1996) *New Agenda for Health*, London: Institute of Public Policy Research.

Crail, M. And Cross, M. (1995) '2020 Visions' *Health Service Journal*, 31st August, 105(5468): 8–11.

Curtice, J. and Jowell, R. (1996) 'The sceptical electorate' in R. Jowell *et al.* (eds) *British Social Attitudes: the 12th Report 1995–1996 edition*, Aldershot: Dartmouth Publishing.

Dawson, D. and Maynard, A. (1996) 'Private finance for the public good?' *British Medical Journal*, 313: 312.

Department of Health (1995) *NHS Responsibilities for Meeting Continuing Health Care Needs*, HSG(95)8 LAC(95)9.

—— (1996a) *Primary Care: the Future Choice and Opportunity*, London: HMSO.

—— (1996b) *A Service with Ambitions*, London: HMSO.

Duggan, M. (1995) *Primary Health Care: A Prognosis*, London: Institute of Public Policy Research.

Earl-Slater, A. (1996) 'Privatising medicine in the National Health Service' *Public Money and Management*, Jan–March, 16(1): 39–44.

Financial Times (1996) 'Beef crisis to cost taxpayer £3.3 bn' 27th November, p. 13.

Foster, A. and Laming, H. (1992) *Implementing Caring for People*, EL(92)13 C1(92)10 London: Department of Health.

Gosden, T. and Maynard, A. (1996) 'He who pays the piper' *Health Service Journal*, 31st October, 106(5527): 18.

Griffith, B., Iliffe, S and Rayner, G. (1987) *Banking on Sickness*, London: Lawrence and Wishart.

Hacking, J. (1996) 'Is it worth the weight?' *Health Service Journal*, 18th Jan, 106(5486): 26–7.

Hancock, C. (1996) 'Let's split the difference' *Health Service Journal*, 7th November, 106(5519): 17.

Hancock, T. (1991) 'National and international health goals and healthy public policy' in P. Draper (ed) *Health Through Public Policy*, London: Merlin Press.

Harrison, A. (1995) *Health Care UK 1994–95*, London: King's Fund Institute.

Healthcare 2000 (1995) *UK Health and Health care services: Challenges and Policy options* (publisher not given).

Health Service Journal (1996a) 'Yet another darkest hour' Editorial, 105(5526): 17.

—— (1996b) 'Private finance not meeting capital spending shortfall' 11th July, 106(5502): 7.

House of Commons Health Select Committee (1995) *Priority Setting in the NHS: Purchasing*, London: HMSO.

House of Commons Health Select Committee (1996) *Long Term Care: NHS Responsibilities for Continuing Health Care Needs*, London: HMSO.

Hensher, M. and Edwards, N. (1996) 'Driving range' *Health Service Journal*, 106(5519): 19.

Henwood, M. (1995) *Making a Difference? Implementation of the Community Care Reforms Two Years On*, Leeds/London: Nuffield Institute for Health, Community Care Division/King's Fund Centre.

Henwood, M. (1996) 'Silent progress' *Health Service Journal*, 106(5530): 24–5.

Henwood, M., Wistow, G. and Robinson, J. (1996) 'Halfway there? Policy, politics and outcomes in community care' *Social Policy and Administration*, 30(1): 38–53.

Honigsbaum, F., Calltorp, J., Ham, C. and Holmstrom, S. (1995) *Priority Setting Processes for Healthcare*, Oxford: Radcliffe Medical Press.

Jencks, S. and Schieber, G. (1991) 'Containing health care costs: what bullet to bite?' *Health Care Financing Review Annual Supplement*, 1–12.

Kingman, S. (1994) 'Freeman Hospital: the will to survive' *British Medical Journal*, 309: 461–4.

Klein, R. (1994) 'Can we restrict the health care menu?' *Health Policy*, 27: 103–12.

—— (1995) 'Priorities and rationing: pragmatism or principles?' *British Medical Journal*, 311: 761–2.

Labour Party (1995) *Renewing the NHS*, London: Walworth Road.

Lenaghan, J. (1996) *Rationing and Rights in Health Care*, London: Institute of Public Policy Research.

Light, D. (1994) 'Managed care: false and real solutions', *The Lancet*, 344: 1197.

Limb, M. (1996) 'Nothing to declare?', 5th December, *Health Service Journal*, 106(5532): 11.

National Association of Health Authorities and Trusts (NAHAT) (1995) *Reshaping the NHS: Strategies, Priorities and Resource Allocation*, Birmingham: NAHAT.

—— (1996) *The 1996–97 Contracting Round: NAHAT Survey of NHS Providers and Purchasers*, Birmingham: NAHAT.

Maynard, A. (1996) 'At the leading edge', *Health Service Journal*, 25th April, 106(5500): 25.

Milio, N. (1995) 'Health, health care reform and the care of health' in M. Blunden and M. Dando (eds) *Rethinking Public Policy-making: Questioning Assumptions, Challenging Beliefs*, London: Sage.

Moore, W. (1996) 'All stressed up and nowhere to go', *Health Service Journal*, 5th September, 106(5510): 22–5.

Moran, M. (1997, forthcoming) 'Explaining the rise of the market in health care' in W. Ranade (ed) *Markets and Health Care: a Comparative Analysis*, London: Addison Wesley Longman.

New, B. and Le Grand, J. (1996) *Rationing in the NHS: Principles and Pragmatism*, London: King's Fund.

Newchurch and Company, Health Service Briefing (1995) *Strategic Change in the NHS 3 – Acute Services: A Prognosis for the Millenium*, London: Newchurch.

Observer (1997) '*Virgin MPs set a radical agenda*', 11th May, p. 24.

Organisation for Economic Cooperation and Development (OECD) (1995) *Health Data File 1995*, Geneva: OECD.

Roberts, C. *et al.* (1996) 'The wasted millions', *Health Service Journal*, 10th October, 106(5525): 24–7.

Ruddle, S. (1991) *Rationing Resources in the NHS*, Southampton: Institute of Health Policy Studies, University of Southampton.

Saks, M. (1994) 'The alternatives to medicine' in J. Gabe, D. Kelleher and G. Williams (eds) *Challenging Medicine*, London: Routledge.

Salter, B. (1995) 'The private sector and the NHS: redefining the welfare state', *Policy and Politics*, 23(1): 17–30.

Saltman, R. (1997 forthcoming) 'Sweden' in W. Ranade (ed) *Markets and Health Care: a Comparative Analysis*, London: Addison Wesley Longman.

Saltman, R. and Figueras, J. (1996) *European Health Care Reforms: Analysis of Current Strategies: Summary*, Copenhagen: World Health Organisation Regional Office for Europe.

Smith, C. (1996) 'A Health Service for a New Century: Labour's proposals to replace the internal market in the NHS', Speech by Shadow Secretary of Health, 3rd December.

Stewart, J. (1993) 'The rebuilding of public accountability', in *Accountability to the Public*, London: European Policy Forum.

Taylor-Gooby, P. (1995) 'Comfortable, marginal and excluded: Who should pay higher taxes for a better welfare state?' in Jowell *et al.*

Terry, F. (1996) 'The Private Finance Initiative – overdue reform or policy breakthrough?', *Public Money and Management*, January–March, 16(1): 9–15.

Timmins, N. (1996) 'A different sort of welfare state', *Financial Times*, 27th November, p. 14.
Wall, A. (1997) 'Labouring under delusions', *Health Service Journal*, 2nd Jan, 107(5534): 16.
Watt, I., Freemantle, N.B. and Mason, J. (1994) 'Purchasing and public health: the state of the union', *J. of Management in Medicine*, 8(1): 6–11.
Whitehead, M. (1995) 'Tackling inequalities: a review of policy initiatives' in M. Benzeval, K. Judge and M. Whitehead (eds) *Tackling Inequalities in Health*, London: King's Fund.
Wistow, G. (1995) 'Continuing Care: Who is responsible?' in A. Harrison (1995).
Wordsworth, S., Donaldson, C. and Scott, A. (1996) *Can We Afford the NHS?*, London: Institute of Public Policy Research.

Appendix 1 – Specification for Maternity Services 1995–96 – A summary

1 Mission Statement – sets out what the health authority aims to achieve as service outcomes for its users, and the professional, consumer, and other forms of advice and guidance which inform the specification e.g. 'Changing Childbirth', reports by local CHC, Commission for Racial Equality Code of Practice for Maternity Services, etc.

2 Population to be served.

3 Parameters of the service (how 'maternity services' are defined).

4 Principles and Values – which will inform purchasing decisions e.g. central importance of a woman-centred service; choice; cultural sensitivity; information; accessibility; continuity of care, etc.

5 Implementing 'Changing Childbirth':
All providers must demonstrate effective progress towards meeting the principles and targets set out in the report, according to the timescales agreed with the purchaser. These are set out in detail.

6 Choice of maternity care:
Sets out the kind of choices the purchasers wishes to be available for women giving birth either now or according to agreed timescale e.g. shared care, domino delivery, home births, etc.

7 Essential components of maternity services and quality standards:
Discusses detailed components of maternity services that should be in place and how they should be provided in relation to guiding principles and values. These range from preconceptual services and family planning, to antenatal and postnatal health promotion, education and support for mothers; from the handling of miscarriages, still births and terminations to provision for intensive neonatal care. This is the most detailed part of the specification.

8 Professional/Statutory requirements – that must be adhered to e.g. professional standards of the Royal Colleges, all relevant National Health service legislation, circulars, Codes of Good Practice etc;

provisions of the 1989 Children's Act and procedures and policies laid down by the local Child Protection Committee.

9 Quality monitoring and audit procedures.
Specifies procedures and data required including clinical and consumer audit, visiting access for CHC and local Maternity Consumer groups.

INDEX